S0-ACN-678

The Yankee Cook Book

The Yankee

by
Imogene Wolcott
additions by
Elinor Shepard Beckwith

Revised Edition

The Stephen Greene Press
Lexington, Massachusetts

This edition published by special arrangement
with David McKay Company, Inc.
Reprinted 1985

Produced in the United States of America.

Published by The Stephen Greene Press, Lexington, Massachusetts
Distributed by Viking Penguin Inc.

Library of Congress Cataloging in Publication Data

Main entry under title:

The Yankee cook book.
Reprint. Originally published: New York: I. Washburn, 1971.
Includes index.
1. Cookery, American—New England. I. Wolcott, Imogene B.
TX715.Y174 1981 641.5974 81-6413
ISBN 0-8289-0456-1 (pbk.) AACR2

To my granddaughters,
Cindy,
Peggy,
Allison,
Helen,
Sally,
Bonnie,
and Kate

Acknowledgments

The editor is deeply indebted to *Yankee* magazine for permission to reprint "Rhode Island Clambakes," by Horace G. Belcher; "Sap's Risin,'" by Sydney Wooldridge; as well as many of the recipes and anecdotes.

The editor is likewise sincerely appreciative of the permission given by First National Stores Inc. to reprint recipes submitted both to the printed and to the radio edition of the *First National News*. The staff of the New England Council also deserves especial thanks for its valuable suggestions and encouragement.

Contents

Foreword

THIS book is a record of the delicious recipes that have been the mainstay of Yankee cooking since the days of the Pilgrims. Many were first copies from the yellowed pages of books that have been used by generations of New Englanders. I have substituted exact measurements for directions such as "a scoop of flour" and "a trickle of molasses" and other vague amounts. Oven temperatures and up-to-date cooking methods have been added to make preparation easier and more precise.

In this latest edition of *The Yankee Cook Book,* some of the regional articles have been retained, and new ones have been added. For instance, a description of country fairs and the story of an Indian ancestor offer the reader in search of a recipe pleasant browsing. New recipes have been added in various chapters, and, of course, the chowders, fish cakes, lobster and native fish, cranberry dishes, johnnycake, baked Indian pudding, pies, dumplings, and hundreds of other authentic recipes that have made Yankee cooking famous are still included.

In a sense Yankee lore and Yankee cooking are national rather than regional, for wherever New Englanders went they carried with them their folk tales and beliefs and customs and their cooking know-how, so that they are now a part of our Yankee heritage. Today there is a welcome interest on the part of young people in cooking, and one hopes that with the help of recipes such as these there will be oncoming generations of expert Yankee cooks.

Imogene Wolcott

East Sandwich, Mass.
June, 1970

1

Soups, Chowders, and Stews

Clam Chowder, New England Style

[*Old Bay State recipe*]

1 quart shucked clams
¼ pound salt pork, diced
1 large onion, finely sliced
3 medium-sized potatoes, sliced thin
½ teaspoon salt
⅛ teaspoon pepper
4 cups milk
6 split common crackers
2 tablespoons butter

Split the head of each clam so that it is open flat and rinse in clam liquor to remove grit; remove the black cap. Separate the belly or soft part from the firm part, reserving about a cupful of the plumpest clams. With thumb and forefinger squeeze out the dark part of the bellies. Chop or grind the firm body parts coarsely. Strain ½ cup liquor. Try out salt pork, remove when crisp, sauté onion slices; add potatoes, salt, and pepper and sauté slowly, stirring often, for 10 minutes. Add the chopped clams and liquor. Cover with water and cook 20 minutes. Add the cleaned bellies and cook a few minutes longer. If scum forms, skim it off at once. When clams are tender, add milk in which crackers have been soaking. Add butter; place kettle at back of stove, to allow chowder to flavor and "ripen" for about an hour. Serves 6.

Clam Chowder, Copley-Plaza

[*Sheraton Plaza, Boston, Mass.*]

3 quarts Duxbury clams (in shell)
1 stalk celery
2 medium-sized onions
¼ pound salt pork, chopped
2 medium-sized potatoes
1 cup heavy cream
salt and pepper

Steam the clams with stalk of celery in a little water to prevent burning, until a quart of clam broth is obtained. Slice the potatoes; chop the onions fine and sauté in salt pork fat, taking care they do not become brown. Mix in the potatoes, then add the clam broth. Simmer about 30 minutes; remove from the fire, add cream slowly, stirring well. Add a few of the clams (well cleaned) as a garniture. Season and serve with crackers. Serves 4.

Clam Broth

[*Recipe from Duxbury, Mass.*]

1 quart clams
1½ cups cold water

Scrub clams and wash in several waters until free from sand.* Place in large kettle, add water, cover tightly and cook over low heat about 20 minutes or until shells open. Remove clams from broth. When liquor has settled strain carefully. Boiling water or hot milk may be added to make one quart of broth, if desired. Serve hot or cold, with or without whipped cream and dash of paprika. (Old recipes do not call for additional water or milk or for topping of whipped cream.) Serves 4 to 6.

Rhode Island Clam Chowder

3-inch cube fat salt pork, diced
3 onions, sliced
4 cups potatoes, cut in small cubes
1 quart shucked clams (quahogs)
2 cups boiling water
1 cup stewed, strained tomatoes
¼ teaspoon soda
1 cup milk, scalded
1 cup thin cream
2 tablespoons butter
salt and pepper
8 common crackers, split

Try out pork until crisp; remove scraps. Cook onion in fat until lightly browned, remove, add potatoes to fat and stir and cook over low flame 10 minutes. Chop hard part of clams fine and add

*TO CLEANSE LIVE CLAMS OF GRIT: *Put clams in bucket of sea or salted (1 Tb/qt) water; add handful of corn meal. Let stand at least 1 hour. Scrub shells and proceed.*

with onion to potatoes. Cover with boiling water and simmer until potatoes are nearly done. Stir soda into tomatoes and add with soft part of clam. Simmer gently on back of stove at least 30 minutes. When ready to serve add scalded milk, cream, butter and seasonings. Serve over crackers which have been moistened in cold milk or with crackers served dry. Serves 8.

* *The raging clam chowder controversy that has continued almost uninterruptedly in New England for generations centers on the use of tomatoes as an ingredient in its preparation. Rhode Island and Connecticut housewives uphold the tomato. The rest of New England scorn it. A Maine politician claims the addition of tomato to clam chowder "is the work of reds" who seek to undermine "our most hallowed tradition," and suggests that all housewives and chefs adding tomato be forced "to dig a barrel of clams at high tide" as a penalty.*

Even Maine lobsters are said to object to the adding of this red coloring matter, claiming that it poaches on their preserves, and that it may mislead those who have enjoyed a real lobster stew. They claim they have a priority on said color and that the claws of every Maine lobster are raised in protest.

Rhode Island Quahog Chowder

⅛ pound salt pork, diced
2 onions, sliced
5 potatoes, diced
1 quart boiling water
½ pint quahogs, drained and cut small
liquor from quahogs
salt and pepper

Try out salt pork until browned. Add onions and fry until soft and yellow. Add potatoes and fry a little, but not to brown. Add pork, onions, and potatoes to boiling water. Cook until potatoes are done; then add quahogs. Add liquor from quahogs cautiously, to taste. (Take care!) Season and simmer a few minutes or until quahogs are cooked through. Serves 6.

Martha's Vineyard Quahog Stew

½ cup butter
2 tablespoons flour
4 cups milk, heated
salt, pepper, and dash of mace
1 quart shucked quahogs with liquor
2 eggs, well beaten

Cream flour and butter and stir into milk; add seasonings. Heat quahog liquor, skimming off froth. Chop quahogs fine and simmer in heated juice 3 minutes, stir into heated milk. Put eggs into soup tureen, pour in quahog mixture, stir well, and serve. Clams may be substituted for quahogs. Serves 8.

Cream of Quahog Soup

[*A Cape Cod recipe*]

24 quahogs
½ cup liquor from quahogs, strained
2 sliced onions
3 cups milk
1 teaspoon sugar
2 tablespoons butter
2 tablespoons flour
1 cup heavy cream
salt and pepper
minced parsley

Chop the quahogs fine; place in top of double boiler with onion and liquor. Cook over direct heat for 5 minutes. Add milk and sugar and place over boiling water and let stand but do not cook. Blend butter and flour and stir in. Cook 3 minutes; strain and add cream. Serve in bouillon cups with a small round of toast covered with minced parsley on top. Serves 6 to 8.

Smoky Chowder

½ pound fat salt pork, diced
1 large onion, sliced
4 medium potatoes, sliced
water
salt and pepper
1 bay leaf
4 cups milk
1½ pounds smoked fillet of haddock, cubed

Brown pork in skillet; add onion and sauté until onion is transparent. Add potatoes and water to cover, salt and pepper to taste, and bay leaf. When potatoes are almost done, add milk and fish and simmer 10 minutes. Remove bay leaf. Serves 6.

Gloucester Fish Chowder

3½ to 4-pound haddock or cod
2-inch cube fat salt pork
1 medium onion, sliced
4 cups potatoes, sliced
4 cups hot milk
1 tablespoon salt
⅛ teaspoon pepper

Put cut-up fish in 2 cups cold water; cook until done. Cut pork into tiny dice and fry to a light brown. Remove pork scraps. Add onion to fat and cook slowly about 5 minutes. Pick fish from skin and bones. Add fish liquor and potatoes to fat and onions and enough water to cover potatoes. Boil until potatoes are nearly done; add fish, hot milk, seasonings, and pork scraps, if desired. Simmer 10 minutes. Serve with sour pickles and common crackers or pilot crackers. Serves 8.

* *Mrs. A. Stacey Barnes, Boardman Avenue, Melrose Highlands, Mass., says this recipe comes from her grandmother, a "grand cook who came from a family of Gloucester folk, famous for tasty New England fish dishes."*

Daniel Webster's Fish Chowder

"Take a cod of ten pounds, well cleaned, leaving on the skin. Cut into pieces one and a half pounds thick, preserving the head whole. Take one and a half pounds of clear, fat salt pork, cut in thin slices. Do the same with twelve potatoes. Take the largest pot you have. Try out the pork first, then take out the pieces of pork, leaving in the drippings. Add to that three parts of water, a layer of fish, so as to cover the bottom of the pot; next a layer of potatoes, then two tablespoons of salt, 1 teaspoon of pepper, then the pork, another layer of fish, and the remainder of the potatoes.

"Fill the pot with water to cover the ingredients. Put over a good fire. Let the chowder boil twenty-five minutes. When this is done have a quart of boiling milk ready, and ten hard crackers split and dipped in cold water. Add milk and crackers. Let the whole boil five minutes. The chowder is then ready to be first-rate if you have followed the directions. An onion may be added if you like the flavor."

Boston Style Fish Chowder

[*Parker House, Boston, Mass.*]

A 4-pound haddock
8 cups cold water
1 bay leaf
1 spray thyme
1 stalk celery
½ pound ground fat salt pork
2 onions, chopped fine
4 tablespoons flour
3 medium potatoes, diced
2 cups milk
salt and pepper

Cut fish in 1-inch squares, place head and fish bones in a deep kettle. Add cold water, bay leaf, thyme, and celery. Simmer 15 minutes and strain. Try out salt pork in a heavy skillet; remove cracklings and add onion. Cook until onion is transparent, then add flour. Blend thoroughly. Add potatoes and fish bouillon. Simmer for 15 minutes, then add fish cut in cubes. Simmer until fish is done, about 10 minutes; add milk and bring to a boil. Season. Serves 8.

Oyster Stew

[*Union Oyster House, Boston, Mass., Established 1826*]

- 1 pint oysters (with liquor)
- ¼ cup butter
- 1 cup light cream, scalded
- 3 cups milk, scalded
- pepper
- ½ teaspoon salt
- ½ teaspoon paprika

Pick over oysters; then cook in butter and oyster liquor until edges curl. Add cream and milk. Heat to boiling and season. Serve at once with crackers. Serves 4.

* *A century ago in old New England a bowl of piping hot oyster stew formed the traditional Christmas Eve supper. Coming from the Merrie England of their ancestors, the custom of serving oysters on Christmas was quite natural in a country which had an abundance of fat, delicately flavored oysters. In small communities it is still customary to hold Watch Night (New Year's Eve) services at which oyster stew is served during the evening. True New England oyster stew is never thickened.*

Falmouth Clam and Mushroom Bisque

- ½ pound fresh mushrooms
- 3 tablespoons butter
- 3 tablespoons flour
- 3 cups clam broth, strained
- 1 cup cream
- salt and pepper

Clean and chop mushrooms. Sauté in butter, blend in flour, add the clam broth, and simmer slowly for 10 minutes. Add the cream, season, and serve. Serves 4.

Cream of Oyster Soup

[A Rhode Island recipe]

- 1 pint oysters, with liquor
- 4 cups milk
- 1 slice onion
- 2 stalks celery
- sprig of parsley
- bit of bay leaf
- 4 tablespoons butter
- 4 tablespoons flour
- salt, pepper
- croutons, or toast sticks

Chop oysters; add liquor. Heat slowly to the boiling point and press through a coarse sieve. Scald milk with onion, celery, parsley, and bay leaf. Melt butter, blend in flour, add milk. Stir over a low fire or over hot water until mixture thickens. Add the oysters and season to taste. Serve at once with fried croutons or toast sticks. Serves 4.

Greenfield Corn and Oyster Stew

- 1 pint oysters
- ½ cup water
- 2 tablespoons flour
- 2 tablespoons butter
- 3 cups milk
- 2 teaspoons salt
- 2 cups celery, cut and boiled tender
- ⅛ teaspoon pepper
- 1¾ cups whole kernel corn
- 1 cup cream

Cook oysters in water until edges curl. Remove from heat and strain broth. Blend butter and flour, add broth gradually; add milk, simmer 5 minutes, stirring constantly. Add cooked celery, corn, and cream, and simmer 5 minutes longer. Add oysters last. Season. Serves 6.

Nantucket Scallop Chowder

4 tablespoons butter
2 small onions, sliced
1 pint scallops, cut in pieces
2 cups boiling water
1 cup diced potatoes
4 cups milk, scalded
salt and pepper
common crackers, split and toasted

Melt butter, lightly brown onions in butter. Remove onions. Cook scallops in butter 5 minutes. Add boiling water, onion, and potato and simmer 30 minutes. Add scalded milk and simmer 15 minutes more. Season to taste; serve hot with crackers. Serves 5.

Lobster Stew

5 chicken lobsters, boiled
5 tablespoons butter
5 cups top milk (half milk and half cream)
salt, pepper, paprika, and a sprinkling of cayenne

Remove meat from shell and cut in dices about ½-inch square. Sauté in butter 3 or 4 minutes. (The tomalley and coral of the lobster may be added if desired.) Remove from heat and cool slightly. Add the milk very slowly, stirring constantly, and then the seasonings. Serves 5.

✻ *The Maine Department of Sea and Shore Fisheries reports that the important steps in creating the perfect lobster stew are: (1) the partial cooling of the lobster meat before adding the hot milk, a trickle at a time; (2) constant stirring; and (3) "aging" to improve the flavor. This should take place in a cool room for the first few hours, and then under refrigeration for at least 5 hours before the stew is reheated and served.*

Crab Stew

[*Maine Department of Sea and Shore Fisheries*]

2 tablespoons butter
6 small soda crackers
2 cups fresh Maine crabmeat
½ cup water
1 quart rich milk
salt and pepper
1 tall can evaporated milk

Melt butter in kettle. Roll crackers until crumbs are as fine as flour. Place these crumbs and the crabmeat in butter, add water, and let mixture bubble for 1 minute to bring out the luscious flavor of the crabmeat. Pour in milk and stir until it is very hot, but do not boil. Add seasonings and evaporated milk. Reheat, but again do not boil. Serves 6 people who will probably wish there were seconds.

Old-Fashioned Split Pea Soup

2 cups dried split yellow peas
12 cups cold water
1 onion, sliced
1 ham bone
salt and pepper

Pick over peas and soak overnight. Drain, add cold water, ham bone, and onion. Simmer 3 or 4 hours, or until peas are soft. Rub through a sieve and season. If soup is too thick, add boiling water. Serves 8.

* *Mrs. Leonard S. Cress, Lexington, Mass., author of this recipe, wrote that her ancestors, the Pikes, Dows, and Adams of Massachusetts, Vermont, and New Hampshire, were good old-fashioned New England cooks. This pea soup was always served with johnnycake. Some old-time recipes call for the addition of 1 potato, sliced, or 1 stalk of celery, diced.*

Purée of Split Pea Soup

[*Congress Square Hotel, Portland, Me.*]

- 1 cup yellow split peas
- 1½ cups green split peas
- 16 cups cold water
- ¼ pound salt pork, cut in pieces
- 1 small piece of left-over ham
- 2 stalks celery, diced
- 1 carrot, scraped and sliced
- 1 onion, sliced
- ¼ teaspoon pepper
- 1 teaspoon Worcestershire sauce
- 1 clove garlic (optional)
- 3 tablespoons flour
- 3 medium sized potatoes, peeled and sliced
- 1½ cups light cream, scalded

Soak peas in water overnight; drain, add cold water, bring to a boil, and simmer 30 minutes. Sauté salt pork, add ham cut in pieces, celery, onion, carrot; add pepper, Worcestershire sauce, and garlic. Shake in flour and continue to sauté for 15 minutes, stirring constantly. Combine with peas; add potatoes, simmer 2 hours longer, then strain through purée strainer. (If soup is too thick, add boiling water.) Before serving add cream, heat to boiling, season, and serve with johnnycake. Serves 10 to 12.

Boston Black Bean Soup

- 2 cups dried black beans
- 1 tablespoon salt
- 2 quarts water
- 1 tablespoon butter
- 2 tablespoons flour
- ½ tablespoon minced onion
- ⅛ teaspoon black pepper
- ⅛ teaspoon dry mustard
- 1 cup heavy cream
- 6 thin slices of lemon
- 6 cloves
- 1 hard-cooked egg, sliced

Soak beans overnight in water to cover. Drain. Add salt and water and cook 2 hours or until beans are very soft. Force mixture through sieve. Place purée back on stove and simmer 15 minutes.

Melt butter, blend in flour. Add onion, pepper, and mustard. Add cream slowly, stirring constantly until slightly thickened. Add to bean purée, blending well. Heat just to boiling point. Serve in shallow bowls. Place a slice of lemon with a clove and a slice of hard-cooked egg in each bowl. Serve with croutons. Serves 6.

Baked Kidney Bean Soup

2 tablespoons onion, chopped
1 tablespoon celery, chopped
2 tablespoons butter
2 tablespoons flour
1 teaspoon salt
¼ teaspoon pepper
3 cups baked kidney beans
4 cups water

Place onion, celery and butter in skillet, cover and simmer slowly until tender. Blend with flour, salt, and pepper. Simmer beans for 15 minutes in water. (Canned kidney beans or pea beans or yellow eye beans may be used, in which case use 1 tall 28-ounce tin of beans and 1½ tins water.) Combine all ingredients and press through sieve. Reheat and serve with croutons. Serves 5.

Aroostook Potato and Green Pea Soup

2 medium sized potatoes, diced
1 onion, sliced
2 cups boiling water
1 cup canned or fresh cooked peas
2 tablespoons butter
2 tablespoons flour
4 cups milk
salt and pepper
minced parsley or chives (if desired)

Boil potatoes and onion in water until both are tender. Add peas and rub through a sieve with the water in which potatoes and onion were cooked. Blend butter with flour and add hot milk. Cook until thickened, stirring constantly. Add purée and season. Minced parsley or chives may be served on top. Serves 5.

Aroostook Potato Soup

- 4 cups potatoes, diced
- 2 medium onions, finely sliced
- 3 cups boiling water
- 1 tablespoon flour
- 2 tablespoons butter
- 4 cups milk
- 1 teaspoon salt
- ⅛ teaspoon pepper
- sprinkling nutmeg
- chopped parsley or chives

Cook potatoes and onions in water until tender; drain, force through ricer or sieve with the water in which they were cooked. Blend flour and butter, add purée and milk slowly, stirring well; season and garnish with chopped parsley or chives. Serves 6.

Mashed Potato Soup

Left-over mashed potatoes make excellent potato soup. Sauté finely chopped onion in butter, blend with mashed potatoes, add thin cream sauce or rich milk and seasonings. Heat to boil, stirring constantly. Garnish with minced parsley.

Deerfoot Chowder

- ½ cup salt pork, cut in fine shreds
- 1 medium-sized onion
- 1 medium-sized potato
- 2 cups boiling water
- 2 cups canned corn
- 2 cups milk
- 2 tablespoons flour
- 3 tablespoons cold water
- 1½ cups canned tomatoes
- 1 teaspoon sugar
- ⅛ teaspoon soda
- salt and pepper

Try out the salt pork and sauté the sliced onion in the fat. Add the potato and boiling water and cook until tender. Add corn and milk, thicken with flour blended with cold water, and add the tomato heated with the sugar, soda, and seasonings last. Serves 6.

Maine Corn Chowder

- 3 tablespoons fat salt pork, diced
- 1 onion, sliced
- 2 cups potatoes, diced
- 1½ cups boiling water
- 1 cup canned corn
- 1 cup milk
- 1 cup cream
- salt and pepper
- 4 common crackers, split

Try out salt pork, add onion, and cook until a golden brown. Add potatoes, water, and corn, and cook until potatoes are tender. Add milk and cream and reheat. Season. Place a cracker in each dish and pour chowder over crackers. Serves 4.

Vermont Cabbage Soup

Chop fine 1 small head of cabbage. (There should be about 3 cups when it is chopped.) Add water to cover and cook until tender. Drain off all but 1 cup of the water. Add 3 cups milk and 1 cup cream. Season to taste with salt and pepper. Serve hot. Serves 6.

Yankee Succotash Chowder

- ¼ pound salt pork
- 1 dozen ears sweet corn
- 1 quart cranberry beans, shelled
- water
- 1 quart rich milk
- ¼ pound butter
- 2 tablespoons flour
- 4 tablespoons cold water
- salt and pepper

Cut pork into small cubes. Cut uncooked corn from cob. Place beans, pork, and corn cobs into a large kettle and cover with water. Cook until beans are soft and pork tender. Remove cobs, scrape, add scrapings to kettle. Add milk, butter, salt, and pepper.

Add cut corn and simmer 20 minutes. Thicken with the flour that has been mixed with the cold water. Allow the chowder to stand 1 day. Reheat and serve. Serves 8.

Parsnip Chowder

⅛ pound salt pork
1 small onion, sliced
3 cups parsnips, cut in cubes
1 cup potatoes, cut in cubes
2 cups boiling water
1 quart rich milk
4 tablespoons butter
½ cup rolled cracker crumbs (optional)
salt and pepper
minced parsley (optional)

Try out salt pork; remove cracklings. Add onion and sauté gently; add parsnips and potatoes; add water and cook about 30 minutes or until parsnips and potatoes are done. Add milk and butter. Season to taste. Some recipes call for the addition of ½ cup rolled cracker crumbs; others thicken chowder slightly with 2 tablespoons flour mixed with 2 tablespoons cold water and top with minced parsley. Serves 8.

Cream of Parsnip Soup

½ onion, minced
½ cup water
4 cups milk
1 cup cooked parsnips, rubbed through a sieve
3 tablespoons butter
3 tablespoons flour
1 teaspoon salt
⅛ teaspoon pepper
¼ teaspoon paprika

Boil minced onion until tender in water. Scald milk and add onion and parsnip purée. Blend butter and flour and add to hot mixture, stirring for 5 minutes or until smooth. Season. Serves 5.

✱ *Toward the end of February the frost begins to leave the ground in New England. Then it's time to dig the first "mess" of parsnips from the kitchen garden where they have ripened and sweetened all winter. Parsnips were once considered poisonous until after they had been frozen. The fact is, they were not a "keeping" vegetable, and hence were better in the ground than pulled.*

Parsonage Oyster Plant Soup

1 bunch oyster plant (also called salsify)
1 onion, sliced
2 cups rich milk, scalded
2 tablespoons butter
salt and pepper

Wash, scrape and cut the oyster plant in thin slices. Add onion and enough water to keep from burning. Cook until vegetables are tender and water almost boiled away. Put onion and half the oyster plant through food press or sieve; add milk, butter, and seasonings to taste. Add the remainder of the oyster plant and heat. Serves 3.

Connecticut Cream of Onion Soup

3 cups sliced onions
7 tablespoons butter or chicken fat
3 cups boiling water
3 tablespoons flour
3 cups rich milk, scalded
salt and pepper

Sauté onion slowly in 4 tablespoons butter or chicken fat until lightly browned. Add boiling water and simmer 15 minutes or until tender. Rub through a coarse sieve and reheat. Blend remaining 3 tablespoons butter or chicken fat with flour and add hot milk. Cook until thickened, stirring constantly. Add onion purée. Season. Serves 5.

Vegetable Beef Soup

[*Mrs. G. Earl Chick, Augusta, Me.*]

4 pounds shin of beef
10 cups water
½ cup diced onions
¼ cup diced carrots
¼ cup diced celery
¼ cup diced turnip (optional)
2 whole cloves
1 bay leaf
2 teaspoons salt

Put soup bone on to cook in cold water and cook until meat falls from bone. Set away to cool. Remove the fat and bones; cut the meat in small cubes and add the vegetables and seasonings. Simmer until vegetables are tender. Remove cloves and bay leaf. Makes about 2½ quarts.

✱ *In making soup, use whatever vegetables your family likes, whatever is in season, and plenty of imagination. Here is a partial list of vegetables and herbs that may be used to vary the flavor of this soup: ¼ cup diced green pepper, a nip of ground pepper; 1 cup lima beans, ¼ cup shell beans, ¼ cup green peas, dried tops of fresh celery, 2 tomatoes, 2 sprigs parsley, ¼ cup mushrooms, 1 tablespoon catsup, 1 tablespoon of sugar, a dash of nutmeg, 1 tablespoon of vinegar, 3 sprigs thyme, 1 sprig marjoram, 1 peppercorn.*

Mutton Broth

Substitute 2 pounds breast of mutton for shin of beef in recipe above. Add 2 tablespoons pearl barley, soaked overnight in cold water. Omit turnip and cloves. Strain. Makes 2 quarts.

Martha's Vineyard Chicken Chowder

[*Mrs. Irving F. Maxson, Vineyard Haven, Mass.*]

1 6-pound fowl
2 quarts cold water
¼ pound salt pork, cubed
2 medium-sized onions, sliced
4 cups hot water
8 cups diced potatoes
1 tablespoon salt
4 cups milk, scalded
2 tablespoons butter

The day before this chowder is to be served, clean fowl and cut in pieces, cover with cold water, heat slowly to the boiling point, simmer, covered, 3 hours, or until tender. When done, remove chicken, cut meat in dice. Allow liquor to become cold, remove fat, then return chicken meat to the liquor.

The following day try out salt pork, remove cracklings, add onions and cook very slowly until onions are light brown. Place onions and pork fat in a large kettle, add hot water, potatoes, and salt. Simmer until potatoes are tender. Bring chicken liquor and meat to a boil and boil (not simmer) for 10 minutes. Add milk and butter. Combine the two mixtures. Some Islanders thicken the chowder slightly. Others do not. Serves 12.

✻ *During the summer months the Farmers' Co-operative Market opens twice a week in the Agricultural Hall in West Tisbury, Martha's Vineyard. The farmers supply Islanders and summer guests with fresh fruits and vegetables. Their wives offer cooked foods for sale which are distinctive to the Island, such as beach plum preserves, pastries, cakes, cookies, hot breads, and chicken chowder, one of the most famous of all Island dishes.*

Cream of Turkey or Chicken Soup

[A Vermont recipe]

½ cup finely chopped celery
3 cups turkey or chicken stock
2 tablespoons flour
2 tablespoons butter
½ cup cream

Simmer the celery in the turkey or chicken stock until celery is tender. Thicken soup by blending butter and flour and adding soup gradually. Simmer 10 minutes. Add cream, heat, and serve. Serves 4.

Rhode Island Clambakes

Horace G. Belcher

It has been said that the chief contribution of the Indians to the New England pioneers was the clambake.

All along the shore line from Maine to Connecticut are found heaps of buried shells of the soft shell clam-heaps marking the old gathering places where the tribes assembled for their feasts of shellfish. For the Indians of all the New England tribes went down to the shore in summer for clambakes, just as the New England farmers did later. And the Indians enjoyed their bakes just as much.

While the white man has elaborated the bake, its essentials and the method of making it remain unchanged from those that the Red Man enjoyed. In the Indian clambake the clams, fish, and corn were all cooked in the steam from the clams and from rock-weed spread on hot stones; this was covered over to confine the steam. In the centuries since the first white man tasted the delectable results of this rude open-air cooking he has not improved on it.

The Indian and then the farmer went to the shore, dug his clams in flats exposed at low tide, found stones in the fields and with them made his bake. Later, some of the country churches began making an annual bake as a summer outing and several of these bakes are continued to this day. The Antiquarian Society bake, a Rehoboth, Massachusetts, fixture, used to draw 1500 or more, served in relays in a great tent; it is now reduced to about one third of that number. The Frenchtown bake, another annual Rhode Island feature in what is popularly known as South County although its official name is Washington County (formerly King's), is a popular one. And there are others. Many a political career has been boosted by speeches at some of these bakes.

Each bake has its own bakemaster who serves year after year, sometimes for half a lifetime. He supervises its preparation from the building of the fire to the placing of the clams and the rest of the bake. His judgment fixes the time for the opening bake and to him goes credit for its success. Bakemaking is an art not given to everyone and a good bakemaster is much sought after and proud of his skill.

But these country bakes came only once a year and Rhode Islanders and their visitors pined for an opportunity to enjoy this feast whenever they felt like it. The fame of the Rhode Island bake spread and with it a demand. And so in the latter part of the last century and in the earlier years of the present, the shores of upper Narragansett Bay were dotted with clambake resorts where bakes were served daily. These resorts were reached by big fleets of Bay steamboats running out of Providence and in their heyday many excursions were run to them from neighboring states.

The automobile has driven the sidewheel passenger steamboat of a more leisurely period from Narragansett's waters. Where once stood Field's Point, whose chowder was famous, is now a Providence municipal dock. But two of these old clambake resorts—Rocky Point and Crescent Park, both near Providence—still serve bakes daily in the summer, and the secret of the Field's Point chowder has not been lost.

The Clambake Club at Newport is an adjunct to Bailey's Beach where Society bathes; and the Squantum Association and the Pomham Club, both just outside Providence, serve weekly bakes to their members. Squantum, where Presidents and titled guests have dined, has another famous clam chowder, still made as it was when this exclusive organization was founded during the time that Grant ran for re-election. Guest registers of Squantum and Pomham contain the names of many of the nation's most distinguished men. But their bakes differ only in detail and in their elaboration from the public bakes; and wherever you may get your bake you will find it made in the same way.

Opinions may differ as to whether a clam chowder should be made with milk or should include tomatoes; two propositions good for an argument wherever chowder and bakes are known, but no one ever disputes the old Indian method of making a bake.

The Rhode Island bake is made with soft-shell clams preferably about two inches long. On a layer of stones, each about the size of a man's head, is built a fire of cordwood which is allowed to burn until the stones are heated white hot. Then the embers are removed with six-tined potato diggers and pitchforks, the stones are swept clean of ashes and a thick layer of rockweed, a marine growth found along the shores of Rhode Island, is thrown on the hot stones. A good fire will have the stones white hot and ready in about an hour. At clambake resorts the stones are heated on a cement platform.

In rapid succession the ingredients of the bake are placed on the steaming rockweed whose salty moisture cooks them and whose flavor permeates them. First the clams, then another layer of rockweed, then white and sweet potatoes still in their skins, sweet corn covered with a thin layer of husks, fish in cloth or paper bags (bluefish by preference although mackerel will do), small sausages or buckworsts similarly wrapped, lobsters or chickens or both, although strictly speaking the chicken does not belong in a Rhode Island bake.

Then the whole is covered with a thick wet canvas which is

kept wet during the baking. The steam from the moisture of the clams and the rockweed permeates, "tenderizes," and flavors everything. This steam is carefully confined, for the edges of the canvas are kept covered with rockweed and held down with stones. Even then, the mouth-watering odor of the bake escapes during the forty-five minutes or more it takes to cook the bake.

On the tables you will find sliced cucumbers, sliced tomatoes, sliced raw onions, brown bread, white bread, butter, pepper, salt, vinegar, pepper-sauce, small pitchers of melted butter. The first course is clam chowder, which may be made of soft-shell clams alone, or of the hard-shell clam, which here is known by its Indian name of quahog, or of both. In most cases your clam chowder is made from quahogs, but the best chowder is from equal portions of both soft- and hard-shell clams, flavored with the quahog liquor and with the results of trying out minced salt pork.

With the chowder are served hot clam-cakes or clam fritters, delectable concoctions of dough containing chopped quahogs that give them an incomparable flavor. Dropped from a spoon, the cakes, which take odd, irregular shapes, are fried in deep fat to a golden brown. Properly made they are light, and eaten hot they fairly melt in your mouth. A clam-cake in the left hand and a spoonful of chowder thickened with pilot bread (a flaky hard cracker of nutty flavor) in the right is the proper procedure, repeated to taste; and there is something wrong with your appetite if you do not have a second helping of chowder from the big tureen set on the table. At private bakes chowder, clam-cakes, and little-necks (young quahogs about the size of a half-dollar) are served for luncheon, the bake being opened in the late afternoon, five or six o'clock.

When the bake is opened, tin dishes holding two quarts of clams are served to each guest. You spread the clam shells apart with your fingers, remove the covering of the clam snout, take the clam by the snout and dip it in a small dish in which you have placed a quantity of hot melted butter with a little vinegar or perhaps a dash of pepper-sauce. Then you eat the clams with the exception of the snout, which is tough. The taste is something to remember.

Between times you may drink a cup or so of the clam broth, which you will find fit for the gods and a stomach-settler. After the hot clams come more hot clams—and all the other good things that were in the bake. If the bake is properly made, you will find you can eat clams until the cows come home. When you feel you cannot eat another mouthful, watermelon or, if you are especially fortunate, baked Indian pudding made of Indean meal, molasses, and milk and baked long in a slow oven, is brought on. And at the clambake clubs the bake ends with clear coffee. It is a meal you will never forget—and if you do your duty by the bake you will not need another meal that day.

A family bake or one for a small group may easily be made in a barrel. The best barrel bake I know of is that of Captain Herbert M. Knowles, long superintendent of the Third Life Saving District before the U. S. Life Saving Service was incorporated in the Coast Guard. Here is Captain Knowles' bake:

"Make cheesecloth bags for clams, sweet and Irish potatoes, corn and everything except lobsters, chicken, and fish provided you include these. The bag for clams should be broad enough to allow the clams to spread out over the barrel. The fish should be split in half and placed on shingles wrapped in cheesecloth, so each piece may be handled by unwrapping the cloth and sliding onto a platter. Lobsters may be thrown in the bake in any way.

"Stones about the size of two bowls put together are about the right size. Wood should be packed up crossways, with shavings, etc., underneath, and the stones packed in with the wood up toward the top of the barrel before lighting. Then add wood until the stones get hot. They turn white when of the proper heat. Set the barrel as deeply into sand as you wish. You cannot get it too deep. Put about three inches of sand or gravel in the bottom of the barrel and place pieces of scrap sheet iron around the sides of the barrel. These scraps can be had at any tin shop without cost. The sand and scrap iron prevent the stones from burning the bottom and sides of the barrel. The stones are picked up with a six-tine fork when hot and packed around well. If hot enough they will break and stow well.

"Be sure to have everything for the bake ready to go in the barrel as soon as the stones are put in. The green corn husks should be soaked in salt water and added with the first layer of rockweed over the stones. Then lay in the clam bag, spreading it out as much as possible. Pack your lobsters around this; then lay in the potatoes, fish, chicken, and such other things as you may add.

"Spread a wet or moist bag over the bake and fill the barrel up tightly with wet sea weed. If you have a washtub handy turn it over the top of the barrel and apply wet seaweed around it to hold in the steam.

"Hold your ear to the side of the barrel when you hear the ingredients of the bake growling, which should be within a few minutes after steam starts making; you will know that all is well. The bake should be ready to open in about forty-five minutes to an hour from that time. I never saw one cooked too long and I once had one in about three hours. To my surprise, it turned out to be one of the best bakes I ever had.

"Saving the corn husks, and soaking them to lay over the stones with the seaweed, gives the bake a sweetness which cannot be obtained in any other way."

Albert A. Slocum, who served bakes daily at his place on Pawtuxet Cove, Rhode Island, gave these suggestions for a barrel bake:

"In building the fire, put a flat stone under the lower ends of the wood for a draft, first placing the wood in the form of a square, and then crossing the other sticks east and west. Pile stones on the wood. Avoid granite stones which crumble in heat. Have the stones white hot.

"Put a foot or so of rockweed over the stones in the barrel, first cutting a hole four inches long in the bottom of the barrel for drainage. The hole must be near the point where the head joins the staves, and the barrel must be tipped to aid flow of drainage. Put six inches of rockweed in bottom of barrel, then stones, then a big handful of rockweed over the hot stones. Turn in the clams, a bushel being necessary to furnish sufficient steam for cooking all the features of a bake. Then add sausage, corn, and the rest and cover all with a piece of clean canvas, binding down the edges to keep steam in. A dozen stones of fair size will cook anything. Cook a half hour or more.

"Be sure to permit free egress of water from the bake, through the hole made in the bottom of the barrel for that purpose. This water will rush out in a stream, the presence of which is a sure sign of success for the bake."

Try it yourself sometime—if you can get the necessary fixings. If not, come to Rhode Island, where we know how to make clambakes.

Fish: Shell, Salt, and Fresh

Broiled Fish

Broiled fish has an especially fine flavor. Brush whole fish with vegetable oil and lay on broiler rack. (Fillets and steaks should be laid directly on well-greased broiler pan, either side up.) Season with salt, pepper, and paprika.

Broil fish 3 to 4 inches from heat. Do not overcook or fish will be dry. Test with a fork; when fish flakes easily, it is done. Lean fish should be basted frequently with butter.

Broil fillets, thin steaks, fish sticks, and split fish 4 to 8 minutes. Do not turn.

Broil steaks 3 to 5 minutes; turn, broil 8 to 10 minutes longer.

Broil whole fish 5 minutes; turn, broil 8 to 12 minutes longer. Dot fish with butter and garnish with parsley and lemon wedges.

Whole frozen fish and thick steaks are best defrosted before broiling.

To remove fish from broiler use pancake turner or slide carefully off foil.

✻ *Foil-Broil: To save the bother of scrubbing a messy broiler, line a pan with aluminum foil cut ½ inch larger than pan. (This may be a broiler pan—rack removed—or any shallow pan.) Put 2 or 3 tablespoons vegetable oil on foil. Swish fish in oil, coating it on both sides. Season and broil according to directions above. When done, throw away foil and give three cheers at dishwashing time!*

Baked Stuffed Fish

[*For a whole fish weighing 3 to 5 pounds, dressed*]

Foil-line and add shortening to a baking pan (as above). Season inside of fish; stuff lightly with stuffing (½ recipe page 94). Sew edges with coarse thread. Cut 2 or 3 gashes across top of fish to hold its shape while baking. Dot fish with butter, using at least 4 tablespoons; or insert gashes with fat salt pork or bacon slices. Sprinkle with paprika. Gather foil loosely around fish, keeping top uncovered to brown. Bake 40 to 60 minutes at 350° F. Spoon drippings over fish, season, and serve with lemon wedges.

Shallow-Fried Fish

[*To get a crisp golden crust as in deep-fat frying. For small whole fish, fillets cut in serving-size portions, and fish sticks*]

In a deep skillet or saucepan heat ⅛ inch fat very hot but not smoking. Dip seasoned fish in slightly beaten egg mixed with 1 tablespoon water; then dip in either cornmeal, flour, bread or cracker crumbs, or pancake mix. Fry until brown on both sides, 5 to 10 minutes. Drain on absorbent paper. Serve piping hot with your favorite fish sauce.

Deep-Fat Fried Fish

Bread fish as you would for shallow-fried fish. Fry in hot deep fat (375° F.) in deep kettle, using frying basket. Fish will become crisp and brown in 2 to 8 minutes, depending on thickness. Drain.

Poached Fish

Place fish steak or fillets in skillet with simmering water that barely covers. Season with salt, parsley, celery, onion, and peppercorns. Simmer, covered, until fish flakes easily with a fork, 8 to 12 minutes. Serve with a rich sauce. A 1-pound fish serves 2 or 3.

Super Swordfish

[*A modern Yankee recipe.*]

Squeeze juice of ½ lemon over a 1-inch-thick swordfish steak. Add salt and pepper and a slice of Velveeta cheese; cover with buttered bread crumbs. Bake ½ hour in moderate oven, 350° F.

* *Fish may be wrapped in cheesecloth to handle more easily. Cod, flounder, haddock and halibut are excellent poached.*

Fluffy Fish Cakes

1½ cups shredded codfish
4 medium-sized potatoes
⅓ cup light cream
1 egg, beaten
½ teaspoon pepper

Freshen codfish (page 31). Peel and dice potatoes, then add to fish and boil until potatoes are soft. Drain. Add egg, pepper, and cream and heat until fluffy. Form into balls or cakes, roll in finely crushed cornflakes, and pan-fry or fry in hot deep fat until golden brown. Drain. Makes 16 balls.

* *If time is a factor, use ½ package instant mashed potatoes cooked according to directions. Cook fish until tender before adding the packaged product.*

Eating fish balls for Sunday morning breakfast is part of Boston's tradition, like taking visitors to see the glass flowers.

New England Salt Fish Dinner

[*"Picked Fish"—it's sometimes called*]

2 pounds salt cod
8 medium sized potatoes
6 medium sized beets
½ pound fat salt pork
4 tablespoons flour
2 cups milk

* *There are two ways to freshen salt cod:*

I

Place fish on wooden strips (clothespins will do) or silverware in a large kettle of water. The flesh side should be down so that salt, when extracted, can sink to the bottom of the kettle. Do not allow water to become more than warm. Soak overnight or until sufficiently fresh.

The other way:

II

Place fish in a kettle of cold water, heat water to a point just below boiling; pour off water and start all over again. Three changes of water is usually enough. Tasting is the only sure way to tell exactly how many changes of water are required. After fish has been freshened, simmer until tender in water just below the boiling point. This takes only a very few minutes. Do not at any time boil fish, as boiling makes it tough. Fish is done when it will flake if broken.

Boil the potatoes. Boil and dice the beets. Slice the salt pork into thin strips and cut in fine pieces. Try out slowly, drain, and return 4 tablespoons of the fat to the frying pan. Blend the flour with the hot fat, add the milk slowly, stirring so that gravy will be smooth. Season to taste with salt and pepper. Keep hot.

Place freshened fish on a hot platter with a generous sprinkling of bits of crisp, fried salt pork on top. Surround the fish with a red border of diced buttered beets. Serve potatoes and gravy separately. Complete the meal with squares of golden corn bread flanked by cottage cheese and boiled apple cider sauce. Boiled onions and boiled carrots are sometimes served with this dinner. Serves 6 to 8.

* *Codfish used to come in huge, whole fish that were hung in the cellarway or nailed to the barn door of New England farm homes. Pieces were freshened and made into salt fish dinner, fried with salt pork scraps, served with egg sauce, or made into fish cakes or chowders. Pieces were also broiled over the coals, then boiling water was poured on them, to soften, and they were sent to the table dripping with butter.*

Never cut salt fish; tear it apart.

Red Fish Hash

1 cup cold boiled or baked potatoes
1 cup boiled beets
1 cup left-over cooked salt cod
¼ cup milk
pepper

Chop potatoes, beets and codfish to a fine hash; moisten with milk; season. Brown in a skillet well greased with butter. Serves 4.

* *Fish Hash, another famous Yankee dish, is made according to this same recipe, omitting the beets.*

Scalloped Cod Cheeks and Tongues

Dip cheeks and tongues in milk, roll in flour, and pan-fry in butter until a golden brown. Over them pour freshly browned butter, flavored with lemon juice. Add a sprinkling of chopped parsley. One pound of codfish cheeks and tongues serves 4.

Baked Salt Mackerel

Freshen mackerel (page 31). Drain, place in a foil-lined greased pan, skin side up. Bake in a moderate oven (350° F.) 15 minutes. Pour off any liquid that may be in the pan; add 2 cups thin cream and bake 15 minutes longer, or until fish is light brown and flakes easily with a fork. Allow ½ pound mackerel per person.

Baked Fresh Mackerel

Clean and split large mackerel and rub with salt and pepper. Place skin side down on foil-lined greased baking pan. Pour 1 cup milk over fish. Bake uncovered in moderately hot oven (375° F.) 20 to 25 minutes. Mackerel is also delicious broiled. (See page 28 for easy directions.)

✻ *Boston mackerel is a fat fish and should not be fried, nor should fat be added in the cooking process. It should be boiled, broiled, or baked.*

Eight or nine years ago mackerel almost entirely disappeared. There was a prediction that this branch of the industry had passed out. However, within the past four or five years larger schools of fish have made their appearance than at any time during the past twenty years. It is nothing unusual for fishermen to report acres and acres of swimming, feeding mackerel through which their boats plow their way, literally pushing the fish aside as they go. A net almost a mile long and one hundred twenty-five feet deep is run around the "school"—the ends brought together and a rope in the bottom pulled—causing the net to take the shape of a saucepan and entrap the whole "school." Quite often mackerel fishermen will leave Boston Fish Pier one day and return the next with a large trip of fish that have scarcely stopped wiggling.

Jimmie's Finnan Haddie

Order a split smoked haddock (not individual fillets) cut in individual servings. Place skin side down in shallow baking dish and add enough rich milk to partially cover fish. Dot with butter. Sprinkle with pepper. Place shallow pan under flame of pre-heated broiler and broil until fish is tender, about 20 minutes. Baste with hot milk before serving. Allow ½ pound of fish per person. The milk remaining in the pan makes a delicious bouillon.

* *This recipe comes from Jimmie's Harborside, Boston. Although this restaurant is run by "Jimmie, the Greek," epicures agree that some of the best sea food in Boston is served here. Jimmie is particularly famous for his finnan haddie. Some restaurants serve it with egg sauce or oyster sauce.*

Finnan haddie is, strictly speaking, a Scotch and not a Yankee dish. It gets its title from the reputation of the haddock cured around Findon, a fishing village near Aberdeen, Scotland. Once our American supply was almost entirely imported, but now the great bulk of it, and some of the very finest, comes from New England.

Finnan Haddie Pie

Cover 1 pound finnan haddie with milk and soak 1 hour. Bring slowly almost to the boiling point, cool, drain, and flake. Add to 2 cups medium white sauce, made without salt. Pour into a buttered baking dish. Cover with individual baking-powder biscuits rolled ½ inch thick. Bake in hot oven (400° F.) 15 to 20 minutes or until biscuits are brown. Serves 4.

Two chopped hard-boiled eggs may be added to cream sauce.

Creamed Salt Codfish

Freshen 1 cup salt codfish (page 31). Simmer gently about 5 minutes, or until fish is tender. Drain, reheat fish in 1 cup thin white sauce with salt omitted. Season; serve with baked or boiled potatoes. Hard-boiled eggs may be sliced over the creamed fish.

✻ *It is said that fishermen originally believed the cod became "the sacred cod" because it was the fish that Christ used when He multiplied the fish and fed the multitude, and even today the marks of His thumbs and forefingers are plainly visible on the codfish. His Satanic majesty stood by and said he, too, could multiply fish and feed multitudes. Reaching for one of the fish it wriggled and slid through his red-hot fingers, burning two black stripes down its side and thus clearly differentiating the haddock with its stripes from the sacred cod. These markings, in actual practice, do distinguish one variety from the other. These two fish contribute to the greater portion of the New England catch and are similar in taste and texture. For many years, haddock was not considered a suitable fish for marketing and very little of it was caught, but recently its popularity has increased, until today in New England, there is approximately three times as much haddock marketed as cod.*

Fillet Broiled with Puffy Sauce

[*Mrs. Carl Sullivan, Foxboro, Mass.*]

Foil-broil 2 fillets of flounder, sole, or any white-meat fish (page 28). Combine ½ cup mayonnaise, 3 tablespoons chopped parsley, 3 tablespoons chopped pickle and a dash of cayenne. Beat 1 egg white until stiff and fold into mayonnaise mixture. Spread over fillets and place again under broiler just until sauce becomes puffy and light brown. Serve immediately. Serves 4 to 6.

Creamed Fish

- ¼ cup butter
- ¼ cup flour
- 2 cups milk
- 2 cups cooked or canned fish, flaked
- 2 eggs, beaten
- 2 tablespoons chopped green pepper
- salt and pepper

Melt butter, blend in flour, add milk slowly. Stir and cook until sauce is thickened. Add fish and cook slowly until fish is heated. Add eggs quickly, stirring constantly and taking care that mixture does not boil. Add green pepper, season to taste, and remove from heat. Serves 4.

* *A variety of fish or seafood may be used in this recipe. Cod, haddock, finnan haddie, crab, shrimp, salmon, lobster, and tuna are among the possibilities. Serve over rice, noodles, or toast. A green salad is a fine accompaniment.*

Tunaburgers

- 3 English muffins, split
- 1 7-ounce tin tuna
- ½ cup mayonnaise
- ¼ cup chopped green pepper
- ¼ cup chopped celery

Place muffin halves on cookie sheet, cut side up, toast lightly and butter. Blend remaining ingredients and spread on muffins. Broil 4 inches from heat until mixture begins to bubble, 6 to 8 minutes. Serve with wedges of tomato or deviled eggs. Serves 3.

Baked Fish with Sour Cream

[*A modern Yankee recipe from Mrs. Gordon Shand, East Sandwich, Mass.*]

¼ cup butter
½ cup grated Parmesan cheese
1 cup sour cream
1 pound flounder fillets

Melt butter, stir in the cheese and cream. Spoon half this sauce over half the fillets in buttered baking dish. Repeat. Bake at 375° F. 12 to 15 minutes, uncovered, or until fish flakes easily with a fork and sauce is golden. Serves 4 to 6.

Connecticut Kedgeree

2 cups cooked rice
2 cups cooked flaked fish
4 hard-cooked eggs, chopped
2 tablespoons minced parsley
½ cup top milk
salt and pepper

To hot rice add remaining ingredients and reheat in double boiler. Serve immediately. Serves 5.

* *Many dishes identified with New England had their origin in foreign lands and were brought to this country by our sea-faring forebears. This particular dish may be traced back to the Armenian dish, Kidgeri. Yankee housewives, unacquainted with eggplant, in long-ago days, evidently thought eggs would do just as well. Then someone tried fish instead of lamb. By such steps this recipe evolved, and in its present form has been handed down in a Westport, Conn., family since the days of Clipper ships.*

Warwick Molded Salmon

1 cup milk, scalded
1 cup bread crumbs
1-pound can salmon
3 eggs, beaten
½ teaspoon salt
1 teaspoon lemon juice

Combine milk and crumbs and cook until mixture is smooth. Flake salmon, remove skin and bones. Combine remaining ingredients and pour into oiled bread pan. Place in pan of hot water and bake in moderate oven (350° F.) 1 hour. Unmold and serve with Egg Sauce (page 39) or Cucumber Sauce. Serves 4.

CUCUMBER SAUCE

Whip ½ cup heavy cream; add 1½ tablespoons tarragon vinegar and 1 cucumber, pared, chopped, and well drained. Season with salt and a dash of cayenne. Sour cream may be substituted for whipped cream, but go easy on the vinegar.

✻ *Everyone knows the Yankee is ingenious. A Yankee left his native soil, traveled out to the West Coast, and went to look at the big salmon-canning factories. Smart Westerners saw a chance to unload a "dead horse" on the newcomer. They were running a cannery that unfortunately was not making money—most of the salmon readily available to it was of the pink variety, rather than the red that John Q. Public, for no good reason, has come to think of as being the only first-class kind. Well, the Westerners sold their factory to the Yank and went off chuckling. But not for long. Reports began to get around that he was making money hand over fist. How come? Quite simple, really. He had pink salmon to sell and being a Yank, he found out how to sell it. Every can bore the label—"Finest Pink Salmon—guaranteed not to turn red in the can."*

Boiled Salmon

Wrap a fresh salmon steak in cheesecloth. Simmer gently in 1 quart of boiling water to which has been added ½ teaspoon salt and 2 teaspoons vinegar. Simmer 6 to 8 minutes per pound of fish. Serve plain with Egg Sauce or Cucumber Sauce (page 38). For each person to be served, allow ½ pound of steak.

EGG SAUCE

Add 2 cubed hard-cooked eggs to 1 cup of medium white sauce.

* *The correct menu for the Fourth of July in some parts of New England, particularly around Boston, is fresh salmon, new peas, and boiled potatoes. Strawberry shortcake is served for dessert.*

"Cape Cod Turkey" with Egg Sauce

Remove head and tail from a 4-pound haddock or codfish; split and wipe with wet cloth. Sprinkle inside with a cup of salt. Let stand overnight. In the morning remove salt, rinse thoroughly, tie in cheesecloth and simmer gently about 30 minutes, or until fish is done. Place fish on a platter, surround with boiled potatoes of uniform size and small boiled buttered beets; also with fried salt pork scraps. Serve with egg sauce made by adding hard-cooked eggs to drawn butter or according to Egg Sauce recipe above. Serves 6.

* *Dishes of mashed summer or winter squash, boiled onions, and hot corn bread were often served with this dinner. Left-over fish was made into a dish called "Picked Fish." Bits of the fish were flaked, heated in cream sauce, sprinkled with parsley, and served over mashed potato*

or buttered toast. Salt Fish Dinner (see page 31) was also referred to as "Picked Fish."

The origin of the name "Cape Cod turkey" is obscure. It has come to mean cooked fish; what kind doesn't matter unless you are literal. If you are, it means baked stuffed codfish well-larded with salt pork.

One explanation of the term centers about Thanksgiving. The traditional food for that day was, and still is, turkey. Turkey meant thankfulness to God for his bounty. However, without the fishing industry the colonists would have had very little to be thankful for. No doubt the term "Cape Cod turkey" was started by some wit, which shows that even in early times life was not all drab.

Both the Pilgrims who settled at Plymouth and the Puritans who settled in Boston turned to fishing as a means of livelihood, and codfish was the most profitable product of the deep.

When some of the Plymouth group made money enough to settle in Boston with established businesses, they were referred to as "codfish aristocracy." Although the codfish were a great source of trade, references were derogatory.

Then, too, the Irish in and around Boston used the term "Cape Cod turkey" to refer to their Friday meal of fish. Fish, and particularly salt fish, seemed to taste better if it bore the more aristocratic name "Cape Cod turkey."

Fillet of Halibut—Point Shirley Style

[*Parker House, Boston, Mass.*]

Fillet the halibut, removing skin and all bones. Season with salt and pepper. Dip in melted butter and sprinkle with bread crumbs. Lay in richly buttered pan. Baste each fillet with butter and bake in moderately hot oven (375° F.), until tender, about 20 minutes. Serve with own juice and a freshly boiled potato.

Broiled Scrod

[*Sheraton-Plaza, Boston, is famous for this dish*]

Select a young, fresh codfish and scrape to remove the scales, being careful not to break the skin. Cut into fillets without removing the skin. Season lightly to taste with salt and pepper, and then sprinkle with melted butter. Dip in fresh bread crumbs; sprinkle again with a little more melted butter. Start the broiling with the flesh side down, and when broiling with the skin side down, use care not to allow the skin to break. Serve very hot with a bowl of melted butter with a little lemon juice stirred in. Allow ½ to ¾ pound of fish for each person to be served.

✱ *The sacred cod, six-foot emblem of the Commonwealth of Massachusetts, hangs in the Spectators' Lobby of the State House, in Boston, where it is viewed each year by thousands of sightseers. Only once in over 240 years has this august plaque been absent from its accustomed place. In April, 1933, a group of Harvard students carried it off as a prank. When it was reported lost, hell broke loose in Boston. Twenty-four hectic hours passed and the police had no clue. Then came a tip that the fish was in a crate in an M.I.T. building. Investigation did, indeed, disclose a huge crate, but upon being opened the crate contained not the six-foot cod, but a sardine! Several days passed. The sacred cod was front-page news in the Boston newspapers; the Harvard "Lampoon" offered a reward. At last it was found. It was thrown from a speeding car into the arms of an astonished policeman. Whether the "Lampoon" was responsible for its disappearance, or the little green men who live at the bottom of the Charles River, no one dares to state positively.*

Broiled Scrod

[*Parker House, Boston, Mass.*]

Split a young codfish and remove all bones. Sprinkle with salt and pepper and dip in olive oil. Again sprinkle with salt and pepper and dip in bread crumbs and broil on a medium fire (charcoal is best) about 20 minutes, or until tender. Put on hot platter and cover lightly with butter to which chopped parsley and a little lemon juice have been added. One-half to ¾ pound scrod serves 1 person.

* *In the fish industry, scrod has come to mean haddock under 2½ pounds. The correct definition of scrod is a small fish prepared for planking.*

Baked Striped Bass

Place a 3-pound dressed fish (striper, lake trout, cod, haddock, or other delicately flavored fish) in baking dish lined with well-buttered foil. Season fish inside and out with salt, pepper, and a little onion salt. Sift a thin film of flour over fish. Pour on 2 cups rich milk or undiluted evaporated milk and dot generously with butter. Bake at 350° F. 40 minutes, or until fish flakes easily with a fork and milk is cooked down to a thick sauce. Serve with a sprinkling of paprika. Serves 4.

Martha's Vineyard Eel Stifle

1 quart potatoes
4 onions
2 pounds ells, skinned
salt and pepper
flour
¼ pound salt pork, diced and fried
water

Slice potatoes and onions, cut eels in small pieces, and line a kettle with a layer of potatoes and onions, then a layer of eels. Season with salt and pepper, sprinkle a little flour between each layer; top with salt pork scraps and add pork fat. Add water almost to cover. Cook until tender. Serves 6 to 8.

* *All good Island cooks know what Eel Stifle is, and very few visitors ever leave the Island without having a taste of this popular Vineyard dish.*

Fried Eels

Skin and soak ells in salted water for several hours. Wash, skin, and cut in slices. Parboil in skim milk for 5 minutes. Remove, roll in cornmeal, and pan-fry in salt pork drippings until crisp and brown.

* *Eels are occasionally found in New England waters today, but like salmon, shad, and alewives were barred from many rivers years ago by impassable dams. In the early fall eels used to migrate up the rivers and were taken by means of sluiceways that ran into an "eel pot." Hauls of a hundred or more at night were not uncommon at the time of the year when they returned. Now they are available in many Italian fish markets during the winter months.*

Fried Smelts

Clean, wash, and dry smelts. Roll in seasoned flour. Beat 1 egg slightly, add 2 tablespoons water. Dip floured fish in egg, then roll in fine bread crumbs or cornmeal. Fry in hot deep fat (370° F.) until smelts are a golden brown, about 4 minutes. Or pan-fry, turning so that smelts will brown evenly. Drain, serve with Tartar Sauce (page 59). Smelts may also be foil-broiled (page 28).

Trout Over A Campfire

Sharpen a hardwood stick and push it down the backbone of the tiny fin near the tail. Push the other end of the stick into the earth near the embers. Cook until done.

Broiled Trout

Follow directions for Foil-Broiled Fish, page 28.

* *Trout may also be rolled in equal parts of cornmeal and flour and pan-fried in butter or bacon fat, uncovered, to brown; then covered and cooked slowly until done. No fish is more fitted to grace a silver platter garnished with yellow half moons of lemon and crisp cress. Brook trout is equally at home cooked over the embers of a fisherman's campfire where its tantalizing odor drifts away to blend with the spice of balsam thickets.*

Trout with Almonds

Dust 4 trout with flour; make a small slit in the thickest part of the fillet. Season; brown in frying pan in 6 tablespoons butter. Lay fish carefully on platter. Add 1 cup of slivered blanched almonds to butter in pan; cook slowly to brown. Add juice of ½ lemon and pour mixture over trout. Sprinkle with finely chopped parsley. Serves 2.

Crabs, Hard and Soft Shell

* *All crabs have a hard shell except during the moulting season when the shell is soft. Crabs are at their best in late summer. Watch out for your fingers when you catch them. The little rascals can nip like the dickens!*

Boiled Crabs

Place 12 hard-shell live crabs in 3 quarters salted, boiling water, handling them with tongs. Cover and return to boil. Simmer for 15 minutes. Drain. Serve hot or cold with Lemon Butter (below) or mayonnaise. Serves 2 or 3.

* *Six crabs yield about 1 cup meat.*

Fried Soft-Shell Crabs

Cut off face, just back of eyes. Remove apron and spongy parts under the points of the body covering. Rinse and drain. Follow directions for Shallow-Fried Fish or Deep-Fat Fried Fish (page 29). Twelve crabs serve 4.

Quick Creamed Crab Meat

Combine 1 cup crab meat (canned, frozen, or fresh) with 1 can frozen shrimp soup or 1 can mushroom soup. Serve over toast or rice or as a sauce for poached fish. Serves 3. Add 1 tablespoon dry mustard to this recipe for Deviled Crab.

COLD BUTTER DRESSING FOR FRIED FISH

Cream ½ cup butter; gradually work in ¼ teaspoon salt, sprinkling of pepper, and 2 teaspoons lemon juice. When well blended, work in 1 teaspoon minced parsley or cress. Form into balls and place in refrigerator to harden. Serve one with each portion of fish.

LEMON BUTTER

6 tablespoons melted butter
½ teaspoon salt
⅛ teaspoon pepper
2 teaspoons lemon juice

Blend and serve hot with seafood, fish, or vegetables.

Connecticut Stuffed Baked Shad

1 large shad, about 5 pounds
1 cup cracker crumbs
¼ cup melted butter
¼ teaspoon salt
¼ pound bacon strips
¼ teaspoon pepper
1 small onion, minced
1 teaspoon sage
1 cup hot water

Leave head and tail on fish; clean and dry. Make a dressing of the cracker crumbs, melted butter, salt, pepper, onion, and sage. Stuff shad and sew the edges together. Place on foil-lined pan, well buttered, or rack in baking pan. Add water. Fasten strips of bacon (or salt pork) on the fish with toothpick. Bake in a hot oven (400° F.) for 10 minutes. Then reduce heat to moderately slow (325° F.) and bake for about 35 minutes, basting frequently to keep fish tender and well browned. Serve on hot platter. Serves 6.

Broiled Shad Roe

Dip shad roe in melted butter and lay on foil-lined broiler pan, well buttered. Broil 8 to 10 minutes, turning once and basting frequently with melted butter. Season with salt and pepper. (Worcestershire is optional.) Serve with crisp bacon. Three shad roe will serve 6.

* *Shad is one of the fish that run up the New England rivers in spring. The blooming of the shad bushes, all snowy white, is supposed to herald their coming in northern New England. In southern New England they come in March. Like salmon, shad look for fresh water to spawn. Shad average about 1½ feet long and weigh about 4 pounds. The flesh is dark pink in color and has a distinctive flavor. The roe is exceedingly choice.*

Filene's Sea Food Newburg

[*Restaurant operated by Filene's, Boston, Mass.*]

2 littleneck clams
¼ cup lobster meat
¼ cup crab flakes
¼ cup shrimp
paprika
salt and pepper
4 tablespoons butter
1 tablespoon sherry wine
1 cup cream
3 yolks of eggs, slightly beaten
1 tablespoon lemon juice

Sauté clams, lobster, crab flakes, shrimp, and paprika in 2 tablespoons butter for a few minutes. Add sherry wine; toss over fire few minutes more, then add ¾ cup cream, let come to a boil. Add the balance of cream in which the yolks of eggs have been slightly beaten. Keep stirring all the time until thick, remove from fire. Put in lemon juice, salt, pepper, and 2 tablespoons butter. Serve hot on toast or in chafing dish. Do not allow to boil after adding yolks. Serves 2.

Easiest Baked Scallops

[*Maine Department of Sea and Shore Fisheries*]

Wash 1 pound scallops and drain on paper towels. Cut off hard piece on side. Roll in seasoned flour. Set scallops into a greased pie plate. Dot with butter and pour around them coffee cream to come about half way up on the scallops. Bake 30 to 40 minutes at 350° F. Serves 3.

Fried Scallops

[*Union Oyster House, Boston, Mass.*]

Roll a handful of sea or Cape scallops in flour, then dip them in egg wash (1 egg beaten with 1 tablespoon milk). Take the scallops from the egg wash and roll in equal parts of crumbs and flour mixed together. Fry in hot deep fat (375° F.) for 5 minutes, or until brown. Drain. One pint scallops serves 4.

Boiled Live Lobster

Plunge lobster in a large kettle of rapidly boiling water, adding 1 tablespoon salt for each quart water. When water has returned to a full boil, cover kettle and simmer 20 minutes for a 2-pound lobster. Remove and place on back to drain. Cut in half lengthwise with a sharp knife and crack claws. Take out intestinal vein and stomach but do not discard green liver or coral roe. Serve with Lemon Butter (page 45). Allow 1 small lobster per person. Corn pudding (page 107) is a delicious accompaniment to either hot or cold lobster.

✱ *Mrs. Kenneth Cushman, Falmouth, Maine, says Down-Easters like to boil lobsters in salt water right out of the ocean. It often pays to buy a 15- or 20-pound lobster, cook it, and freeze the meat. A large lobster is done when long, red head "feelers" are easily pulled from socket.*

Lobster À La Newburg

[*Union Oyster House, Boston, Mass.*]

Melt 1 tablespoon of butter in a pan, then add ¼ pound lobster meat. Stir until the meat is braised, about 5 minutes. Add 2 tablespoons sherry.

In another bowl, mix the yolk of an egg and 2 tablespoons of cornstarch. Dissolve this mixture in a pint of milk and then add it to the braised lobster meat. Put on low fire and let simmer, stirring constantly. Season and serve on hot toast. Serves 1 or 2.

Broiled Live Lobster

[*Toll House, Whitman, Mass.*]

If possible have lobsters split at the market. Otherwise hold large claws firmly. With a sharp pointed knife begin at mouth and make incision, then split the shell the entire length of the body and tail. Remove the stomach and intestinal canal and a small sac just back of the head. Crack the large claws and lay the lobster as flat as possible. Brush the meat with melted butter. Season with salt and pepper. Place in a broiler, shell side down. Broil slowly until a delicate brown, about 20 minutes. Serve hot with melted butter. Allow ½ large or 1 small lobster per person.

Baked Stuffed Lobster

2 1-pound lobsters
2 cups soft bread cubes
4 tablespoons melted butter
1 tablespoon grated onion

If lobsters have not been split at market, prepare as directed in recipe above. Remove and save green liver and coral roe. Combine bread cubes, butter, onion, green liver, and roe. Place in body cavity and over surface of tail meat. Bake in hot oven (400° F.) for about 20 minutes or until stuffing is lightly browned. Serves 2.

✻ *The early settlers found large numbers of lobsters along the northern Atlantic coast. When the lobster is taken from the water its shell is a dark bluish-green. This color changes rapidly to "lobster-red" during cooking. Discard lobsters that are not alive and active at time of cooking. Chicken lobsters weigh ¾ to 1 pound; jumbos, over 2½ pounds.*

Lobster Salad

- 2 cups lobster meat, cut in small pieces
- 2 tablespoons mayonnaise
- 3 tablespoons chopped celery

Mix thoroughly and chill. Season to taste. Serve on lettuce with a sprinkling of paprika. If desired, top with a whole lobster claw removed from the shell. Serves 3.

Lobster Roll

Follow directions for lobster salad. Split and grill 4 hamburger or hot dog rolls. Fill with lobster salad, add a piece of crisp lettuce and serve. Serves 4.

Mussels on the Half-Shell

[*Maine Department of Sea and Shore Fisheries*]

- 4 dozen mussels
- 1 tablespoon minced onion
- ⅓ cup water
- juice ½ lemon
- 3 tablespoons butter
- salt and pepper
- 1½ teaspoons flour
- 1 teaspoon parsley, chopped

Scrub mussel shell. Place in a saucepan with water and lemon juice. Cover and boil 5 or 6 minutes or until shells open. Discard top shell of each mussel and arrange bottom halves on serving plates. Strain liquid and reduce by boiling. Melt butter in small skillet, blend in flour and seasonings. Add ⅓ cup liquid and bring to a boil. Pour over mussels. Serves 4.

* *This is a dish to be used as a first course but, accompanied by a hearty vegetable, salad, and some crisp green things, can make the grade as a main dish—good to the last mussel!*

Panned Oysters

[*A Rhode Island recipe*]

1 pint oysters
4 tablespoons butter
2 tablespoons lemon juice
Worcestershire sauce (if desired)
pepper
salt
lemon slices

Drain oysters, place in a heavy frying pan with butter, and cook over a low fire until the edges curl. Add lemon juice, pepper, and salt to taste. A dash of Worcestershire sauce may be added if desired. Serve on hot toast and garnish with lemon. Serves 4.

Lemon juice may be omitted and a wine glass of sherry added before serving.

* *When the first settlers came to America, one of the most impressive indications of the richness of the new country was the great abundance, large size, and excellence of the oysters they found along the coastline. They observed that the Indians also enjoyed large quantities of this delicious shellfish.*

Oysters are entirely edible, easy to prepare and serve. They may be enjoyed raw on the half-shell with a cocktail sauce (page 59), in soup or stew (pages 9, 8), baked, broiled, scalloped, creamed, or added to bread stuffing for fish or poultry.

Deep Dish Oyster Pie, made by topping creamed oysters (page 55) with biscuit dough and baking in a hot oven until biscuits are done, is a famous Rhode Island recipe.

To retain the delicate flavor of oysters, do not overcook or they will cease to be plump and tender.

In recent years shucked oysters have been quick frozen, a process which makes them available every month of the year. Frozen oysters should not be thawed until ready to use. Once thawed, they should never be refrozen.

Scalloped Oysters

½ cup bread crumbs
1 cup cracker crumbs
¼ cup melted butter
2 cups rich milk or cream
1 pint oysters, drained
salt and pepper
4 tablespoons oyster liquor

Mix bread and cracker crumbs and stir in melted butter. Put a thin layer of crumbs in bottom of a buttered, shallow baking dish; cover with oysters and sprinkle with salt and pepper. Add half of the oyster liquor and milk or cream; repeat, cover top with remaining crumbs. Bake 20 minutes in a hot oven (400° F.). Serves 4.

Oysters or Scallops on Skewers

Alternate large oysters and small squares of bacon on skewers. If scallops are used, wash, drain, and dip in seasoned crumbs, eggs, and again in crumbs. Pour melted butter over them or alternate with bacon squares. Place skewers under a broiler 5 or 10 minutes, or until bacon is crisp. Turn to brown evenly. Serve with tartar sauce (page 59). Sweetbreads, oysters (or scallops), bacon, and mushrooms may be alternated.

Scalloped Mussels

[*Maine Department of Sea and Shore Fisheries*]

Wash 1 quart mussels, cover with hot water and bring quickly to a boil, cook 5 or 6 minutes to open shell. Drain and remove meat.

Combine 2 cups bread crumbs with ¼ cup melted butter. Place a layer of the crumbs in a buttered casserole. Add a layer of mussels, sprinkle with minced green pepper, and season with salt, pepper, and onion salt. Repeat until crumbs and mussels are all used. Put in enough milk to moisten and sprinkle buttered crumbs on top. Bake 30 to 40 minutes at 350° F. Serves 4.

Oyster and Mushroom Mousse

12 large oysters
1 pound mushrooms
2 tablespoons butter
3 tablespoons flour
4 egg yolks, beaten
1 teaspoon salt
dash of pepper
1 cup heavy cream, whipped stiff
2 egg whites, whipped stiff

Put oysters and mushrooms through food chopper. Melt butter, stir in flour. Lightly sauté the mushrooms and oysters in this mixture. Remove from fire, add egg yolks, salt, pepper. Fold in cream and egg whites. Butter a 9-inch ring mold. Fill it ⅔ full with the mousse. Cover with buttered paper. Place in a pan of hot water. Bake in a slow oven (325° F.) for 1 hour. Invert the mousse onto a platter. Fill the center with buttered peas. Serves 6.

Oysters Baked in Green Peppers

6 small green peppers	½ cup oyster liquor (about)
7 common crackers, rolled fine	⅓ cup butter, melted
1 tablespoon butter	salt and pepper
24 large or 48 small oysters	1 tablespoon minced parsley

Cut thin slice from stem end of peppers. Remove seeds and inner membrane. Parboil 10 minutes in salted water. Drain and place upright in a buttered baking dish.

Mix crackers with melted butter. Sprinkle inside of peppers with salt, put a thick layer of crumbs in each pepper. Add 2 large or 4 small oysters. Season with pepper and salt and a sprinkling of parsley; moisten with a little of the oyster liquor. Add another layer of crumbs, then 2 or 4 more oysters. Season and top with crumbs. Moisten with a little more of the oyster liquor and dot with bits of butter. Bake in a hot oven (400° F.) about 20 minutes or until crumbs are browned. Serves 4 to 6.

Oysters with Tripe

1 pound honeycomb tripe	1 cup milk
1 tablespoon butter	25 large oysters
1 small onion, chopped	½ teaspoon salt
1 tablespoon flour	¼ teaspoon pepper

Boil tripe until tender. Cut into dice. Melt butter in saucepan. Add the chopped onion. Cover saucepan and cook until onion is soft but not brown. Sprinkle in the flour and mix. Add the milk, stir until boiling; then add tripe and oysters. When oysters are cooked sufficiently to curl the gills, add salt and pepper; serve at once. Serves 6.

Oyster Fritters

1½ cups oysters
2 eggs, slightly beaten
1 cup milk
2 cups flour, sifted
2 teaspoons baking powder
½ teaspoon salt

Chop the oysters. Make a batter of the eggs, milk, flour, baking powder, and salt. Stir the oysters into the batter and drop by spoonfuls into deep hot fat (375° F.). Turn the fritters over to brown evenly on both sides. Drain. Serves 4.

Pigs in Blankets

12 large oysters
salt and pepper
bacon
toast

Sprinkle oysters with salt and pepper. Encircle each oyster in a strip of bacon. Secure bacon firmly with a toothpick. Broil 8 minutes or until bacon is crisp. Serve on rounds of well-buttered toast.

Creamed Oysters

[*A Rhode Island recipe*]

4 tablespoons butter
4 tablespoons flour
½ teaspoon salt
pepper
2 cups milk
1 pint oysters with liquor
1 cup diced celery, cooked
1 slice pimiento

Melt butter, stir in flour, salt, and pepper; when well blended add milk. Stir over a low fire until smooth and thick. Add oysters, celery, and minced pimiento. Cook gently about 3 minutes or until the edges of the oysters curl. Serve at once on hot toast or in toasted bread cases or patty shells. Serves 4.

Oysters and Macaroni

- 4 ounces elbow macaroni
- 25 large oysters
- 1 teaspoon salt
- ¼ teaspoon black pepper
- 1 cup soft bread crumbs
- 1 tablespoon butter
- ½ cup grated cheese
- 1 cup milk

Place the macaroni in a kettle of boiling salted water. Cook until tender. Pick over the oysters. Drain. Grease a baking dish. Cover the bottom with the boiled macaroni; then a layer of oysters; season with salt and pepper. Continue until the dish is full, having the top layer macaroni. Sprinkle the cheese over the top; then the bread crumbs. Dot the top with pieces of butter. Pour on the milk. Bake 20 minutes in a hot oven (425° F.) and serve at once. Serves 4.

Chatham Oyster Shortcake

Bake a shortcake dough (omitting sugar) in two layers, one on top of the other. Split and spread with butter.

FILLING

Scald 1 quart oysters in their liquor. Remove oysters and keep hot. Strain 1 cup of the liquor into saucepan. Mix 2 tablespoons flour with 3 tablespoons cold water. Stir into oyster liquor and season to taste with salt, pepper, and celery salt. Cook slowly for 5 minutes, stirring constantly. Add 3 tablespoons heavy cream and the oysters. Stir until well heated, then place between and on top of the shortcake and serve. Serves 6.

Steamed Clams

* *See Clam Broth. Steamed clams are served in soup plates accompanied by cups of clam broth and individual dishes of melted butter.*

Succulent steamed clams, dripping butter all the way from plate to lips, are among earth's choicest contributions to man's gastronomic pleasure.

New Hampshire Shore Dinner

Clam or Fish Chowder

Crackers—Celery—Sour Pickles

Steamed Hampton River Clams

with

Clam Bouillon and Drawn Butter

Broiled Rock Cod—Fried Clams

Broiled Lobsters—Potato Chips

Corn on the Cob—Tomato and Cucumber Salad

Rolls

Apple Pie—Cheese—or Ice Cream

Coffee

Maine Shrimp

Maine shrimp are smaller than the Gulf variety and are meaty and sweet. Break off the heads and cook in boiling salted water until the shells are red, about 2 minutes from the boiling point. Cool, peel off shell. These shrimp do not have to be deveined. Proceed as usual for shrimp cocktail or creamed and casserole dishes. One pound fresh shrimp in shell makes about ½ pound cooked and peeled shrimp.

Baked Shrimp

Place cooked, shelled shrimp close together on a buttered pan. Cover with fine buttered bread crumbs, season with salt and pepper. While baking, baste several times with equal parts of melted butter and lemon juice. Bake 6 to 8 minutes in a 400° F. oven. Allow 8 to 12 shrimp per person.

"Fannie Daddies"

[*The Cape Cod name for Fried Clams*]

- 3 dozen clams removed from shells (about 1 quart)
- 1 cup fine bread crumbs, cracker crumbs, or cornmeal
- ½ teaspoon salt
- pepper
- 1 egg, beaten with 1 tablespoon water

Drain clams; dip in seasoned crumbs, then in egg-water mixture, then again in crumbs. Fry in deep fat (375° F.) 2 or 3 minutes, until golden brown. Or pan-fry 5 to 8 minutes in hot (but not smoking) fat. Drain on absorbent paper and serve with Tartar Sauce. Serves 4. Oysters are prepared in the same way.

TARTAR SAUCE

½ cup mayonnaise
1 tablespoon minced pickles
1 teaspoon minced onion
1 tablespoon minced olives
1 tablespoon minced parsley

Combine and serve on lettuce leaf.

COCKTAIL SAUCE FOR SEAFOOD

1 cup catsup
2 tablespoons vinegar
½ teaspoon salt
1 tablespoon each: horseradish, minced celery, minced onion
few drops Tabasco sauce
1 teaspoon Worcestershire sauce

Blend all ingredients and chill.

Scalloped Clams

4 tablespoons butter
3 tablespoons flour
1 tablespoon chopped parsley
1 teaspoon scraped onion
½ teaspoon dry mustard
½ teaspoon salt
pepper
1 cup milk
2 cups clams, removed from shell
2 hard-cooked eggs, minced
½ cup buttered bread crumbs

Melt butter, add flour, and stir until blended; add seasonings and milk, stirring until smooth. Add clams and eggs. Pour into buttered scallop shells or a shallow baking dish. Cover with buttered crumbs. Bake in a moderately hot oven (375° F.) 20 minutes or until crumbs are brown. Serves 4 to 6.

Clam Cakes

[*In Maine and on Cape Cod they make them this way*]

1 quart clams, shucked
1 cup fine cracker crumbs (about)
½ cup clam liquor
2 eggs, well beaten

Drain clams and save ½ cup liquor. Remove the black from soft part. Put the necks through a food chopper. Put clams in a dish, add clam liquor and enough cracker crumbs to absorb all the moisture. Let stand 10 minutes. Add eggs. Shape into flat cakes. Drop into hot deep fat (375° F.) and cook until a golden brown. Drain. Serves 4.

Deep Sea Clam Pie (Cape Cod Style)

[*Mrs. Emma Cross, Onset, Mass.*]

¼ pound salt pork, cut in slices
1 tablespoon butter
2 tablespoons flour
1 cup clam broth
½ cup water
4 large sea clams
pepper
pastry crust

Try out the salt pork, add butter; blend in flour, add the clam broth and water, and cook until broth is thickened. Grind the meaty portion of the clams (discarding the tough portions) and add the broth. Season with pepper—no salt is required. Line a deep dish with a rich pastry crust. Pour in clam mixture and cover with top crust. Cut a hole in the center and surround hole with a twist of crust. Bake in a hot oven (450° F.) for 15 minutes; then reduce heat to moderate and bake 20 minutes longer. Serves 4.

Easy Cheese and Shrimp Souffle

[*A modern Yankee recipe*]

In a double boiler melt ½ package Velveeta cheese and 1 tin of frozen shrimp soup. Cool, add 6 well-beaten egg yolks; then fold in 6 egg whites beaten until they stand in peaks. Bake at 360° F. 37 minutes. Serves 5.

Martha's Vineyard Quahog Fritters

1 pint shucked quahogs
2 cups flour, sifted
3 teaspoons baking powder
½ cup quahog liquor
⅓ cup milk
2 eggs, separated
⅛ teaspoon salt
⅛ teaspoon pepper

Chop quahogs; mix and sift dry ingredients; add quahog liquor, milk, egg yolks, and clam mixture, stirring until smooth. Fold in egg whites, beaten until stiff. Drop by spoonfuls into hot deep fat (375° F.) and cook 3 minutes, or until brown. Drain. Serves 8.

✱ *This recipe comes from West Tisbury, Martha's Vineyard. Clams or oysters may be substituted for quahogs. Scallops, cut in quarters and parboiled, may also be used, substituting milk for the quahog liquor.*

"Boat Steerers"

[*Clam Fritters is another name*]

1 quart shucked clams
1 egg, slightly beaten
2 tablespoons olive oil (or melted butter)
½ cup milk
1 cup flour, sifted
4 teaspoons baking powder
¼ teaspoon salt
⅛ teaspoon pepper

Put shoulder and rim of clams through food chopper, leave soft parts whole. Add egg, olive oil, and milk. Mix and sift dry ingredients and add to clam mixture, stirring until smooth. Drop by spoonfuls in deep hot fat (375° F.) and cook until golden brown. Drain. Serves 8.

Martha's Vineyard Clam Boil

1 quart medium sized potatoes
1 large bunch carrots
6 small onions
½ peck small clams
1 pound frankfurters
1 pound link sausages
6 ears corn
1 quart water

Place potatoes in their jackets in the bottom of a large kettle or boiler, add carrots cut in halves, onions, and clams in the shell that have been thoroughly washed. On top place the frankfurters, sausages, and the ears of corn. Pour on water. Tightly cover the kettle or boiler and steam-cook until tender, about 45 minutes. Serves 6.

* *A clam boil may be prepared at home on the kitchen stove, but it tastes better on a moonlight night on the beach.*

Clam Pie

2 dozen clams
3 medium onions, sliced
2 medium potatoes, cut in ¼ inch slices
3 tablespoons butter
2 tablespoons flour
2 cups rich milk or thin cream
salt and pepper
1 tablespoon minced parsley
3 common crackers

Scrub clams thoroughly. Place in saucepan, adding 1 cup hot water. Simmer until shells open slightly. Remove clams from shells, reserving water in which clams were steamed. Chop clams fine. Strain liquor and cook sliced onion and potatoes in this broth until tender, but not broken. Melt 2 tablespoons butter, stir in flour. Add milk gradually, stirring until thickened. Add clams, potatoes, onions, and liquid in which they were cooked. Season, simmer 2 minutes, pour into well-buttered glass baking dish, and sprinkle with parsley. Split crackers and soak in cold milk until softened. Arrange over clam mixture. Dot with remaining tablespoon butter, sprinkle with paprika, and bake in a moderately hot oven (425° F.) until crackers are lightly browned. Serves 6.

Mistress Howe's Clam and Chicken Pie

1 dozen tiny onions
2 tablespoons butter
2 dozen clams, chopped
1 cup diced cooked chicken
2 hard-cooked eggs, diced
1 cup diced cooked potatoes
½ cup chopped celery
1 teaspoon salt
½ teaspoon pepper
¼ cup sherry
1 tablespoon flour
½ cup cream
pastry for one-crust pie

Sauté onions in butter until soft. Add clams, chicken, eggs, potatoes, celery, seasonings, and sherry. Simmer about 5 minutes. Mix flour and cream into a paste and blend in. Simmer another 5 minutes. Pour into baking dish, cover with pastry, rolled thin and slashed to permit escape of steam. Bake 15 minutes at 400° F. and an additional 15 to 20 minutes at 350° F. Serves 6.

* *This classic Yankee recipe comes from Longfellow's Wayside Inn at Sudbury, Mass. In early days The Inn was called Howe's or The Red Horse. This recipe has been popular for 280 years.*

The Perfect Church Supper

C. M. Webster

Father was a tolerant man who excused dull sermons and forgave bad amateur plays—the ministers and actors had done their best, he said—but he asked for perfection in a church or Grange supper. Since preaching and acting were pleasures that he could not enjoy in his own home, he was willing to be lenient in judging them, but when a man forsook his own wife's excellent cooking, changed his clothes, hitched up and drove two miles, and then paid twenty-five cents for a meal, he had a right to expect a lot. Father was almost always disappointed in the suppers he went to; something he wanted was not there, or the food he got was not seasoned right; but on one historic occasion he was completely satisfied.

I was home from college for Easter vacation, so I know all about that perfect supper. It was held in April on a Friday night. By the time spring came, Father was a trifle bored by home cooking, no matter how good it was; and Friday was better than Saturday as a night for suppers, for he liked to have plenty of time to take a bath and then study his Sunday School lesson for the next day. That Friday evening was just right for the season of the year and held no menace of too warm or too cold weather to come; the going was good, and our Morgan gelding passed Seth Osgood's rig on the way to the village. Little things like those helped put Father in a pleasant mood.

After he had bought our tickets from the minister's wife, Father spent a profitable five minutes selling Jerome Ennis a load of hay at the top market price; then he looked around for a seat. At least two suppers had been partially ruined by poor neighbors, but tonight he found a place next to Oscar Tillinghast, a man who did not talk too much and passed things promptly. After a few polite remarks about health and the weather, Father's face became sober as he wondered what there was to eat and who was waiting on this table.

The jolly and buxom Mrs. William Moseley brought a big dish of baked beans. Father took an experimental helping and tasted critically. Yes, they were yellow-eyes and baked to the right consistency with New Orleans molasses and none of that heretical brown sugar. He took a real helping and looked to see what went with the beans. There was a dish of pork—slices of melting softness with a crisp edge. Father ate three and then discovered the brown bread. That was as it should be; a church supper was no place for fragile rolls or biscuits or uninteresting white bread. There was a quarter of a pound of Mrs. Elijah Holcomb's butter to go with the brown bread. Father ate a slice and finished half of his beans before he reached for the rest of the supper.

So far everything had been perfect, but he was fussy about salads. This one suited him; the potatoes were tender and yet escaped being an indefinite mush; not too many onions spoiled the taste of the slices of hard-boiled eggs that matched the potatoes in a ratio of one to three, and the mayonnaise was good. Father ate a big spoonful and continued his search, for a good supper meant more than beans, bread, and salad.

Young Mrs. Moseley's bare round arm put a steaming cup of coffee beside his plate, and after the thick cream and sugar and the first swallow, Father remarked: "Some women I could mention didn't have a hand in making that coffee; it's too good."

Then he asked for the cole slaw. A minor crisis was at hand. Had mayonnaise been used? No, only vinegar, cream (not milk), and sugar, and not too much vinegar. The critic ate a little of it; took another helping of yellow-eyes, and began to relax. Now was the time for the extra dishes that turned an adequate supper into a real good one. Father sampled and liked the sweet pickles and the watermelon rind in its thick juice spotted with cloves, but he approved most of the green tomato relish.

"Must be yours, Mrs. Tillinghast," he said. "Nobody else gets quite this flavor."

"I'm glad you like it. But you just try these pickled beets I brought and see what you think of them."

Father accepted a very small beet and ate it cautiously. "Umm. Pretty fair." A second . . . "Good!" and he took two larger ones for leisurely consumption.

"They seem to have a new flavor that I can't remember ever happenin' on before," he remarked.

"That's because I use a few bay leaves the way my grandmother did," explained Mrs. Tillinghast.

Father often jeered at the way some women spoiled a good dish by sticking in some funny thing, but this time he welcomed the exotic.

"I don't generally take to new dishes, but those pickled beets go good with baked beans," he said.

Father took a bite more of beans, a dab of cole slaw, a slice or two of green tomatoes, a touch of salad, and another beet before he looked expectantly at the pretty Mrs. Moseley.

"We've got punkin, mince, 'n' apple pie," she announced.

"Do you know whose apple pies they are?" asked Father.

"Mrs. Dwight Porter brought two."

"She uses cinnamon," said Father dourly.

"And I guess one of Mrs. Lincoln's is left."

"Good!" said Father. "You might bring me a piece. She puts a dash of nutmeg in her pies."

Father scarcely looked at his pie when Mrs. Moseley brought it; he was interested in the last vital question—would there be cheese, and if so, what kind? Of course he knew what he wanted, but no supper he had ever gone to had as yet given it to him. But this one was different, for there beside the pie was a large rectangle of sage cheese tastefully marbled with delicate streaks of green. When he had very slowly eaten the pie and cheese, Father allowed himself to be argued into having a second cup of coffee and a small piece of mince pie.

"Wouldn't you like a bite more of that sage cheese?" asked Mrs. Moseley.

"It is about the best I've tasted in a long time," admitted Father.

Five minutes later he sighed and remarked to Oscar Tillinghast, "That's what I call an A-One supper."

"It might've been a whole lot worse," agreed Oscar.

For the next quarter of an hour, Father and Oscar and Seth Osgood and Jerome Ennis discussed farming, the weather, Jerome's new Ayrshire bull, and, in lowered voices, the tendency of the minister to shout and wave his arms in the pulpit. Then Father remarked that tomorrow was a day of work and he'd better be getting along home.

While we drove through the April evening, Father forgot the caution of Puritanism and its fear of open praise and talked lovingly about each dish in that perfect supper.

"Yes, sir," he said at last. "Everything was there that should be, and it was all good. Got real satisfactory service, too, and could look twice at the woman who was giving it. And it seemed kind of good to talk things over for a minute with some men. In a way you might say that everything sort of fitted together into as good a supper as a man has any right to expect."

Meat, Poultry, and Game

Cooking Game Birds

Two rules are important to follow in cooking all wild birds: wrap the breasts of all but wild duck and goose (which are fat birds) with larding pork or strips of bacon. Take care not to overcook game birds, as this makes them stringy and spoils the flavor. Cook only until joints move easily.

WILD DUCK AND WILD GOOSE

Stuff with quartered onions and apples or stalk of celery. Discard before serving. Roast breast side up in a 425° F. oven, basting every 5 minutes with drippings or equal parts drippings and red wine. A wild goose is larger than a wild duck and a 4- to 6-pound goose may need as long as 3 hours to cook. Duck cooks at 12 minutes per pound for very rare duck with the juice red.

PHEASANT, GROUSE, AND PARTRIDGE

Rub each bird with soft butter or place a slice of bacon over the breast. Equal parts of melted butter and white wine may be used for basting. Baste frequently until a golden brown. If birds are brown before joints move easily, reduce heat, cover loosely with foil and continue roasting.

QUAIL AND SQUAB

Place bacon slices over breast. Roast at 325° F. 20 to 40 minutes, basting every 5 minutes. Cooking time varies with the age and size of bird.

Mrs. Vallée's Spiced Beef

[Kay Vallée Lenneville, Westbrook, Me.]

4 or 5 pounds chuck roast
cider vinegar to cover meat
2 onions, ground
1 teaspoon cinnamon
1 teaspoon allspice
1 teaspoon cloves
1 teaspoon salt
1 teaspoon pepper
2 onions, sliced
4 carrots
1 medium-sized yellow turnip

Cover the meat with the vinegar, ground onions, and spices and let stand overnight. Remove meat from liquid; place in a covered roaster, add ½ cup of the vinegar liquid and 2 cups water. Place sliced onions over meat. Roast in slow oven (275° F.), about 3 hours. When meat is nearly done, before the last half hour, put carrots and turnip through food chopper and fry in equal parts of vegetable shortening and butter until golden brown. Cover top of meat with these vegetables and cook until done. Serves 8. Serve with mashed or baked potatoes.

* *This recipe comes from Rudy Vallée's paternal grandmother, a Vermonter, who gave it to Rudy's mother.*

Yankee Pot Roast

4 pounds beef—round, chuck, or rump
salt, pepper, flour
⅛ pound salt pork
1 bay leaf
sprig parsley
5 or 6 raisins
6 carrots
6 onions
6 potatoes
1 small turnip, sliced (optional)

Wipe meat with a clean damp cloth. Sprinkle with salt, pepper, and flour. Try out a small piece of salt pork in an iron pot. Put in meat and brown on all sides. (Roll it over, so as to keep juices in. Do not insert fork.) When brown, add enough boiling water to cover the bottom of the pot. Add bay leaf, parsley, and raisins. Cover and simmer slowly for 3 hours, keeping about 1 cup water under the meat. The last hour of cooking add carrots, onions, turnip (if desired); add the potatoes the last half hour. Serve on a platter with the vegetables arranged around the meat. Mix about 2 tablespoons flour in ¼ cup cold water to a smooth paste to thicken gravy. Season a little more if necessary. Serves 8.

✻ *Generations of Yankee cooks have been taught that sometime during the cooking, a pot roast should "catch on" (stick to the pot just enough to brown) thereby giving the gravy richness and savor.*

Vermont Corned Beef

4 or 5 pounds corned beef
whole cloves
½ cup maple syrup

Cover corned beef with water and bring to boiling point. Drain, cover with hot water, and let simmer until done, allowing about 40 minutes per pound. When done place on a rack in an open roasting pan. Stick with whole cloves in diagonal design. Pour maple syrup over meat and put in moderate oven (350° F.) to brown and glaze. Baste occasionally with maple syrup. Serves 8.

Maine Corned Beef Hash

[*This was a favorite recipe of Kenneth Roberts, the author, who lived in Kennebunkport, Me.*]

3 cups boiled potatoes
4 cups corned beef
¼ cup butter
¾ cup boiling water
pepper

Place cold potatoes and cold corned beef (free from gristle and fat) in chopping bowl. Chop until both meat and potatoes are in very small pieces. Melt butter in heavy skillet. Add boiling water. Add chopped meat and potatoes seasoned with pepper. Fry over very low heat for about 15 minutes or until brown crust has formed on lower side of hash; then fold over as omelet is folded. Serves 4 to 6.

New England Boiled Dinner

[*Mrs. William D. Eddy, 52 High Street, Jamestown, R.I.*]

Select a 4- or 5-pound piece of corned beef, preferably brisket, corned between 4 and 7 days without saltpeter. Place in a large kettle, cover with cold water and boil slowly. After cooking 2 hours add ½ pound salt pork. When beef is almost done (3 to 4 hours) add the following vegetables: onions, cabbage quartered and cored, medium-sized white turnip pared and quartered, and last carrots and potatoes. When potatoes are done, place meat in center of a large platter and arrange vegetables around meat. Beets are served with a boiled dinner but should be cooked separately. A 4-pound piece of corned beef serves 8.

* *For corned beef and cabbage omit all vegetables except cabbage.*

Aunt Dilly's Savory Meat

3 pounds corned beef, chopped fine
8 crackers, rolled
2 eggs, beaten
½ cup warm water
pepper
½ teaspoon sage or parsley

Mix ingredients well and pack into 2 greased loaf tins, 5 x 4 x 3 inches. Bake in a moderately hot oven (375° F.). When cold, slice and serve with mustard pickles. Serves 8. One medium-sized onion, minced, may be added if desired.

Red Flannel Hash

1 tablespoon butter
1 cup chopped cooked corned beef
3 cups chopped boiled potatoes
1 cup chopped cooked beets
½ chopped onion

Heat butter in frying pan. Spread mixture smoothly over the bottom of the pan. Brown slowly. When crust forms, turn as an omelet. Serves 4.

* *The best Yankee cooks state positively that the meat and potatoes used to make hash should always be chopped separately in a wooden chopping bowl, by hand, never put through the food grinder. A little cream may be added to moisten.*

A sauce made by blending 2 tablespoons freshly grated horseradish with ½ cup whipped cream is excellent with hash. Sliced green tomato pickles are a perennial favorite.

Original Plymouth Succotash

4 pounds corned beef
4 or 5 pound fowl
1 quart pea beans
1 turnip, sliced
6 potatoes, sliced
salt
2 quarts hulled corn, cooked

Boil the meat and fowl together the day before the dish is to be served. Soak the beans overnight, then cook until soft enough to mash. Reheat the meat and fowl, then remove both and skim the fat from the broth. Add to the broth slices of turnip and potato, cook slowly, and when nearly done add the mashed bean pulp and the hulled corn. Stir often so that vegetables will not burn on the kettle. Unless the broth is very salty it will be necessary to add salt to season properly. Serve the meat and fowl on a large platter and the vegetables in a large tureen. Serves 12.

✱ *This dish was made by the Pilgrims and handed down through succeeding generations. It is served by every true Plymouth family on Forefathers' Day—December 21st. This dish keeps well and is improved with each warming over.*

From a Rotary Club luncheon comes the story of a conversation between a Westerner and a New Englander. In the course of their talk, the Yankee had occasion to use the expression "New England conscience" several times and finally the Westerner, somewhat puzzled, asked him to define it. "Well," said the Yankee, "the way I see it, a New England conscience doesn't prevent your doing anything, but it does prevent your enjoying it."

"Joe Booker"

[A stew famous in the vicinity of Booth Bay Harbor, Me.]

½ pound salt pork, diced
2 cups lean veal or beef, diced
2 cups turnip, diced
2 cups potatoes, diced
1 cup onions, sliced
2 cups carrots, diced
8 cups water
salt and pepper

Try out salt pork; remove the cracklings. Add to the fat the meat, vegetables, and water. Simmer 2 hours, or until meat is tender. Season to taste. This hearty stew may be served with dumplings or not, as desired. Serves 8.

Salt Pork with Milk Gravy

[A New Hampshire recipe]

Cube and fry until crisp ¾ pound lean salt pork. Remove from fat. Drain off excess fat, leaving 2 tablespoons in pan. Add 2 tablespoons flour and blend until smooth. Add 1 cup cold milk. Heat, add pork cubes, and serve over hot baked or mashed potatoes. Serves 2 or 3.

Homemade Beef-and-Pork Sausage

[A New Hampshire recipe]

10 pounds pork (the cheeks, small chin segments, mixed fat and lean scraps)
5 pounds lean beef strips
3 ounces salt
1½ ounces black pepper
1 ounce sage
¼ ounce summer savory
¼ ounce sweet marjoram
¼ ounce thyme

Grind meat, then add seasonings; mix with a wooden paddle. Press mixture down in the pan. Stand in a cold place. Use only top quality meat. Dry the herbs in the oven and "fine up" before using.

* *Nothing tastes finer on a zero morning than sausage and fried apples, sausage and scrambled eggs, sausage and griddle cakes, or even honest-to-goodness fried sausages with golden gravy and baked potatoes.*

Sausage and Hominy

1 pound little link sausages
water
2 cups cooked hominy
¼ cup melted butter
1 tablespoon sugar
parsley garnish

Place sausages in frying pan and cover with cold water. Let come to a boil. Pour off water and let cook until brown. Place in the center of platter a mound of hominy which has been cooked in boiling salted water and seasoned with melted butter and sugar. Arrange the sausages around the hominy and garnish with parsley. Serves 3 or 4.

Fried Sausage

With wet hand shape sausage meat into flat cakes; pan-broil in hot frying pan about 15 minutes, pouring off fat as sausage fries. Drain on absorbent paper; 1 pound sausage meat makes 8 small cakes. Serve with Apple Rings.

APPLE RINGS

Core and pare cooking apples. Slice into rings about ½ inch thick. Dip rings into milk and roll in flour. Fry in sausage fat. When lightly brown, remove and sprinkle with confectioners' sugar.

Apples Stuffed with Sausage

Mash 1 pound of lightly seasoned sausage meat in a skillet. When it has browned, add enough fresh bread crumbs to absorb the fat. Core, but do not peel 6 or 8 Greenings. Fill centers with sausage meat and bread crumbs. Bake in a moderately hot oven (375° F.) about 40 minutes, or until apples are tender. Serve with cornbread and custard pie for lunch. Serves 3.

Hog's Head Cheese

[*Also called Souse Meat*]

1 pound fresh pork scraps (ears, feet, nose or pig's head)
1 pound neck of beef
water
1 teaspoon salt
1¼ tablespoons poultry seasoning
½ teaspoon pepper

Simmer pork and beef in small amount of water until meat falls from bone. Remove bones, lift meat from kettle and chop. Stir in seasonings; add broth in which meat was cooked and mix thoroughly. Heat through, pack in bread tins (or milk pans) and place overnight in a cool place. Remove fat that rises to top of loaf and slice. Serve with fried Baldwins and baked potato.

✱ *Some prefer vinegar gravy with their meat but it is generally served plain. This recipe came from an 1850 bride of a Maine pioneer and is still used in the family of Mrs. Pearl Ashby Tibbetts, Bethel, Maine. Additional broth remaining after making head cheese is sometimes thickened with corn meal and made into mush. It is sliced, browned in hot fat, and served for breakfast. Yankees call it Panhas.*

Stuffed Pork Chops

- ½ cup chopped celery
- 2 tablespoons finely chopped onion
- 2 tablespoons chopped parsley (optional)
- 1 cup soft bread crumbs
- 1 tablespoon melted butter
- 1 cup cranberry sauce (canned or homemade)
- 1 teaspoon salt
- pepper
- 6 pork chops, 1 inch thick
- flour
- 2 tablespoons fat

Combine the celery, onion, parsley, crumbs, cranberry sauce, and butter. Add salt and a dash of pepper. Cut pockets in the pork chops and stuff; sprinkle with salt and pepper and dredge with flour. Brown lightly in fat, then bake uncovered in a moderate oven (350° F.) about 60 minutes or until tender. Serves 6.

New England Pork Chops

- 4 pork chops, well trimmed of fat
- flour
- 4 medium-sized onions, sliced
- 2 tablespoons butter or vegetable shortening
- water
- salt and pepper

Sift flour over pork chops, covering both sides. Fry onions in butter until light brown. Place chops in skillet with onions. Brown quickly on both sides; season. Add water enough to cover, and cook over low flame for 45 minutes, tightly covered. Chops will be tender with a slightly thick brown gravy. Serves 2 to 4.

Ham Baked in Cider I

[*A Vermont recipe*]

Center slice of smoked ham,
cut 2 inches thick
16 whole cloves
2 tablespoons dry mustard
½ cup maple syrup
½ cup cider (or apple juice)

Stick whole cloves into fat and rub mustard over ham. Lay in casserole and pour maple syrup and cider over ham. Bake in moderate oven (350° F.) until tender, about 1½ hours. A 1½ pound slice of ham serves 3.

Ham Baked in Cider II

[*A delicious Colonial dish*]

1 smoked ham about 10 pounds

Marinate ham overnight in 1½ quarts sharp cider. Remove from cider and place it, uncovered, in a roasting pan in slow oven (300° F.) and roast 3 hours, basting with cider. Remove rind from ham. Cover with a mixture of equal parts of brown sugar and bread crumbs. Stick whole cloves into surface and brown in oven about 1 hour longer, or until ham is tender. Serve hot or cold with cider sauce made from juices in pan. Serves about 25.

RAISIN SAUCE FOR HAM

1 cup seedless raisins
water
1 cup sugar
¼ cup cider vinegar
½ teaspoon salt
⅛ teaspoon clove
1 glass currant or grape jelly

Soak raisins in lukewarm water until plumped. Pour off water. Add remaining ingredients. Heat before serving. Good with hot or cold ham.

Ham Apple Pie

In a buttered baking dish place 3 alternate layers of ham sliced about ¼ inch thick and 3 Greenings, peeled, sliced, and sprinkled with 1 tablespoon brown sugar. Sprinkle the juice of half a lemon over the top layer. Place in a moderately hot oven (375° F.) for 45 minutes. The dish should be covered until the last 30 minutes of cooking. The juice should cook down thick. Serves 4.

Bertha's Ham Loaf

1 pound uncooked ham (string end)
1 pound fresh pork
1 onion, chopped fine
1 cup fine bread crumbs
1 egg
¾ cup milk
pepper

Grind ham and pork together twice. Blend all ingredients thoroughly and turn into an oiled bread tin. Bake 1½ hours in a moderate oven (350° F.). Unmold and serve with mustard sauce.

MUSTARD SAUCE

1 egg
½ cup prepared mustard
1 bouillon cube
⅓ cup sugar
½ cup mild vinegar

Beat the egg; heat the remaining ingredients and when bouillon cube is dissolved, pour onto the egg. Serve hot without allowing sauce to boil. Two tablespoons butter may be added just before serving.

Fried Ham with Apple Rings

[*A Connecticut recipe*]

- 1 slice ham, 1 inch thick
- 4 red cooking apples
- 1 egg, beaten
- ¼ cup milk
- ½ cup flour
- ¼ teaspoon salt
- brown sugar
- cinnamon

Rub frying pan with ham fat and brown ham on both sides; cover, cook slowly 30 minutes, turning several times. Core, but do not peel apples. Cut thick rings crosswise. Combine egg, milk, flour, and salt, dip apple rings in this batter and fry in ham fat, after removing slice of ham, adding more ham fat or bacon fat so that fat is about 1 inch deep in frying pan. When brown, drain and sprinkle apple rings with brown sugar and cinnamon and serve in an overlapping ring about the ham. Serves 4.

✽ *Although older recipes did not call for it, 2 teaspoons of brandy added to the batter gives a special flavor to the apples.*

Windsor Pie

- 1½ cups chopped cooked ham, some fat included
- 3 cups drained, cooked macaroni
- 6 common crackers, crushed
- 2 tablespoons butter
- 3 cups milk (about)

Place the chopped meat in well-buttered baking dish. Place cooked macaroni on top of meat, then crackers. Pour milk over the crackers, slowly wetting the whole top surface. Add milk until all of mixture is covered. Dot with butter. Bake in a slow oven (300° F.) about 1 hour, or until milk is absorbed and the top nicely browned. Serves 4. Serve with coleslaw.

Corned beef or well-seasoned chopped cold meat of any kind may be used in place of ham. Minced onion and seasonings should be added to chopped beef or lamb.

Bean Pot Stew

1 pound beef (bottom of round) cut in cubes
1 onion
2 tablespoons fat
2 small carrots, sliced
1 small turnip, sliced
1 cup peas, fresh or canned
4 tablespoons rolled oats
1 teaspoon salt
water to cover
pepper
3 potatoes, cubed

Brown meat and onion in fat; add carrots, turnips, and peas. Turn into greased bean pot or casserole. Add remaining ingredients except potatoes, cover with water, and bake in moderate oven (350° F.) 4 hours. Add potatoes the last hour of cooking. Serves 4.

Easy Beef Stew

[*Not strictly a Yankee recipe but so popular it is included*]

2 pounds of stewing beef, cut in cubes
1 can condensed onion soup
1 can condensed mushroom soup

Remove any fat from cubes of beef. Place in a large casserole. Pour on soups. Bake in a slow (300° F.) oven for 3 hours. Add ½ cup red wine. It is not necessary to brown the meat; do not add liquid to condensed soup. This stew has a rich, brown gravy and should be eaten with hot garlic bread and a tossed green salad for a delicious, easy meal. Can be made ahead of time and reheated, adding wine. Serves 6 to 8.

Church Supper Meat Loaf

6 pounds beef, ground
2 pounds pork, ground
3 teaspoons salt
4 large onions, finely chopped
6 cups soft bread crumbs
2 cups water
1 teaspoon pepper
5 eggs, lightly beaten

Combine ingredients and turn into four greased loaf pans. Bake in moderately hot oven (375° F.) for 40 minutes. Serve plain or with tomato sauce. Serves 24.

* *For a tastier meat loaf, add fresh or dried basil, chopped green pepper, chopped celery, and chopped parsley. Cover top with bacon slices, or baste with tomato juice or melted butter to keep loaf moist.*

New Hampshire Church Supper Menu

Chicken Pie or Meat Loaf or Other Cold Meat

—Scalloped Potatoes—

Mixed Vegetable Salad—Whole Wheat and White Rolls

—Pickles—

—Washington Pie—

—Coffee—

Hamburg Loaf

1 egg, beaten
2 pounds hamburg
1½ teaspoons salt
½ teaspoon pepper
10 soda crackers, rolled
1 can mushroom soup (12 oz.)

Mix the egg into the hamburg; add seasonings and crackers. Lastly add the can of mushroom soup. Bake in a moderately hot oven (375° F.) 40 minutes. Serves 6.

Beef Steak and Oysters

[*A Rhode Island recipe*]

Broil a steak until nearly tender. Cover with drained oysters, dotted with butter. Bake in a moderate oven (375° F.) until oysters are plump. Season oysters. Serve with lemon butter and chopped parsley sauce. Allow ½ pound steak per portion.

Meat Balls with Cranberry Sauce

- 1 pound ground beef
- ½ cup dry bread crumbs
- 1 egg
- 2 tablespoons finely chopped onion
- 2 teaspoons salt
- ⅛ teaspoon pepper
- 1 cup strained cranberry sauce (canned or homemade)
- 1 8-ounce can tomato sauce
- ½ cup water

Combine the beef, crumbs, egg, onion, and seasonings. Form into small balls and allow to stand for a few minutes. Brown in fat. Make a sauce by mashing the cranberry sauce and mixing it with the tomato sauce and water; pour over the meat balls; cover and simmer for 1 hour. Serves 5.

Veal Pot Pie I

- ½ pound fat salt pork
- 2 pounds veal from the breast
- water
- salt and pepper
- dumpling dough (recipe page 90)
- ½ pint cream
- 1 tablespoon butter

Cut salt pork in ½ inch pieces. Slice into a deep kettle, cover kettle, and let salt pork fry a light brown. Add veal, cut in small cubes; cook for ½ hour, turning often to brown on all sides. Add boiling water to cover the meat to the depth of 1 inch. Season. Cover kettle and simmer until meat is tender, about 45 minutes. Make dumpling dough; carefully drop in dumplings. Cover and let cook until dumplings are done. Lift dumplings from the kettle, lay around edges of a hot platter. With a skimmer lift out the veal and lay in the center of the platter. Add cream to the liquid in the kettle. Thicken gravy. Stir in 1 tablespoon butter. Pour gravy over veal on the platter and serve at once. Serves 6.

* *This recipe is a treasured family recipe belonging to one of the oldest families in Norwich.*

Veal Pot Pie recipes called for a deep baking dish lined with baked pastry crust. Rice was placed over the crust so that it would keep its shape. The veal was then added and topped with pastry or cream of tartar biscuits, soda biscuits, or dumplings. The veal was browned in a variety of herbs from the kitchen garden, parsley, a little thyme, a bay leaf; also a dash of cayenne. Sometimes vegetables were omitted and diced oysters and hard-boiled egg yolks added to the veal.

Veal Pot Pie II

[*A New Hampshire recipe*]

- 1½ pounds veal
- 6 tablespoons flour
- 1 teaspoon salt
- dash of pepper
- ¼ cup fat
- boiling water
- 2 small onions, finely cut
- 2 carrots, diced
- soda biscuits (recipe page 159)

Cut veal in 1-inch dice. Dredge with seasoned flour and sauté in fat until well browned, turning frequently. Cover with boiling water and simmer, covered, 1½ hours or until tender, adding onions and carrots the last ½ hour of cooking. Thicken with paste of a little additional flour and water, if gravy is not thick. Place meat, gravy and vegetables in a deep baking dish. Cover with small rounds of soda biscuits rolled ½ inch thick. Bake in hot oven (450° F.) about 15 minutes. Serves 5.

Liver Loaf

- ¼ pound salt pork
- 1 pound liver
- 20 crisp soda crackers
- 1½ cups hot stock (or water)
- 2 eggs, beaten
- 1 tablespoon minced onion
- 1 teaspoon poultry seasoning
- 1 teaspoon salt
- ¼ teaspoon pepper
- 1 tablespoon butter

Pan-fry the salt pork. Remove from pan. Add liver to the fat. Sear on both sides. Coarsely grind the liver and pork together. Pour the hot stock over crumbed crackers. Combine meat, crackers, eggs, and seasonings. Shape into a loaf and dot with butter. Bake in a hot oven (425° F.) for 25 to 30 minutes. Serves 6.

Braised Breast of Lamb with Spinach Stuffing

Simmer a breast of lamb in salted water to cover until tender, about 20 minutes per pound. Remove from broth, slip the bones out at once and allow the meat to cool. Spread out breast of lamb, cover with a thin layer of spinach stuffing, roll and tie at both ends with clean, white string. Place rolled meat in a baking pan, sprinkle lightly with flour and pour ¼ cup of the broth around it and brown in a hot oven (400° F.).

SPINACH STUFFING

- 2 cups dry bread crumbs
- ½ pound spinach leaves
- 4 tablespoons butter
- 2 tablespoons celery, chopped
- 1 tablespoon green pepper, chopped
- 1 tablespoon onion, chopped
- ½ teaspoon salt
- ¼ teaspoon pepper

Wash spinach thoroughly, cut in fine pieces, and place in a saucepan with celery, green pepper, onion, and 2 tablespoons butter. Cook to wilt the spinach slightly, about 2 minutes, stirring constantly. Push spinach to one side of the pan, melt remaining butter in empty part of pan and add the bread crumbs. (This is an easy way to butter the crumbs.) Mix spinach and crumbs. Season.

Fried Pickled Tripe

Parboil pickled honeycomb tripe about 3 minutes. Dry thoroughly and dip in beaten egg. Roll in flour and fry in a well greased skillet until brown on both sides.

Broiled Tripe

[*Famous recipe of the Parker House, Boston, Mass.*]

Cut honeycomb tripe in pieces about 4 by 6 inches. Season with salt and pepper. Sprinkle with flour, then dip in olive oil and sprinkle generously with sifted bread crumbs. Broil slowly 2 or 3 minutes on each side or until the crumbs are brown (a charcoal fire is best). Serve with mustard sauce.

MUSTARD SAUCE

Sauté 1 tablespoon minced onion in 3 tablespoons butter. Add 2 tablespoons cider vinegar and simmer 5 minutes. Moisten 2 teaspoons dry mustard with 1 tablespoon water and blend; then add 1 cup brown gravy. Let simmer a few minutes and strain. Serve very hot. Makes 1¼ cups sauce.

New Hampshire "Old Home" Chicken Pie

1 recipe plain pastry
1 fowl (about 4 pounds)
3 cups chicken gravy
salt and pepper

Line an earthen baking dish with the pastry rolled about ¼ inch thick. Lay into this unbaked shell pieces of hot boiled chicken, seasoned to suit the taste, and pour gravy over it. Put on the top cover, rolled ⅛ inch thick, and gashed to allow the steam to escape. Bake in a hot oven (450° F.) for about 15 minutes, then reduce heat to moderate (350° F.) and continue baking about 30 minutes longer. This recipe makes 6 servings.

PLAIN PASTRY

2½ cups sifted flour
¾ teaspoon salt
¾ cup shortening
⅓ cup cold water (about)

Mix and sift flour and salt. Cut in shortening. Add water in small amounts, stirring with a fork and laying dough to one side as it is formed. Use water sparingly. Roll dough ¼ inch thick, and form bottom and top of pie as suggested above.

Potted Chicken

[In Plymouth, Mass., they call it "tendering a fowl"]

Cut up a fowl as for fricassee. Roll each piece in seasoned flour. Pack closely in a large bean pot and cover with boiling water and bake 3½ hours. Cover after water begins to boil.

Cape Cod Chicken

2 slices of fat salt pork
1 fowl cut in pieces for stewing
6 slices of turnip
6 onions
6 potatoes
salt and pepper
dumplings

Try out pork in large kettle and then lay in the chicken pieces. Cover with boiling water and boil ½ hour. Then lay in the turnip slices and the onions. When nearly done add potatoes. Twelve minutes before serving put in the dumplings or steam separately. Put chicken on large platter surrounded by vegetables and dumplings; make the gravy and serve in bowl. Serves 6.

DUMPLINGS

2 cups flour
¾ teaspoon salt
3 teaspoons baking powder
1 cup rich milk

Sift dry ingredients together 4 times. Add milk, stirring quickly to make a soft dough. Drop by spoonfuls on top of chicken gravy or stew, making sure the dough rests on pieces of meat or vegetables and does not settle in the liquid. Cover tightly and steam 12 minutes without removing cover. Dumplings may also be dropped on a plate and cooked in a steamer over rapidly boiling water for 20 minutes. Makes 12 dumplings. If *rich* milk is not available cut in 2 tablespoons shortening as for baking-powder biscuits.

* *A clever New England way of making a tough chicken tender enough to fry is to soak it overnight in buttermilk. The buttermilk also gives it a delicious flavor.*

Chicken Smothered in Oysters

[*Famous "company dish," 300 years old*]

Clean and cut young chickens into quarters. Season. Heat butter in a skillet and sauté chicken. Place in a baking dish. Pour over ½ cup milk for each chicken. Cover dish and place in a moderately hot oven (375° F.) for 1 hour. Baste frequently. Add 1 pint small oysters and 1 cup cream for each chicken and roast 15 minutes longer. Remove chicken to hot platter. Pour oysters and cream around and serve.

Creamed Chicken and Rice

Singe and wash one 5-pound chicken. Tie drumsticks and wings close to body. Place in kettle with 1 carrot, 1 cup celery, ¼ teaspoon salt, 3 quarts of water and simmer gently 1½ hours.

For the cream sauce, melt 2 tablespoons butter, blend well with 3 tablespoons flour, add 2 cups of broth from the chicken pot, stirring all the while. Add 1 cup of cream last, and season with salt and pepper, to taste. Add mushrooms to sauce if desired.

Disjoint chicken, place in sauce and keep warm till serving time. Serve with boiled rice molded in ring, piling the chicken in the center with the sauce. Serves 6.

Hen and Beans

[An old New Hampshire recipe]

Cut up a tough old rooster as for fricassee. Prepare Boston Baked Beans according to recipe on page 104. Smother pieces of chicken under the beans and proceed as for Boston Baked Beans.

Maine Chicken Stew

2 3½-4 pound chickens
6 potatoes, sliced
3 onions, sliced
cold water
2 tablespoons butter
1 cup thin cream or rich milk
salt and pepper
minced parsley
6 to 8 common crackers

Cut chicken for stewing. In an iron kettle place alternate layers of chickens, slices of potato, and thinly sliced onion. Cover with cold water. Simmer gently until chicken is tender. Add butter in small bits and cream or milk. Season with salt and pepper and minced parsley. Split crackers, moisten in cold milk, and reheat in stew. Serves 8.

Hartwell Farms Creamed Chicken

½ cup chicken fat or butter
1½ cups flour
1 tablespoon salt
½ teaspoon white pepper
1 cup fresh mushrooms, sliced
2 cups milk
2 cups cream
1 cup chicken soup
2 cups diced chicken

Blend chicken fat or butter, salt, pepper, and flour in top of a double boiler. Beat thoroughly with a whip; add milk and cream.

Continue beating with a whip until it begins to thicken. Add the chicken soup. Set this mixture aside until it cools. Add the diced chicken and mushrooms. Heat for serving. Do not cover while reheating. Serves 8 to 10.

* *By not sautéeing the mushrooms, the sauce is not darkened. The mushrooms will be cooked but not overdone as the mixture heats for serving. This was one of the very popular recipes of The Hartwell Farms, Lincoln, Mass., and came from Marion Fitch who now makes it to sell for the Women's Exchange in Lincoln.*

Vermont Roast Turkey

Singe, clean, and rub inside with salt; stuff and truss. Rub entire turkey well with olive oil, butter, or cooking oil. Place breast side up in an ordinary dripping pan with a rack in the bottom. Do not cover. In such a roaster any steam that forms will go off into the air and not stay inside to draw juices from the turkey and make it dry.

Roast turkey at a moderately slow temperature (325° F.). Do not sear. Keeping the temperature constant throughout the cooking gives a finished bird that is cooked evenly. There will be little or no sputtering and the drippings will be just right for making a nice brown gravy. Allow 25 to 30 minutes per pound. A young turkey weighing between 10 and 14 pounds, market weight, requires 3 to 3½ hours roasting at 325° F. (Market weight means picked but not drawn and including head and feet.)

Turn a turkey cooked in an open roaster breast side down the last 30 minutes of roasting. To turn without breaking the skin, pick the turkey up by the neck and legs using several folds of soft clean cloth as a "holder."

To determine if turkey is done, run a steel skewer or cooking fork into the thickest part of the breast and also into the thigh next to the breast. If the meat is tender and the juice does not look red, the turkey is roasted enough. Basting is not necessary if the bird is fat. Otherwise baste every 30 minutes with pan drippings or water and butter.

✻ *In buying a turkey allow ¾ pound for each person to be served. That is as the bird is weighed when bought, undrawn with head and feet attached. A 15-pound turkey will make 20 generous servings.*

BREAD CRUMB STUFFING

- 5 cups bread crumbs
- 1 onion, minced
- 1 cup finely chopped celery
- ¾ cup butter, melted
- 1 teaspoon salt
- ¼ teaspoon pepper
- ½ teaspoon poultry seasoning or thyme, marjoram, or sage

Mix bread crumbs, onion, celery, seasonings, and melted butter with a fork. Makes stuffing enough for a 10-pound turkey. Halve this recipe for 5-pound chicken or fish.

✻ *A half-cup fat salt pork (put through the meat grinder) was often substituted for the melted butter. Certain New England recipes call for the addition of ½ teaspoon grated nutmeg.*

BUTTERNUT STUFFING

- 1½ cups butternut meats, chopped
- 4 cups bread crumbs, sifted
- 1 teaspoon dried powdered sage
- ½ teaspoon summer savory
- ½ teaspoon thyme
- 1 egg, well beaten
- ½ cup cream
- 4 cups hot mashed potatoes
- 1 teaspoon salt
- ½ teaspoon pepper

Mix well nuts, bread crumbs, and dried powdered herbs. Combine well-beaten egg with cream. Add this to the freshly boiled mashed hot potatoes. Add salt and pepper and beat. Put the mixtures together and stuff bird. Makes stuffing enough for a 13-pound turkey. Butternut stuffing was an old-time favorite, and too good to be forgotten.

Roast Venison

[*A Maine recipe*]

Roast venison in the same manner in which lamb is roasted, allowing 25 minutes to the pound for cooking (in an oven 350° F.) as venison is served rare. If venison is lean, place a few slices of salt pork over the roast. Serve with currant sauce and fried hominy. (See recipe page 96.)

CURRANT SAUCE

1 cup hot gravy
¼ glass currant jelly

Combine and serve.

Venison Steaks and Cutlets

Broil or pan-fry in the same manner in which chops are broiled, first brushing with olive oil. If venison is strong, marinate with French dressing for 1 hour before broiling. Venison from a freshly killed deer should ripen for 2 weeks before being eaten.

Shoulder cuts of venison may be braised with celery, onion, or carrot. Add 1 tablespoon vinegar and cook about 2½ hours. Serve with grape jelly.

VENISON SAUCE

½ tablespoon chicken fat or butter
1 cup barberry, wild currant, or grape jelly
⅛ teaspoon salt
1 tablespoon cider or cider vinegar
½ teaspoon ground cloves
½ teaspoon cinnamon

Let butter melt (but do not let it brown) in skillet. When melted, add the jelly, salt, cider, and spices. Simmer slowly until mixture thickens slightly.

* *This sauce may be made ahead of time. When desired for use, reheat in double boiler. The above quantity is for a 6-pound haunch of venison, a good-sized chicken, a roast partridge, pheasant, or roast lamb. This recipe is 180 years old and comes from Kent, Conn.*

FRIED HOMINY

[*To serve with roast duck and birds and venison*]

2 cups cold cooked hominy
2 egg yolks
½ teaspoon salt

Combine hominy, egg yolks, and salt. Shape in croquettes and fry in hot deep fat (370° F.) for 5 minutes until delicately browned, or pan-fry. Serves 3 or 4.

Squirrel Pie

Dress 4 squirrels and cut into suitable pieces to serve. Soak overnight in lightly salted water. Wash well and parboil 15 minutes. Rinse well with hot water and simmer in 2 cups water until tender, about 1 hour. Remove meat to a pastry-lined deep dish (which has an inverted cup in the center). Thicken and season the gravy, adding 2 tablespoons butter, and pour over meat. Top with tiny baking powder biscuits or a pastry crust. Bake in a hot oven (450° F.) until crust is well browned. At least 4 squirrels are needed to fill a 2-quart dish. Four squirrels serve 6. Bottom crust may be omitted.

✱ *To dress squirrels, cut off forefeet at first joint; cut skin around first joint of hind legs, loosen it, and with a sharp knife slit the skin on the under side of legs at the tail. Loosen the skin and turn it back until it is removed from the hind legs. Draw the skin over the head, slipping out the forelegs when reached. Cut off the end of nose and thus remove the entire skin. Wipe squirrel with a damp cloth, remove entrails (heart and liver are edible). An ingenious way to remove skin readily is to slip tip of bicycle pump under the skin of legs. The pressure of the air does the trick neatly.*

Coot Stew

Skin 2 coots (do not pick). Wash in salt and water and let stand overnight in solution of ¼ cup salt and water to cover.

Place in stew kettle and boil for 10 minutes. Remove and pour off water. Return to kettle. Add 1 teaspoon salt, ¼ teaspoon pepper and fresh water to cover.

When tender enough to break at joints, remove. Add to liquor 4 medium-sized onions, chopped, 6 large potatoes, diced, 1 sweet potato, diced, 1 cup diced turnip, and cook until almost done, then add coots, which have been cut in pieces. Thicken slightly and serve. Serves 6.

The Country Fair

A country fair is a kaleidoscopic collection of special sights and sounds. Everywhere there is color and action and everywhere you feel the pull of prideful competition.

The father of all fairs in this country was Elkorah Watson of Pittsfield, Mass., who is said to have bought a pair of prize merino sheep that he wanted to show off to his neighbors. To summon an audience he tethered the sheep in the town square and rang a loud ship's bell. The interest that was shown in his animals gave Mr. Watson the idea of organizing a small fair in his home town in 1810, the first of its kind in this country.

Now there are hundreds of thousands of fairs all over America in which amateurs, Grange and 4H members, housewives, and even local merchants and large corporations take part. Many are sponsored by the county agricultural society and cooperate with the state department of agriculture.

The largest of the Yankee fairs is the Eastern States Exposition held each fall in Springfield, Mass., and attended by half a million people. But if you like a small fair you'll find one of the most delightful is the Barnstable County Fair on Cape Cod which was first held in 1853 and has been going strong ever since.

It goes on for four days in July and about 20,000 people are there.

At the heart of the fair is the exhibitor who has worked for months to bring his cattle, fruits, vegetables, flowers, arts and crafts, clothing, and embroidery to the peak of perfection.

Even children exhibit. Prizes are awarded for the best original drawings and paintings by 9- to 13-year-olds and a popular pet show is scheduled for youngsters in which cats, dogs, pet ducks, and even turtles vie for blue ribbon awards.

The vegetables, fruits, and flowers draw big crowds. Take the green beans, for example: you'll see exactly fifteen green beans to a packet, each faultlessly like every other in size, color, and shape—neither too small nor too large—and scrupulously free of even the smallest blemish. Row upon row of colorful vegetables —all perfect—tomatoes, summer squash, lettuce, turnips, Green Mountain potatoes, cucumbers, beets, and many others delight the eye.

Nearby is the fruit exhibit featuring polished McIntosh apples, pears, crabapples, purple plums, luscious blueberries, red, ripe raspberries, and fat strawberries—a marvelous medly of nature's brightest colors and textures.

The color and beauty of the flower exhibits in the next stall include old-fashioned bachelor buttons, calendulas, cosmos, nasturtiums, hollyhocks, and zinnias that make up a real Yankee garden.

The display of baked goods at any fair is one of my favorites: cherry pies, yeast breads, rolls, flaky baking powder biscuits, muffins, cupcakes, brownies, light and dark cakes, fancy decorated party cakes, each wrapped in transparent paper and accompanied by a 3 x 5 recipe card. There's even an award for the best-packed school lunch! All this food is usually sold each night at seven o'clock and freshly baked items appear next morning.

Many fairs have row upon row of homemade pickles, jams, jellies and preserves as well as Mason jars filled with homegrown fruits and vegetables, expertly canned and ready for the long winter.

The rules governing food competition state that "no package mixes may be used." Nor are synthetic materials usually permitted in needlework contest, and for rugs and sweaters only 100 percent wool yarns are accepted.

Here and there around the fairgrounds are food booths where you can buy delicious bowls of fish chowder or plates of potato salad, lobster rolls, coffee, and doughnuts as well as other classic dishes prepared by the best cooks of a local church. And what food experts these ladies are!

Soft drinks are on sale at all fairs as well as crackerjack, popcorn, candy-coated apples, and tantalizing pink spun-sugar candy!

But I skip lightly over such carnival foods as they are not to be mentioned in the same breath with real Yankee cooking.

When the fair ends, it does so with a swish and a bang! On the final night, the sky blazes with a mammoth display of fireworks. Thus the country fair, a bit of yesterday, is over for the year, but with any luck it should be with us next summer.

Vegetables: Individual and Collective

Boston Baked Beans

1 quart pea beans
½ pound fat salt pork
2 teaspoons salt
1½ tablespoons brown sugar
¼ cup molasses
½ teaspoon dry mustard
boiling water

Wash and pick over beans. Soak overnight in cold water. In the morning, drain, cover with fresh water, and simmer until skins break; turn into bean pot. Score pork and press into beans, leaving ¼ inch above the beans. Add salt, sugar, molasses, and mustard. Add boiling water to cover. Cover and bake in slow oven (250° F.) for about 8 hours without stirring, adding water as necessary to keep beans covered. Uncover during last half hour to brown. Serves 8.

✱ *The secret of delicious baked beans is to keep them covered with water at all times except the last hour of baking. Cape Cod cooks add ½ cup cream to baked beans the last half hour of baking. A large onion nestled in the center of the bean pot is popular with Connecticut cooks. A bay leaf hidden here and there also adds flavor. In the early days, beans were left to bake all night in the slow steady heat of the great brick oven.*

The Puritan housewife baked her beans all day Saturday, served them fresh for the Saturday night meal (the beginning of Sabbath); warmed them over for Sunday breakfast, and served them warm or cold, depending on the heat-holding qualities of her oven, for Sunday's noonday lunch, providing she did not consider it necessary to fast from breakfast until sundown on Sunday.

Of all the Puritan influences that fastened themselves on New England, the Saturday night baked bean supper is one of the most lasting and widespread in its effect on other parts of the country. Beans are still eaten every

Saturday night and Sunday morning by thousands of New Englanders. All religious significance has been lost many years ago, but the baked bean holds popular favor in its own right.

Baked Beans with Maple Syrup

[*A Vermont recipe*]

- 1 quart pea beans
- ½ pound fat salt pork
- 1 onion
- ½ cup maple syrup
- ½ teaspoon dry mustard
- 2 teaspoons salt
- boiling water

Soak beans overnight. In the morning put on to cook in fresh water. Let simmer until skins burst, 1 to 1½ hours. Drain beans. Put an onion in bottom of bean pot; add beans. Mix syrup, mustard, and salt and sprinkle over beans. Put pork down into beans so that only the rind is above the surface. Pour on boiling water to cover. Bake in a slow oven (250° F.) for 6 to 8 hours, adding water, a little at a time, to keep beans covered. Serves 6.

New Hampshire Baked Yellow Eye Pork and Beans

- 1 quart dried yellow eye beans
- ½ pound salt pork (streaked with lean)
- 1 tablespoon sugar
- ¾ cup brown sugar
- 1 teaspoon mustard
- ¼ teaspoon pepper
- ½ teaspoon ginger
- ½ cup tomato catsup
- 2 teaspoons salt
- boiling water

Wash and pick over beans. Soak overnight in cold water to cover. In the morning drain, cover with fresh water, and simmer for 1 to 1½ hours, or until the skins wrinkle. Turn into beanpot. Add sugar, brown sugar, mustard, pepper, ginger, catsup, and salt. Score the pork and press it down into the beans. The rind should be uppermost and projecting ¼ inch above the beans. Pour on boiling water to cover. Cover and bake in a slow oven (250° F.) about 8 hours. During the baking add boiling water so that the beans are covered with water. Uncover during last half hour to brown. Serves 8.

Serve sliced green tomato pickles or sharp cucumber pickles with the beans.

Baked Beans, Maine Lumbercamp Style

[*From Howard Reynolds's series on camping on the Allagash printed August, 1923, in the Boston* Post]

"First a hole is dug in the ground, fairly free of rocks, 2 feet deep by 18 inches in circumference. In the hole kindling of soft wood is first placed, and over the hole a cobhouse of split hard wood is built. When the fire is lighted in the kindling the cobhouse catches fire, and as the air circulates freely through it, the hard-wood sticks, being of uniform size, all burn down together.

"In the meanwhile over the campfire a pail of beans (about 2 quarts dried beans) has been parboiling so that their skins crack when dished out in a spoon and exposed to the air. The water from these is drained off and they are poured into another pail on the bottom of which has been placed several thick slices of fat salt pork. On the top of the beans is placed a piece of pork weighing about a pound, the rind of which has been well gashed. Over all is poured a teaspoonful of salt, 3 tablespoons of molasses, 2 of sugar and a dash of mustard, dissolved in hot water. The pail is then filled with enough boiling water to cover the beans.

"Next the coals are raked out of the hole and the pail, covered tight with an empty corn-can put on top and wedged in so as to keep the pail upright, is placed in the hole. The live coals are then shoveled around it and over it, together with a few inches of earth tramped down tight and allowed to remain alone all night. In the morning dig the pail out and serve."

Frozen Bean Porridge

Put 3 cups of dry red kidney beans to soak overnight, parboil them in the morning until the skins crack; drain. Cook 3 pounds soup bone (beef with marrow) until the bones may be removed and the meat cut in pieces. Add enough water to the amount the meat was boiled in to make 6 quarts; add the beans, 2 tablespoons salt, ¼ teaspoon black pepper, and cook until the beans are tender but not mushy. Add 1 cup yellow corn meal, wet with water, and cook 30 minutes, stirring often to avoid "catching on" (sticking and burning). Set out to freeze. Small amounts are cut from this as needed and "het" boiling hot. An iron kettle is best but any heavy kettle will do.

✻ *This porridge was made in huge iron kettles and hauled on ox sleds into the wilderness for a staple food when men and boys went to clear the land and build a cabin for their families, who would follow in the spring. Without doubt, much of New Hampshire was "settled" on frozen bean porridge.*

Martha's Vineyard Green Corn Pudding

[*Mrs. Charles L. Foote, W. Tisbury, Mass.*]

24 ears of corn
milk
3 eggs, well beaten
2 tablespoons butter, melted
1 teaspoon salt
4 tablespoons sugar

Cut each row of corn lengthwise through each kernel. Then grate with grater and scrape each ear, taking care not to scrape too close to the cob. Sometimes the corn will be milky, at other times dry. The amount of milk to add depends on the corn. The mixture should be about the consistency of corn bread mixture after the milk, eggs, butter, salt, and sugar are added. There will be about 4 cups of the mixture. Turn into a greased baking dish. Bake 2 to 3 hours in a very slow oven (250° F.) or until pudding is set and light brown. It should be dry enough when done to cut into squares. Butter each individual serving. Serves 6 to 8.

Oven Roasted Corn

[*A New Hampshire recipe*]

Place ears of corn (with husks) in a moderate oven (350° F.) and bake for 30 minutes. Remove husks and silk and serve hot with butter. Oven-roasted corn has the flavor of corn served at corn roasts or clambakes.

> * *One of the commonest faults of cooking corn on the cob in water is overcooking it. Drop corn into boiling, salted water. When water returns to boil, turn off heat and let stand in water exactly 5 minutes.*

Corn Oysters

[*Mrs. Nellie Barrett, West Sumner, Me.*]

½ cup flour, sifted
½ teaspoon baking powder
½ teaspoon salt
1 cup canned corn
1 egg, well beaten
2 tablespoons melted butter
1 tablespoon milk

Sift dry ingredients. Combine the corn and milk and mix thoroughly. Add egg and butter and mix well. Drop from tip of spoon into hot fat in skillet. These little fritters should be the size of large oysters. Sauté until brown, turning to brown both sides. Makes 12 to 16 oysters.

If pulp from corn-on-the-cob is used, score the kernels on the cob down the middle with a sharp knife, and press out the pulp using the dull back of the knife. Make a batter of the remaining ingredients adding flour in small quantities until the consistency is that of pancake batter. If the corn is not milky, add an additional tablespoon of milk.

Hulled Corn—Old Method

Boil white wood-ashes in an iron kettle with plenty of water until the mixture is stout enough to float an egg. Drain it off from the ashes. Place the shelled corn in the liquid. Boil the corn carefully until the hulls rub off. Rinse in several waters so that no lye remains. Boil again in salted water until tender.

Hulled Corn—New Method

Pick over 1 quart dried, yellow corn. Cover with 2 quarts cold water to which has been added 2 tablespoons soda. Soak overnight. Boil in the same water, adding more as needed, until the hulls are loosened, about 3 hours. Drain, wash, rub off the hulls between hands. Boil corn again in clear water. Change the water, add a teaspoon of salt and boil gently until corn is tender, about 4 hours. Serve hot with milk or butter. One quart corn makes 4 quarts when cooked.

* *Hulled corn is a favorite old New England dish. It is made from yellow corn, whereas hominy, another venerable dish, is made from white corn. Both hulled corn and hominy (samp) may be purchased today in two forms—*

hulled and ready to cook (about 4 hours cooking time required) or in tins, all cooked, ready to heat and serve. Hulled corn or hominy is an excellent change from potatoes. It may be warmed up by frying in butter.

Many New Englanders recall peddlers who used to sell hulled corn and horseradish.

Succotash

2 tablespoons butter
2 cups cooked beans (lima or kidney)
2 cups corn (fresh scraped from the cob or canned)
½ cup water
1 teaspoon salt
⅛ teaspoon pepper
1 teaspoon sugar
¼ cup rich milk

Melt butter; add the beans, corn, and water and the seasonings. Cook over low heat. Stir in the milk as water is absorbed. Heat thoroughly, but do not boil after milk is added. Serve very hot. Serves 6.

Nine Potato Recipes from Aroostook, Me.

[*Pearl Ashby Tibbetts, the busy wife of a very busy country doctor in Bethel, Me., contributes all nine*]

POTATOES AND PEPPERS IN CREAM

Cut 6 Maine potatoes, boiled in skins, into small cubes. Parboil 1 sweet green pepper, remove seeds, and chop. Place cubes of potato and chopped pepper in top of double boiler with 1 cup top milk and cook 15 minutes. Then place in casserole with 2 tablespoons grated cheese. Cook about 20 minutes in moderate oven (350° F.). Serves 4 to 6.

POTATOES IN HALF SHELL

Bake even-sized Maine potatoes. Slice lengthwise. Carefully scoop out interior of each. Mash well and add butter, salt, pepper, and hot milk or cream. Beat vigorously and when fluffy return to shells. Sprinkle with paprika and chopped parsley, brown in the oven, and serve.

SMALL POTATOES

Peel and wash 8 small Maine potatoes. Boil quickly and drain. Add 3 tablespoons butter; 1 tablespoon lemon juice and 2 tablespoons minced parsley. Serve with any cooked fish. Serves 3 or 4.

PUFF BALLS

- 6 medium potatoes
- 3 tablespoons butter
- ½ cup hot milk
- salt and pepper
- egg
- bread crumbs
- ¼ cup mild grated cheese

Pare and boil potatoes. Drain and mash very smooth and light. Add butter, hot milk, grated cheese, salt and pepper to taste, and beat until fluffy. While hot, shape into little balls, roll in egg and bread crumbs, place on a well-buttered tin, and brown delicately in a hot oven (450° F.). Serve immediately. Serves 4.

PANNED POTATOES

Put 2 tablespoons butter in a baking pan; pare and slice 6 Maine potatoes as for frying, put in pan, sprinkle with salt and pepper, and cover with rich milk. Cook in moderate oven (350° F.) about 40 minutes until potatoes are tender and milk absorbed. Serves 4.

SAVORY SUPPER DISH

Slice a layer of raw onion in bottom of buttered baking dish. Fill dish with thin slices of raw Maine potatoes. Add salt and pepper. Nearly cover with water, place cubes of salt pork on top and cook slowly 3 hours in an oven 250° F.

MASHED MAINERS WITH MINT

Boil and mash Maine potatoes; add salt, butter, and hot milk. Beat until fluffy and add 2 tablespoons finely chopped fresh mint leaves. Excellent with roast lamb.

POTATO BROWN MOUND

Pile mashed potatoes lightly in greased baking dish. Pour over ½ cup heavy cream and sprinkle with ½ cup dry bread crumbs. Bake in hot oven (450° F.) until crumbs are brown. Serve with cold sliced meat.

MAINE SOUFFLÉ

Combine 3 cups hot boiled and mashed Maine potatoes, ¼ cup melted butter, yolks of 2 eggs, a little cayenne pepper, and 1 cup hot milk. Stir well and then fold in the beaten whites of the eggs. Pile in well-buttered baking dish and bake 15 minutes in a moderate oven (350° F.). Serves 4.

Grandmother's Potatoes

Pare large potatoes and cut a tunnel through the center of each one with an apple corer. Draw a small sausage through each one; place potatoes in the pan and lay a slice of salt pork or bacon on each one. Bake in a moderately hot oven (375° F.), about 50 minutes or until done, basting with hot water when necessary.

"Necessity Mess," "Potato Bargain," or "Tilton's Glory"

[*From a book of Vineyard recipes*]

"To make this dish properly," according to Joseph C. Allen, Cape Higgon, Mass., "an iron pot should be used. Otherwise it must be started in a frying pan. ½ pound mixed pork, 3 onions the size of duck eggs, 1½ quarts potatoes, peeled and cut in slices ½ inch thick. Slice the pork about ¼ inch thick. Peel and slice onions very thin. Place in the pot and fry briskly until very brown. Then put in the potatoes and fill the pot with water until it is about an inch above the potatoes. Boil slowly until the potatoes are thoroughly cooked but not enough to crumble. Thicken the gravy, using about 3 tablespoons flour and serve in one dish. A small turnip, a carrot, or both, may be added, as may also dumplings. But as these are not, properly speaking, 'necessities,' I have not included them in the recipe."

Scootin'-'Long-the-Shore

¼ cup bacon fat
1 cup onions, sliced
4 cups raw potatoes, sliced

Heat bacon fat in a skillet; stir in the onions and potatoes. Cover and cook slowly, stirring occasionally until the fat is absorbed and the potatoes are tender. Uncover when brown and crusty on the bottom. Serve with fried or boiled fish. Serves 4.

Halleluia

¼ pound salt pork, sliced
2 cups hot water
4 large onions, sliced
4 potatoes, sliced
1 tablespoon flour
¼ cup cold water
½ teaspoon salt
½ teaspoon sugar
⅛ teaspoon pepper

Try out the pork; add water, onions, and potatoes. Cook slowly 50 minutes, or until vegetables are soft. Before serving thicken with flour dissolved in cold water; add salt, sugar, and pepper. Serves 5.

Maple Candied Sweet Potatoes

[*A Vermont recipe*]

- 6 medium-sized sweet potatoes
- ½ cup maple syrup
- 1 tablespoon butter
- 1 teaspoon salt
- 1 cup apple cider (or apple juice)
- ½ cup water

Boil potatoes in jackets until nearly done. Peel, slice, and put into baking pan. Let maple syrup, butter, salt, cider, and water come to a boil. Pour over potatoes and bake in slow oven (300° F.) for 1 hour or until potatoes are glazed and syrup of desired consistency. Serves 6.

Baked Sweet Potato and Apple Slices

[*A Vermont recipe*]

- 2 large apples
- 2 large cold cooked sweet potatoes
- ½ teaspoon salt
- 2 tablespoons butter
- ¼ cup maple syrup

Select tart, perfect apples; core, pare and cut in crosswise slices and sauté each slice in butter until nearly soft. Brown well, but do not allow the slices to break. Cut the potatoes into rather thick crosswise slices, sprinkle with the salt and place a slice of fried apple on each slice of potato. Arrange in a shallow baking dish, slightly overlapping one another. Pour the maple syrup over all and dot with the butter. Bake in a moderately hot oven (375° F.) about ½ hour, or until the potato absorbs nearly all the syrup and the apples are quite brown. Serves 4.

Jerusalem Artichokes

Pare, boil in salted water about 30 minutes, or until tender; drain, add melted butter, minced parsley, and a few drops lemon juice. Serve in place of potatoes.

Mashed Turnip

[*A Connecticut recipe*]

Wash and slice 2 medium-sized yellow turnips (rutabagas). Boil in salted water until tender. Drain, mash; season with butter, salt, pepper, and a little cream. Serves 8 to 10.

Hashed Turnip

- 2 cups turnips, white or yellow
- 1 teaspoon salt
- 1 tablespoon butter or salt pork fat or sausage fat
- freshly ground pepper to taste
- 4 tablespoons water

Wash, peel, and slice turnip. Cook until done, about 30 minutes, in unsalted water. When done, chop coarsely and measure. Add other ingredients.

Cook slowly in spider or saucepan stirring constantly about 4 minutes. Serve at once. Serves 4.

✻ *Young white turnips peeled, diced, cooked, and buttered are delicious with pork.*

Baked Turnip Puff

2 cups hot mashed potato
2 cups hot mashed turnip
2 tablespoons melted butter
½ teaspoon salt
⅛ teaspoon pepper
2 tablespoons sweet cream
1 egg, well beaten

Mix potato and turnip. Add other ingredients in the order given. Turn into a well-greased baking dish and bake in a hot oven (400° F.) for 20 minutes. Serve hot in same dish. Serves 6.

Pickled Beets

½ cup vinegar
½ cup water
4 whole cloves
1 stick cinnamon
2 teaspoons sugar
1 teaspoon scraped onion
salt and pepper
2 cups hot cooked beets, sliced

Combine all ingredients, except beets, in a saucepan. Simmer about 8 minutes. Pour over beets, and let stand until cold.

Harvard Beets

¾ tablespoon cornstarch
¼ cup sugar
⅛ teaspoon salt
½ cup vinegar
¼ cup beet liquid
2 cups cooked cubed beets
2 tablespoons butter

Mix cornstarch, sugar, and salt. Add vinegar and beet liquid gradually until blended. Stir and cook until thickened. Add beets and butter. Serve hot. Serves 4.

Pan-Fried Tomatoes

Slice green or firm ripe tomatoes in thick slices, without peeling. Sprinkle with salt and pepper. Dip each slice in flour. Pan-fry in a small amount of fat until brown on both sides. Pour off excess liquid from tomatoes while frying. Excellent served with cold meat.

Scalloped Tomatoes

- 2 cups canned tomatoes
- ½ small onion, scraped
- 1 teaspoon salt
- 1 teaspoon sugar
- pepper
- 2 cups dried bread crumbs
- 4 tablespoons butter

Mix tomatoes and seasonings. Arrange tomatoes and crumbs in alternate layers, in buttered baking dish, having bread as top layer and dotting each layer with butter. Bake in a moderately hot oven (375° F.) about 20 minutes. Serves 5.

* *Tomatoes were introduced into New England gardens almost 200 years ago and were called "love apples." They were chiefly eaten sliced raw with sugar, or stewed with a little water, salt, pepper, and a generous lump of butter. Sugar was sprinkled over them.*

Fried Cucumbers

Peel cucumbers and slice lengthwise, making about 8 wedge slices to one large cucumber. Put in ice water until ready to cook. Dip in beaten egg and then in wheat germ and sauté until lightly browned. Serves 4.

Summer Squash

Summer squash may be boiled or steamed. Wash, cut off stem, but do not pare. Cut in slices; place in steamer (or top of double boiler) or in rapidly boiling salted water. Cook until tender (15 to 30 minutes). If boiled, drain well, mash, and drain again. Turn into a serving dish, season with melted butter, salt, and pepper.

Baked Squash

[*As Vermonters prepare it*]

Cut a Hubbard squash in pieces. Remove seeds and stringy parts. Place in a covered pan. Bake 2 hours in a slow oven (300° F.). Remove from shell, mash, season to taste with butter, salt, pepper, and maple syrup.

Parsnip Fritters

[*A Vermont recipe*]

Wash and scrape 10 medium-sized parsnips. Cook in boiling, salted water for 45 minutes. Drain and mash; season with butter, salt, and pepper. Shape into small, flat, round cakes. Roll in flour, fry lightly and quickly, turning frequently. Serves 4 to 6.

Parsnip Stew

8 parsnips
6 potatoes
¼ pound salt pork
salt and pepper
water

Parboil parsnips and potatoes; peel and slice in fairly thick pieces. Place alternate rows crosswise and at an angle in a casserole with thin slices of salt pork between. Season with salt and pepper. Fill dish ⅔ full of water. Bake in a slow oven (300° F.) about 30 minutes, or until potatoes and parsnips are done. Serves 6.

✱ *Parsnips were a familiar dish long ago. As early as 1600 the phrase "soft words butter no parsnips" came into existence.*

Mushroom Soufflé

½ pound mushrooms
4 tablespoons butter
½ teaspoon salt
pepper
4 tablespoons flour
1 cup milk
3 egg yolks, beaten
3 egg whites, beaten stiff

Peel mushrooms; chop fine. Cook in butter until slightly brown. Add salt, pepper, flour; brown lightly. Add milk; cook until thick, stirring constantly. Cool. Add egg yolks and fold in egg whites. Pour into a greased baking dish; bake in a moderate oven (350° F.) 50 minutes. Serve immediately. Serves 4.

Broccoli

Cut off large outer leaves, peel woody outer skin of thick stems. If stems are large, split. Stand with blossoms uppermost in kettle and cook uncovered in boiling salted water 15 to 30 minutes, or until just tender. Drain, season with salt, pepper, and melted butter to which an equal amount of lemon juice has been added. Allow ½ pound broccoli per person.

Vinegared Carrots

[A Vermont recipe]

Wash and scrape 12 medium-sized carrots. Boil until tender. Cut lengthwise in quarters. Place in heated shallow serving dish. Season with salt, pepper, paprika, and 2 tablespoons melted butter. Pour over carrots ⅓ cup hot cider vinegar. Serves 6 to 8.

Stuffed Eggplant

[A Connecticut recipe]

1 medium-sized eggplant
1 cup uncooked mushrooms
½ cup chopped onion
4 tablespoons butter
1 cup minced ham
¼ teaspoon salt
⅛ teaspoon pepper
¾ cup bread crumbs

Cut eggplant in half lengthwise. Scoop out pulp to within ½ inch of the outer skin. Peel mushrooms. Chop mushrooms and eggplant coarsely, and sauté in butter with onion for 10 minutes. Add ham and seasonings. Fill eggplant shells with the mixture and sprinkle top with buttered bread crumbs. Bake in a moderately hot oven (375° F.) until heated through and brown. Serve with thin strips of pimiento arranged crosswise on top. Serves 6.

Creamed Asparagus

Break asparagus in 1½-inch lengths, reserving tips. Place in boiling salted water. Boil until tender, about 20 minutes, adding tips the last 10 minutes of cooking. Drain, season with butter, salt, and pepper and reheat with a few tablespoons of heavy cream. Many New England cooks prefer asparagus served in this way to the long, awkward stalks.

Great-Great-Grandmother's String Beans

1 quart string beans
cold water
1 tablespoon butter
1/8 teaspoon soda
1 teaspoon sugar
1 1/4 teaspoons salt
pepper
1 cup boiling water
1 cup creamy milk

Break off both ends of beans, pull off strings, if present, and break into small pieces or cut into julienne strips. Let stand in cold water to which 1 tablespoon salt is added for 1 to 2 hours. 30 minutes before dinner, drain. Into a saucepan, put butter and heat to a froth but do not brown. Add beans, soda, sugar, salt, pepper, and boiling water. Cook slowly, being careful that the beans do not burn. They will be tender in 30 minutes and most of the water will have boiled away. Add milk, let boil up once, then set where they will keep hot until served. Makes 3 cups cooked beans.

Stuffed Peppers

[*A New Hampshire recipe*]

6 green peppers
2 cups chopped cooked meat
1/2 cup bread crumbs
1/2 cup stock
1 small onion, chopped
1/8 teaspoon pepper
1/2 teaspoon salt
buttered bread crumbs

Wash peppers. Cut a piece from the stem end of each. Remove seeds. Parboil for five minutes. Stuff with a mixture of the meat, bread crumbs, stock, onion, and seasonings and top with buttered bread crumbs. Pour water around the peppers to cover the bottom of the baking pan. Bake for 45 minutes in a moderate oven (350° F.). Serve with tomato sauce. Serves 4 to 6.

Buttered Connecticut Valley Onions

Peel onions and cook uncovered in boiling salted water about 30 minutes, or until tender. Drain, add butter and cream, salt and pepper.

Edgartown Stuffed Onions

Remove skins from large onions and boil in salted water 10 minutes. Drain and cool. Remove center of onion without destroying shape of outer ring. Make filling by combining equal parts of cold chicken, chopped celery, and finely chopped onion centers. Season with salt and pepper and moisten with cream and melted butter. Refill the cavities and cover top with buttered crumbs. Place in baking dish with a little chicken stock or water and bake in a moderate oven (350° F.) until onions are cooked, about 15 minutes.

Scalloped Eggs and Onions

[*New England Fresh Egg Institute*]

12 small onions
8 slices bacon, cut in pieces
2 cups medium white sauce
6 sliced hard cooked eggs
½ cup buttered bread crumbs

Peel and slice onions. Cook bacon until crisp and break into small pieces. Cover bottom of a well-greased casserole with white sauce; place a layer of raw onions in it. Sprinkle with half the bacon, cover with half the eggs. Repeat, making the last two layers onions and white sauce. Sprinkle with buttered crumbs. Bake in moderate oven (350° F.) for about 1¼ hours or until onions are tender. Serves 5.

Onion Soufflé

[*A Connecticut recipe*]

- 12 silver-skinned onions
- 1½ tablespoons butter
- 1½ tablespoons flour
- 1 cup rich milk
- ¼ teaspoon salt
- ⅛ teaspoon pepper
- ¼ cup soft bread crumbs
- 1 egg yolk
- 3 egg whites, stiffly beaten

Peel onions. Cook in boiling salted water until tender. Drain thoroughly, chop and drain again. Force through a sieve. There should be 1 cup thick purée. Blend butter and flour, add milk to make a cream sauce. Add crumbs, egg yolk, salt, and pepper. Combine with the onion purée. Fold in egg whites. Pour into a buttered baking dish. Set dish in a pan of hot water and bake 40 minutes in a moderate oven (350° F.). Serves 6. Serve as an entrée or with the meat course. Delicious with fowl.

Dock Greens

Dock greens are a long narrow leaf that may be found almost any place alongside of a clump of dandelions in fields or backyards. They have a taste of their own but resemble spinach slightly. Cook the same as spinach, adding a small piece of salt pork for extra flavor. Drain, serve with melted butter, salt, and pepper. One reason they were much used in early days was because anyone could go out and gather them without cost. Dock greens, served with new potatoes rolled in garden parsley and melted butter, with hot cornbread and cup custards, make a tempting but healthful meal.

Stewed sorrel was another old-time favorite. Wash sorrel in several waters. Cook leaves until tender in boiling, salted water. When done, season with butter, salt, pepper, and sweet cream. Sorrel Pie was a popular Maine dish.

Marsh marigold or cowslip greens were still another spring-time vegetable. The greens were gathered when the cowslips were in bud, the pithy stems discarded. The leaves were cooked with a piece of well-scored salt pork until the pork was nearly done. Peeled potatoes were added. When the potatoes were done, they were removed and the greens were drained and served with butter, salt and pepper, or vinegar.

Farmer's Cabbage

Put 1 cabbage through the meat grinder, coarsely. Place in a well-buttered baking dish. Season with salt and pepper. Add 2 cups medium white sauce. Mix well. Cover with buttered bread crumbs. Bake until brown in a moderate oven (350° F.) about 20 minutes. Serves 6.

✻ *Coarsely ground carrots may be added to the casserole.*

Fried Sauerkraut

½ cup sliced onions
4 tablespoons butter
1 pound sauerkraut, drained

Sauté onions in butter until delicately browned. Add sauerkraut and mix well. Cover and simmer gently for about ½ hour. Serves 5.

Yankee Slaw Dressing

1 cup milk
1½ tablespoons flour
½ teaspoon salt
½ tablespoon mustard
2 tablespoons sugar
¼ cup vinegar
1 egg
1 tablespoon butter
2 quarts cabbage, shredded

Scald three-fourths of milk. Measure and sift flour, salt, and mustard and make a smooth paste with remaining cold milk. Add to hot milk and cook thoroughly. Heat vinegar and add slowly to dressing after it has thickened. Beat egg with sugar and add to dressing; stir while adding. Add butter. Pour hot dressing over cabbage. Serve slaw hot or chill and serve cold. Serves 6.

Wilted Lettuce

3 bunches garden lettuce
4 slices bacon
pepper
¼ teaspoon salt
¼ cup vinegar
1 hard-cooked egg, sliced

Shred lettuce into salad bowl. Sauté bacon, remove from the pan, and cut into small pieces. Add vinegar, salt, and pepper to the bacon fat, bring to a boil and pour over lettuce. Mix and serve at once with egg slices and the bacon pieces over it as a garnish. Serves 6.

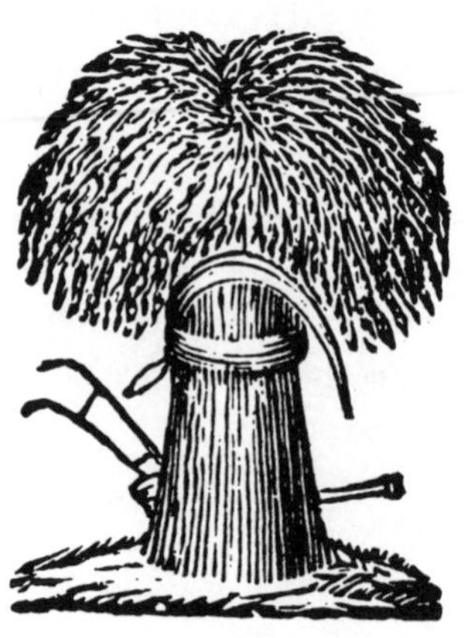

Breads, Biscuits, Gems, Shortcake, and Mush

Ranger Pancakes

1 teaspoon soda
1 cup sour milk
1 egg, beaten
2 tablespoons melted shortening
½ cup cornmeal
2 cups flour
½ teaspoon baking powder
½ teaspoon salt
1 cup sweet milk

Add soda to sour milk. Add egg, shortening, and cornmeal. Sift remaining dry ingredients. Add alternately with sweet milk. Use more or less flour if a thicker or thinner batter is preferred. Beat until free from lumps and bake on a hot greased griddle. Makes about 24 griddle cakes.

* *Griddle cakes taste better to a true Vermonter if they are baked in large thin cakes, spread while hot off the griddle with butter and soft maple sugar and stacked in a pile of 6 or 8 cakes. The stack is cut in pie-shaped wedges and served at once. A topping of whipped cream is optional.*

Mrs. Packard's Pancakes

2 cups flour, sifted
2 tablespoons bread crumbs or shredded biscuit crumbs or yellow cornmeal
2 teaspoons baking powder
½ teaspoon salt
1 cup milk
½ cup cream

Combine the ingredients and beat lightly. Do not beat out all the "nubs" of flour. Fry on a hot, greased griddle. Serve with butter or bacon fat or maple syrup. Serves 5.

Parker House Pancakes

[*Parker House, Boston, Mass.*]

- 2 cups flour, sifted
- 3 teaspoons baking powder
- ½ teaspoon salt
- 1 tablespoon powdered sugar
- 2 eggs, well beaten
- 1¾ cups milk (about)

Mix and sift dry ingredients. Combine eggs and milk; add flour mixture and beat until smooth. Bake on a hot, well-greased griddle. One tablespoon of the mixture makes one cake. This recipe makes about 24 small, thin, delicate cakes.

* *Our great-grandmothers used hard wood ashes (in place of baking soda) to make pancakes rise. They poured boiling water over sifted ashes in a cup, let ashes settle and used the liquid as we use soda that has been dissolved.*

Green Corn Griddle Cakes

[*A Martha's Vineyard recipe*]

- 20 ears sweet corn
- 2 cups milk
- 1 cup flour, sifted
- ½ teaspoon baking powder
- 2 teaspoons salt
- 1 teaspoon sugar
- 2 eggs, beaten separately

Cut each row of corn lengthwise through each kernel. Grate with grater and scrape each ear, taking care not to scrape too close to the cob. Combine ingredients, folding in stiffly beaten egg whites last. Drop by spoonfuls on a well-greased hot griddle. Makes about 12 griddle cakes.

Squash Griddle Cakes

1 cup milk, scalded
1 cup strained squash
1 tablespoon butter
1 tablespoon sugar
½ teaspoon salt
1 egg, beaten
2 teaspoons baking powder
1 cup flour, sifted

Pour the hot milk over the squash. Add the butter, sugar, and salt. When cool add the egg, then the baking powder sifted with the flour. Bake on a hot, greased griddle. Makes about 12 griddle cakes.

Rhode Island Jonnycake

1 cup Rhode Island white jonnycake cornmeal, not bolted (waterground if you can get it)
1 teaspoon salt
1 cup boiling water
½ cup milk (about)

Add salt to cornmeal; scald with boiling water until every grain swells; add milk very gradually until batter is a little thicker than ordinary pancake batter. Bake on slightly greased skillet, allowing more time than for frying griddle cakes. Let cakes cook thoroughly on one side before turning. Turn so that cakes are golden brown on both sides. Makes 16 small cakes.

* *Rhode Island jonnycakes are NOT easy to make. The trick is to get the batter thin enough so that cakes will be about ⅛ inch thick, yet not too thin, or it will be difficult to turn the cakes. The batter should just start to spread when it touches the hot skillet. It is worth experimenting, for the result is a delicate satisfying cake. Some Rhode Islanders add a teaspoon of sugar to the above recipe; some use all water and no milk; some use evaporated milk. Serve with butter only if you are a native son; otherwise serve with butter and maple syrup.*

New Bedford Johnnycake

Follow recipe for Rhode Island Jonnycake, adding 2 tablespoons flour and 1 tablespoon sugar to the cornmeal.

Suet Johnnycake

[*Helen H. Radcliffe, The Galley, Fairhaven, Mass.*]

8 tablespoons Rhode Island white corn meal
boiling water
½ teaspoon salt
3 tablespoons molasses
1 cup suet, chopped
milk

Scald cornmeal until every grain swells. Add salt, molasses, and suet. Thin batter with milk so that it will drop on griddle by spoonfuls, retaining its shape. Fry on griddle slowly until well browned on both sides. Makes 10 griddle cakes.

Fried Indian Cakes

[*Also called Cornmeal Slappers*]

2 cups cornmeal
½ teaspoon soda
½ teaspoon salt
2½ cups boiling water (about)

Mix cornmeal, soda, and salt quickly with boiling water until just stiff enough to form into inch-thick cakes with the hands. Fry in skillet in hot fat, deep enough to cover about halfway up around cakes, turning so that both sides become golden brown. Serve hot with butter and maple syrup and bacon.

Old-Fashioned Raised Buckwheat Cakes

- ½ cake compressed yeast
- 1 cup milk, scalded
- 1 cup water
- 1 teaspoon salt
- 2 tablespoons molasses
- 1 cup flour
- 1 cup buckwheat flour
- ¼ teaspoon soda
- ¼ cup lukewarm water

Crumble yeast cake into lukewarm milk and water, add salt, molasses, and flours to make a batter as thick as cream. Stir until free from lumps. Cover and let rise overnight at room temperature. In the morning, before baking, stir in soda dissolved in water. Pour into small cakes and fry on hot griddle, greased with salt pork. Serve with maple syrup. Makes 20 small cakes.

* *In households where cakes were served every morning a cup of batter was left to "rise" them, instead of fresh yeast.*

Sour Milk Buckwheat Cakes

[*To serve with pork gravy*]

- 1 cake compressed yeast
- 4 cups lukewarm water
- 1 cup cornmeal
- 4 cups buckwheat flour
- 1 teaspoon salt
- 1 cup sour milk (or buttermilk)
- 1 teaspoon soda
- ¼ cup warm water

Crumble yeast into lukewarm water, add cornmeal, buckwheat flour, salt, and milk; beat until a smooth batter is formed. Cover and let rise overnight at room temperature. In the morning, before baking, add soda dissolved in ¼ cup warm water. Mix well and fry on hot buttered griddle. Makes 36 small cakes.

* *If a less pronounced buckwheat taste is preferred, add 1 cup flour and 1 additional cup lukewarm water.*

New Hampshire Ski Snack

Raised Buckwheat Cakes with
New Hampshire Maple Syrup
Broiled Homemade Sausage
Coffee

Waffles

2 cups flour, sifted
3 teaspoons baking powder
½ teaspoon salt
3 eggs, separated
1¼ cups milk
¼ cup melted butter or butter substitute

Mix and sift dry ingredients. Combine well beaten egg yolks and milk, and add to flour mixture. Beat until smooth, then add shortening. Fold in stiffly beaten whites and bake in a hot waffle iron. Makes 6 waffles.

Jolly Boys

[*Also called Rye Meal Drop Cakes*]

1 cup sour milk
½ teaspoon soda
1 egg, beaten
½ cup molasses
2½ cups rye meal (about)

Stir soda into sour milk; combine remaining ingredients, adding rye meal until mixture is about the consistency of doughtnut dough. Drop balls from tip of mixing spoon into hot fat (365° F.). When golden brown drain and serve with maple syrup if desired. Or they may be broken in half and a piece of butter sandwiched between halves. Makes 25 small cakes.

Connecticut Spoon Cakes

1 teaspoon soda
2 cups sour milk
1 egg, slightly beaten
1 teaspoon salt
3 cups sifted flour (about)

Combine soda and sour milk; add egg and salt and enough flour so that batter will "drop off" teaspoon into hot fat without sticking to spoon. Fry in hot deep fat (370° F.) 3 or 4 minutes, or until golden brown. Drain and serve with molasses sauce or maple syrup.

MOLASSES SAUCE

6 tablespoons molasses
1½ teaspoons vinegar

Mix molasses and vinegar and dip each "mouthful" into the sauce.

Holy Pokes

Form bread dough, which has risen once, into balls the size of large marbles. Let rise again until it has doubled in volume. Slip dough balls into a kettle of fat heated to 360° F. and fry until a golden brown. Drain and serve with plenty of butter. Or serve with maple syrup, as a fritter.

Banana Fritters

[*A modern Yankee recipe*]

melted fat or oil
4 medium ripe bananas
¼ cup flour
fritter batter

For shallow frying, have 1 inch of melted fat or oil in frying pan. For deep-fat frying, have deep kettle ½ to ⅔ full of melted fat or oil. Heat fat to 375° F. (or until a 1-inch cube of bread will brown in 40 seconds). Cut bananas crosswise into quarters, halves, or 1-inch thick pieces. Roll pieces in flour, then dip into fritter batter, completely coating the banana with the batter. Shallow fry or deep-fat fry in the hot fat 4 to 6 minutes or until brown and tender. Drain on unglazed paper. Serve very hot. Serves 6 to 8.

FRITTER BATTER

- 1 cup flour, sifted
- ¼ cup sugar
- 1¼ teaspoons salt
- 2 teaspoons baking powder
- 1 egg, well beaten
- ⅓ cup milk
- 2 teaspoons melted fat or oil

Sift together the flour, sugar, salt, and baking powder. Combine egg and milk, and add gradually to dry ingredients, stirring until batter is smooth. Then stir in fat. This is a stiff batter.

Apple Fritters

- 1 cup flour, sifted
- 1½ teaspoons baking powder
- ¼ teaspoon salt
- ⅔ cup milk
- 1 egg, beaten
- 3 large apples, peeled, cored and sliced
- 2 tablespoons powdered sugar
- 1 tablespoon lemon juice

Make a batter by sifting together flour, baking powder, and salt; add milk and egg and beat until smooth. Add sugar and lemon juice to apple slices; dip in batter and fry in hot deep fat (375° F.) until a golden brown. Drain and sprinkle with powdered sugar. Serves 6.

Cape Cod Cranberry Drop Cakes

- 2 cups cranberries
- ½ cup water
- ½ cup sugar
- 1¼ tablespoons melted butter
- ½ teaspoon salt
- dash of cinnamon
- 1 cup cracker crumbs

Wash and pick over cranberries. Add water and cook until berries are soft. Force through sieve. Add sugar to pulp and then add butter and seasonings. Stir in cracker crumbs. Drop by spoonfuls into deep hot fat (370° F.) and cook until browned. Drain and serve hot or cold. Serve with chicken or turkey in place of potatoes or dumplings. Serves 6.

Maine Molasses Doughnuts

- 2 eggs
- 1 cup sugar
- ½ cup molasses
- 1 cup sour milk
- 1 teaspoon soda
- 4 cups flour (about)
- ¼ teaspoon cloves
- ¼ teaspoon ginger
- ⅛ teaspoon salt
- 1 tablespoon melted lard

Beat the eggs, add the sugar and beat well, then the molasses and sour milk to which has been added the soda, then the flour, mixed and sifted with the spices, and last the melted shortening. Handle dough as little as possible. Roll out a few at a time, cut, and fry in deep hot fat (375° F.). Turn frequently as they fry; drain. Makes 36 doughnuts.

✻ *Great-grandmother was less accurate in her measurements than present-day cooks. She did not use a spoon or cup to measure her molasses but measured it by the "plop" or "blurp" as it came from the jug. Old recipes sometimes specified how many "plops" to add.*

Banana Doughnuts

5 cups sifted flour
4 teaspoons baking powder
1 teaspoon soda
2 teaspoons salt
1 teaspoon nutmeg
¼ cup shortening
1 cup sugar
3 eggs, well beaten
1½ teaspoons vanilla extract
¾ cup mashed bananas (about 2 bananas)
½ cup sour milk or buttermilk
½ cup flour for rolling
melted fat or oil

Sift together flour, baking powder, soda, salt, and nutmeg. Beat shortening until creamy. Add sugar gradually and continue beating until light and fluffy. Add eggs and beat well. Add combined vanilla, bananas, and sour milk to creamed mixture and blend. Add flour mixture and mix until smooth. Turn a small amount of dough onto a floured board. Knead very lightly. Roll out with a floured rolling pin to ⅜-inch thickness. Cut with floured 2½-inch doughnut cutter.

Heat fat to 375° F. or until a 1-inch cube of bread will turn golden brown in 40 seconds. Slip doughnuts into fat with spatula. Fry about 3 minutes, or until golden brown, turning frequently. Drain on absorbent paper. Sugar the doughnuts, if desired. Makes about 3½ dozen doughnuts.

Mrs. Scully's Doughnuts

2 eggs
1¾ cups milk
1½ cups sugar
6 cups flour
3½ teaspoons baking powder
½ teaspoon salt
½ teaspoon lemon extract (optional)
¼ teaspoon grated nutmeg
few drops of vinegar

Beat the eggs until lemon colored; add the milk and sugar. Add the flour which has been sifted three times with the baking powder and salt. Beat thoroughly. Add the lemon extract, nutmeg, and vinegar and beat again. Roll out ¼-inch thick on lightly floured board and cut with floured doughnut cutter. Fry in hot deep fat (375° F.) for 2 to 3 minutes, or until lightly browned, turning doughnuts when they rise to top and several times during frying. Drain. Makes 48 doughnuts.

Potato Doughnuts

- 2 tablespoons butter
- ¾ cup sugar
- 2 eggs, well beaten
- ¼ cup sour milk
- 1 teaspoon soda
- 1 cup warm riced potato
- 1½ teaspoons salt
- ¼ teaspoon nutmeg
- 1½ cups flour, sifted (about)

Cream butter and sugar; add eggs, sour milk, soda, potato, salt, nutmeg, and enough flour to make an easily handled dough. Roll, cut into rounds with a doughnut cutter, slip into a kettle of fat heated to 375° F. Do not attempt to fry more than 4 or 5 at a time. As soon as doughnuts rise to the surface turn them. Turn frequently thereafter until they are sufficiently brown. Drain. Makes 18 doughnuts.

Raisin Doughnut Balls

- ½ cup sugar
- 2 egg yolks, well beaten
- ½ cup sour milk
- ½ teaspoon soda
- 2 cups flour
- ½ teaspoon cinnamon
- ¼ teaspoon salt
- ⅓ cup seeded or seedless raisins

Add the sugar to the beaten egg yolks; add the milk to which the soda has been added. Sift the flour, cinnamon, and salt and add. Stir in raisins. Drop by teaspoons in hot deep fat (375° F.). Fry until little balls are lightly browned, turning as they rise to top and several times during frying. Drain. Makes 20 doughnut balls. Serve with sweet cider.

White Bread for Two

- 1 tablespoon lard
- 1 tablespoon butter
- 2½ tablespoons sugar
- 2 teaspoons salt
- 1 cup boiling water
- 1 cup milk, scalded
- 1 package yeast
- ¼ cup lukewarm water
- 6 to 8 cups bread flour, sifted

Place lard, butter, sugar, and salt in a large mixing bowl and pour on the boiling water and scalded milk. When lukewarm add yeast cake crumbled in lukewarm water. Gradually add just enough flour so that dough can be handled easily. The dough should be moist and a little sticky to the fingers. Turn out on floured board and knead until smooth and elastic. Place dough in greased bowl, cover and let rise in a warm place until doubled in bulk (about 4 hours or overnight). Knead, adding more flour if necessary, shape into loaves and place in greased bread pans; cover and let rise in a warm place until doubled in bulk (about 2 hours). Bake in a moderately hot oven (375° F.) 20 minutes; reduce heat to moderate (350° F.) and bake 40 minutes longer. Remove from pans and rub with melted butter and slightly cool. While yet a trifle warm, place in bread box. The crust will be crispy but soft. This is a delicious bread. Makes 2 loaves.

* *The kneading process is simple. Turn dough onto a lightly floured board, fold, press down with heel of hand; turn ball of dough a quarter circle, repeat for 8 to 10 minutes. While bread rises, the dough should be kept as close as possible to 85° F. It may be placed in a large pan filled with lukewarm water. Be sure to add water to keep it warm.*

Anadama Bread

2 cups water
½ cup yellow cornmeal
2 tablespoons shortening
½ cup molasses
2 teaspoons salt
2 packages yeast
½ cup lukewarm water
7½ cups flour (about)

Boil the 2 cups water and add the cornmeal gradually, stirring constantly. Add the shortening, molasses, and salt and let stand until lukewarm. Add crumbled yeast cakes to lukewarm water and add the cornmeal mixture. Stir in the flour to make a stiff dough. Knead well. Place in a greased bowl, cover, and let rise in a warm place until doubled in bulk. Cut through the dough several times with a knife, cover and let rise again for about 45 minutes, or until light. Toss onto a floured board and knead well. Add more flour if necessary. Make into 2 loaves and place in greased loaf tins. Cover, let rise in a warm place until doubled in bulk. Bake in a hot oven (400° F.) for 15 minutes then reduce the heat to moderate (350° F.) and bake about 45 minutes longer, or until done. Brush with melted fat and remove the bread from the pans to a cake rack. Makes 2 loaves.

Oatmeal Bread

[*Helen H. Radcliffe, The Galley, Fairhaven, Mass.*]

4 cups boiling water or milk
2 cups rolled oats (regular)
2 tablespoons lard
⅔ cup molasses
1 tablespoon salt
1 package yeast
½ cup lukewarm water
9 to 10 cups flour, sifted

Pour boiling water or scalded milk over rolled oats and lard, cover, and let stand an hour. Add molasses, salt, and yeast cake (dissolved in lukewarm water). Add flour, gradually, beating it in with a knife. Let rise until double its bulk; cut down, shape into loaves and let rise again. Press into buttered bread tins; let rise again and bake 40 to 45 minutes in a 400° F. oven. Makes 4 loaves.

Oatmeal Bread with Nuts and Honey

✻ *Before Oatmeal Bread goes into oven spread with equal amounts of honey and finely chopped nut meats. This bread has been popular in the family of Mrs. E. W. Beach, Marvel Road, New Haven, Conn., for two generations. It will keep a long time—if you let it!*

Salt-Rising Bread

- 1 cup of milk, scalded
- 4 tablespoons cornmeal
- 2 tablespoons sugar
- 1½ teaspoons salt
- 3 tablespoons melted shortening
- 1 cup lukewarm water
- 5 cups flour (about)

Scald cornmeal, sugar, and ½ teaspoon of salt with milk. Let stand in a warm place overnight or until fermented. Into this "yeast" stir shortening, remaining teaspoon of salt, lukewarm water, and 2 cups of flour. Return to a warm place and let rise until sponge is very light. Gradually stir in remaining flour and shortening. Knead until smooth, shape into loaves, and place in 2 greased bread pans. Cover and let rise until 2½ times its original bulk. Bake in a moderately hot oven (375° F.) for 10 minutes. Lower heat to moderate (350° F.) and bake 25 minutes longer. Salt-rising bread is not as light as yeast bread. It is moist and crumbly. The "yeast" will keep 2 or 3 weeks in cool weather and is not injured by freezing. In warm weather only ⅓ the quantity of yeast is required.

✻ *It is important that the cornmeal mixture be fermented. To hasten fermentation, mixture may be placed in a cov-*

ered jar that is put in a bath of water as hot as the hand can stand. If mixture is not fermented do not use.

Featherbeds

[*A New Hampshire potato roll*]

2 large potatoes
1 teaspoon salt
2 tablespoons sugar
3 tablespoons butter
1½ cups potato water
¾ cup milk, scalded
1 package yeast
7 cups flour, sifted

Boil potatoes until tender; drain and save water. Mash potatoes, add salt, sugar, butter, and beat well. Add potato water and hot milk and cool. When lukewarm, add crumbled yeast cake and stir in 4 cups flour, beating well; then add enough remaining flour to make a dough stiff enough to knead. Knead until smooth and elastic; brush top with melted butter and place in large greased mixing bowl; cover and let rise until doubled in bulk (about 5 hours or overnight). Place on board, pat into ½-inch thick pieces (do not knead); pinch off small pieces and shape into small rolls. Place in greased pan and let rise until very light and more than doubled in bulk; bake in hot oven (400° F.) for 20 minutes or until done. Makes 48 small rolls.

Connecticut Hot Cross Buns

1 cup milk, scalded
½ cup sugar
3 tablespoons melted butter
½ teaspoon salt
1 package yeast
¼ cup warm water
1 egg, well beaten
3 cups flour
½ teaspoon cinnamon
½ cup currants

Combine the milk, sugar, butter, and salt. When lukewarm, add the yeast cake dissolved in the lukewarm water and the egg and mix well. Sift the flour and cinnamon together and stir into yeast mixture. Then add the currants and mix thoroughly. Cover and let rise in a warm place until double in size. Shape the dough into large biscuits and place on a well-buttered baking pan. Let rise again. Beat 1 egg and use to brush the top of each biscuit. Make a cross on each biscuit with a sharp knife. Bake in a hot oven (400° F.) for 20 minutes. Remove from oven and brush over lightly with a frosting made with milk and confectioners' sugar.

Cape Porpoise Squash Biscuits

1½ cups strained squash
1 cup milk, scalded
½ cup sugar
1 teaspoon salt
4 tablespoons butter
½ to 1 package yeast
5 cups flour, sifted (about)

Place squash, milk, sugar, salt, and shortening in a mixing bowl and cool; when lukewarm add crumbled yeast, which has been dissolved in the water, and half the flour and beat thoroughly. Gradually stir in remaining flour, adding just enough to make a dough that can be handled easily; turn out on floured board and knead until smooth and elastic, adding flour as necessary. Place dough in greased bowl and brush with melted shortening; cover and let rise in a warm place overnight or until doubled in bulk. Knead, shape into biscuits, and place in a greased pan, brush with melted shortening, cover, and let rise in a warm place until very light (1 to 2 hours). Shape into biscuits. Bake in a hot oven (400° F.) for about 15 minutes. Makes about 3 dozen rolls.

Sour Milk Rusks

[*Olive Winsor Frazar, Duxbury, Mass.*]

- 2⅛ cups flour, sifted
- 1 teaspoon soda
- ½ teaspoon salt
- 1 teaspoon nutmeg
- 1 teaspoon cinnamon
- ½ teaspoon cloves
- 1 cup sugar
- ½ cup shortening
- 1 egg, beaten
- 1 cup sour milk
- ½ cup raisins

Mix and sift dry ingredients; cream sugar and shortening. Add egg and stir in the milk and dry ingredients alternately. Stir in raisins. Pour into a square tin and bake in a moderate oven (350° F.) 1 hour. Cut in 16 squares.

❋ *Many of the old fashioned rusks were made with yeast dough. Rusks have come to have an entirely different meaning from what they had several generations ago. Today a rusk is looked upon as a dried sweetened bread, not unlike toast.*

Yankee Thrift

❋ *"My mother used to make her own bread," writes J. Almus Russell, Bloomsburg, Pa. "Every week she set a sponge in a large iron-ware bread pan, placed on a small table behind the kitchen stove. One Friday evening she set the sponge as usual, threw a clean remnant of freshly laundered turkey-red tablecloth over the bread bowl, and retired for the night.*

"The next morning as we entered the kitchen, Mother glanced in the direction of the rising bread dough. Strangely enough, the tablecloth was not to be seen although the bowl still remained in its usual place and

position. Then I discovered that Peter, the house cat, becoming chilly during the night, had jumped upon the bowl. His weight had gradually carried the cloth downward into the dough while the sponge had risen high around him, making a warm and springy mattress.

"As ours was a thrifty Yankee family, Mother shooed Peter off the tablecloth, removed the covering, decided that no harm had been done, and baked the bread as usual."

Parker House Rolls

[*Parker House, Boston, Mass.*]

½ cup scalded milk
½ cup boiling water
1 teaspoon salt
1 teaspoon sugar
1 tablespoon butter
½ yeast cake dissolved in ¼ cup lukewarm water
3 cups bread flour, or enough to knead

Put milk, water, salt, butter, and sugar into mixing bowl and mix well. Add yeast. Then add flour until it is stiff enough to knead. Cover and let it rise to double its bulk, shape into balls, put into buttered pan, and cover. Let it rise in a warm place again to double its bulk. With the floured handle of a wooden spoon press the balls through the center, almost cutting in half. Brush one half with butter, fold other half over and press together like a pocketbook. Let rise again and bake in a hot oven (400° F.) for 15 minutes. Brush the tops with butter after baking. This recipe will make about 2 dozen rolls.

* *The origin of Parker House Rolls dates back to the days of Harvey D. Parker, the Maine coachman who founded the now famous hotel in Boston. The legend is that one of the hotel's first guests was an English lady who thought*

her diamonds had been stolen by the chambermaid. She went screaming into the kitchen, accusing the chambermaid, and shouting, "My diamonds! My diamonds!" The cook, who was in love with the chambermaid, was so angry that he picked up pieces of dough in his fists and slammed them into a pan in the oven. When the rolls were baked they were dented in the middle. Meanwhile the lady found her diamonds; but to this day Parker House Rolls (or Pocket Book Rolls, as they are also called) are always dented in the middle.

Banana Bread

- 1¾ cups sifted flour
- ¾ teaspoon soda
- 1¼ teaspoons cream of tartar
- ½ teaspoon salt
- ⅓ cup shortening
- ⅔ cup sugar
- 2 eggs, well beaten
- 1 cup mashed banana (2 to 3 bananas)

Sift the flour, soda, cream of tartar, and salt together 3 times. Rub the shortening to a creamy consistency with the back of a spoon. Stir the sugar, a few tablespoons at a time, into the shortening and continue stirring after each addition until light and fluffy. Add eggs and beat well. Add flour mixture, alternately with banana, a small amount at a time. Beat after each addition until smooth. Pour into a well-greased loaf pan and bake in a moderate oven (350° F.), about 1 hour or until bread is done. Makes 1 loaf, about 8½ x 4½ x 3 inches.

Blueberry Cake

[*Durgin-Park, Boston, Mass.*]

- ¾ cup sugar
- 2 eggs, beaten
- 3 cups flour
- 3 teaspoons baking powder
- ¾ teaspoon salt
- 1¼ cups blueberries, washed and drained
- 1 tablespoon melted butter
- 1½ cups milk

Mix sugar with beaten eggs; sift flour, baking powder, and salt and add; stir in blueberries, melted butter, and milk. Beat just enough to mix; bake in hot oven (400° F.) about 30 minutes. Makes 1 large panful that cuts into 21 squares.

❋ *Durgin-Park originated in the Revolutionary period and is still going strong in the market district of Boston. The clientele sit at tables with red-checked cloths. The house specialties are seafood, slabs of rare roast beef, a mixture known as "bale of hay"—peas, carrots and potatoes, and massive helpings of strawberry shortcake.*

Vermont Graham Bread

- 1½ cups sour milk (or buttermilk)
- 2 tablespoons sour cream (or melted butter)
- ⅔ cup molasses and maple syrup (half of each or alone)
- 2 teaspoons soda
- ½ teaspoon salt
- 1⅓ cups graham flour
- 1⅓ cups flour, sifted
- raisins may be added

Mix in the order given. Bake in greased bread tins in a moderate oven (350° F.) 45 to 50 minutes.

Popdoodle Cake

[*Sometimes called Coffee Cake*]

- 2½ cups flour, sifted
- 2 teaspoons baking powder
- 1 cup sugar
- ½ teaspoon salt
- ½ cup shortening (butter and lard mixed)
- 1 cup milk
- 1 egg, beaten

Mix and sift dry ingredients; cut in shortening, combine with milk and egg, and add. Spread dough on a greased layer pan. Before baking sprinkle top with ½ cup sugar and 2 teaspoons cinnamon, mixed. Bake in a hot oven (400° F.) about 30 minutes. Makes 1 (9-inch) coffee cake.

Auntie's Holiday Breakfast Cake

[*Miss Elizabeth Grindrod, Meriden, Conn.*]

- 2½ cups flour
- 1 teaspoon baking powder
- 1 teaspoon salt
- ⅔ cup shortening
- ⅔ cup brown sugar
- ⅔ cup milk
- 1 egg, beaten
- 1 teaspoon cinnamon
- ½ teaspoon nutmeg

Mix flour, baking powder, and shortening. Add brown sugar, cinnamon, and nutmeg. Mix. Reserve one cup of mixture for top. Add milk and egg. Sprinkle reserve mixture on top. Bake in moderate oven. Delicious warm from oven, or if cool can be sliced and lightly toasted under broiler.

Popovers

1 cup flour
¼ teaspoon salt
2 eggs (3 if small)
1 tablespoon melted shortening
1 cup milk

Sift the flour and salt; add remaining ingredients and beat with rotary beater until smooth. Fill greased custard cups or iron or aluminum muffin pans ½ full and bake in a hot oven 450° F. about 20 minutes; then reduce heat to moderate oven (350° F.) and continue baking 20 to 25 minutes longer. Makes 6 large popovers. Do not peek during first half-hour of baking. It is well to heat cups or pans in oven while mixing the batter.

Vermont Maple Rolls

2 cups flour
2½ teaspoons baking powder
½ teaspoon salt
4 tablespoons shortening
¾ cup milk (about)
butter
½ cup maple sugar

Sift flour once, measure, add baking powder and salt, and sift again. Cut in shortening. Add milk gradually, stirring until soft dough is formed. Turn on lightly floured board and knead 15 seconds, or enough to shape. Roll in oblong piece, ¼-inch thick. Spread with softened butter and sprinkle with maple sugar. Also ½ cup chopped butternuts, walnuts, or pecans may be spread over sugar. Roll as for jelly roll and cut in 1-inch thick slices. Place slices on greased pan or muffin tins. Spread tops of slices with butter. Bake in hot oven (400° F.) 15 minutes. Makes 10 to 12 rolls.

Corn Rolls

[*Parker House, Boston, Mass.*]

⅓ cup sugar
¼ cup lard
1 egg, beaten
¾ teaspoon salt
1 cup milk
1 cup yellow cornmeal
1 cup flour, sifted
3 teaspoons baking powder

Cream sugar and lard; add egg and beat. Add salt and milk and stir; add cornmeal, flour, and baking powder. Bake in greased muffin tins in a hot oven (400° F.) 20 minutes, or until done. Makes 12 rolls.

Corn Bread

[*Durgin-Park, Boston, Mass.*]

¾ cup sugar, sifted
2 eggs, beaten
2 cups flour
3 teaspoons baking powder
¾ teaspoon salt
1 cup yellow cornmeal
1 tablespoon melted butter
1½ cups milk

Mix sugar and beaten eggs; sift flour, baking powder, and salt and add; then add cornmeal, melted butter, and milk. Beat just enough to mix. Bake in a hot oven (400° F.) about 30 minutes. This makes 1 panful that cuts into 21 squares.

✱ *At Durgin-Park's, in the market, straw-hatted butchers and professors from Harvard dine off red-checked tablecloths. Durgin-Park's is as famous for steaks and seafoods as it is for hot breads.*

Best New England Johnnycake

✻ *Don't try to follow this recipe!*

"To make this johnnycake," according to the Model Cook Book, *published in 1885, "take one quart of buttermilk, one teacup of flour, ⅔ of a teacupful of molasses, a little salt, one teaspoonful of saleratus, one egg (beat, of course). Then stir in Indian meal, but be sure not to put in too much. Leave it thin, so thin that it will almost run. Bake in a tin in any oven, and tolerably quick. If it is not first-rate and light, it will be because you make it too thick with Indian meal. Some prefer it without the molasses."*

Granny's Apple Corn Bread

- 2 cups yellow cornmeal
- ¼ cup sugar
- 1½ teaspoons salt
- 2 cups sour milk
- 2 tablespoons shortening, melted
- 2 eggs, beaten
- 1 teaspoon soda
- 1 tablespoon cold water
- ⅞ cup raw chopped apple

Mix in the top of a double boiler the cornmeal, sugar, salt, milk, and shortening. Set over hot water and cook about 10 minutes. Cool, add eggs, soda dissolved in water, and apples. Bake in greased baking pan in hot oven (400° F.) about 25 minutes or until done. Makes 8 large squares.

Maple Corn Bread

1⅓ cups flour
⅔ cup cornmeal
3 teaspoons baking powder
½ teaspoon salt
⅓ cup maple syrup
½ cup melted shortening
2 eggs, slightly beaten

Sift dry ingredients; add the syrup, shortening and eggs. Stir until well mixed, but do not beat. Turn into a greased pan and bake 25 minutes in a hot oven (425° F.). Makes 8 squares.

Crackling Bread

1½ cups cornmeal
¾ cup flour
1 teaspoon baking powder
2 tablespoons sugar
¼ teaspoon salt
1 cup sour milk
1 cup diced salt pork cracklings

Mix and sift dry ingredients; add milk and stir in cracklings. Turn into two large pans or into 16 muffin tins. Bake in hot oven (400° F.) for 30 minutes.

* *Cracklings are thin slices of salt pork remaining after the fat has been rendered. In some households, children ate them as children today eat popcorn or candy. Thin slices of salt pork were laid on brown paper in a baking pan that was placed in a slow oven. When they were hot a little salt was sprinkled over them.*

Scraps left from the leaf in making lard may be substituted in this recipe as they are also known as cracklings. In that case increase the salt to ½ teaspoon.

Muffins

2 cups flour, sifted
3 teaspoons baking powder
3 tablespoons sugar
½ teaspoon salt
1 egg, well beaten
1 cup milk
3 tablespoons butter or butter substitute, melted

Mix and sift dry ingredients. Combine egg and milk, add to flour, and stir only until mixed. Add shortening and blend, but do not beat. Bake in greased muffin tin in a hot oven (425° F.) about 25 minutes. Makes 12 muffins.

Maine Blueberry Muffins

2 cups flour
2½ teaspoons baking powder
½ cup sugar
½ teaspoon salt
1 egg, well beaten
¾ cup milk
¼ cup melted fat
¾ cup blueberries

Sift flour once, measure, add baking powder, sugar, and salt, and sift again. Combine egg and milk, add to flour and stir only until mixed. Do not beat. Add shortening and blend. Fold in blueberries. Mixture will be stiffer than usual muffin mixture. Bake in greased muffin tins in a hot oven (400° F.) 25 to 30 minutes. Makes 12 muffins.

Berkshire Muffins

⅔ cup milk, scalded
½ cup yellow cornmeal
½ cup cooked rice
½ cup flour, sifted
2 tablespoons sugar
½ teaspoon salt
3 teaspoons baking powder
1 egg, separated
1 tablespoon melted butter

Pour hot milk over cornmeal and let it stand for 5 minutes. Add rice. Mix and sift dry ingredients. Combine with cornmeal, rice, and egg yolk, well beaten, then add melted butter. Fold in stiffly beaten egg white. Bake in a hot oven (425° F.) about 25 minutes. Makes about 8 small muffins.

Apple Muffins

2 cups pastry flour
½ cup sugar
4 teaspoons baking powder
½ teaspoon salt
1 cup milk
4 tablespoons melted butter
1 egg
1 cup peeled, chopped apples

Mix and sift dry ingredients. Combine milk, shortening, and egg and add, stirring only until mixed. Add apples and blend but do not beat. Turn into greased muffin tins or custard cups, then sprinkle tops with a mixture of ½ teaspoon cinnamon and 2 tablespoons sugar. Bake at 400° F. for 20 minutes. Makes 12 muffins.

Cranberry Muffins

¾ cup cranberry halves
½ cup powdered sugar
2 cups flour
3 teaspoons baking powder
½ teaspoon salt
4 tablespoons sugar
1 egg, well beaten
1 cup milk
4 tablespoons shortening, melted

Mix cranberry halves with the powdered sugar and let stand while preparing muffin mixture. Sift dry ingredients, add egg, milk, and shortening; then add the sugared cranberries. Mix but do not beat. Bake in a moderate oven (350° F.) for 20 minutes. Makes 12 muffins.

Maine Oatmeal Gems

[*Mrs. Nellie Barrett, West Sumner, Me.*]

2 cups rolled oats
1½ cups sour milk
1 teaspoon soda
¼ cup molasses
pinch of salt
1 egg, beaten
1 cup flour, sifted

Mix rolled oats and milk and let stand several hours or overnight. Add soda, molasses, salt, egg, and flour. Blend well but do not beat. Bake in greased muffin tins in a hot oven (400° F.) 20 to 25 minutes. Makes 12 muffins.

Graham Gems

[*Thorndike Dempsey Hotel, Rockland, Me.*]

½ teaspoon soda
1 cup sour milk
1 egg, beaten
2 tablespoons molasses
2 tablespoons butter
½ teaspoon salt
2 cups graham flour

Stir soda into sour milk; combine with egg, molasses, and melted butter; add graham flour and salt. Blend only enough to mix. Do not beat. Fill greased muffin tins ⅔ full and bake in a hot oven (400° F.) 20 to 25 minutes. Makes 12 muffins.

GLAZE

3 teaspoons milk mixed with 3 teaspoons molasses

After baking, while the gingerbread is still hot, brush over top with the glaze. The gingerbread is a crisp sheet of cooky-like pastry, delicious with a glass of milk. The longer it lasts the better it is.

* *In the early days of New Hampshire, between 1800 and 1850, there were great celebrations known as "Muster and Training Days." These were the heydays of the food peddlers who sold squares of delicious gingerbread, glazed on top. This recipe is just as it was over a hundred years ago. There are as many variations of this recipe as there are variations of corn bread.*

Hard Gingerbread

1½ cups butter
2½ cups sugar
6 eggs
¼ cup milk
1 teaspoon soda
3 teaspoons ginger
1 teaspoon salt
8 cups flour, sifted

Cream butter, add sugar, eggs, milk, and sift in dry ingredients. Spread ¼-inch thick on greased inverted dripping pan. Roll very thin, preferably with a greased rolling pin. Bake in hot oven (400° F.) about 10 minutes. Cut in squares and keep in a covered crock. This gingerbread was made in large quantities every year and served with home-made wines when the minister or a special guest called. Best when 1 day old. Makes 48 squares.

Maine Gingerbread

- ½ cup sugar
- ½ cup shortening (lard, butter, bacon drippings, or any combination of the three)
- 1 cup molasses
- 2 teaspoons soda
- 1 cup boiling water
- 2½ cups flour
- 1 teaspoon ginger
- 1 teaspoon clove
- 1 teaspoon cinnamon
- ½ teaspoon salt
- 2 eggs, well beaten

Cream sugar and shortening; add molasses; dissolve soda in boiling water and add to the sugar mixture. Sift the remaining dry ingredients and add this to the mixture, and beat until smooth. Add the eggs last. Pour into a greased pan 12″ x 8″ x 2″ and bake in a moderate oven (350° F.) about 45 minutes. Makes 1 panful.

Muster Day Gingerbread

- 2½ cups flour, sifted
- 1 teaspoon ginger
- ½ teaspoon salt
- 3 tablespoons butter
- 1 teaspoon soda
- 3 tablespoons boiling water
- 1 cup light molasses

Sift the flour, ginger, and salt together; work the butter into the flour mixture. Dissolve the soda in the water, add to the molasses, and stir in dry ingredients. Knead well together. Let stand in a cold place until dough is thoroughly chilled. Roll out on floured board to ¾-inch thickness, adding just enough additional flour so that dough will roll. Bake in a moderately hot oven (375° F.) about 20 minutes. Makes 2 sheets 7 by 11 inches.

South Glastonbury Gingerbread

- 1 cup lard
- ½ cup sugar
- 3 eggs, well beaten
- 1 cup molasses
- 1 cup buttermilk or sour milk
- 4 cups flour
- 2 teaspoons baking powder
- 1 teaspoon soda
- ½ teaspoon cinnamon
- 1½ teaspoons nutmeg
- 1 tablespoon ginger

Cream shortening, add sugar and cream. Add eggs and molasses. Alternate buttermilk with the sifted dry ingredients. Pour into well-greased floured cake pan and bake 40 to 50 minutes in a moderate oven (350° F.). Makes 2 (9-inch) square cakes.

✱ *More gingerbread is eaten in New England than in any other section of the country. It was probably one of the first breads baked in New England. A gingerbread recipe was brought over on the* Mayflower.

Strawberry Shortcake

[*Mrs. George D. Aiken, Montpelier, Vt. The favorite recipe of Vermont's former governor and his family*]

- 2 cups flour
- 3 teaspoons baking powder
- 1 teaspoon salt
- 2 teaspoons sugar
- ½ cup shortening
- ¾ cup milk (about)

Mix and sift dry ingredients; cut in shortening until well mixed; add milk, stirring quickly to make a soft dough. Turn onto a lightly floured board and pat with hands just enough to shape. Cut in 2 cakes ½-inch thick. Bake in a hot oven (450° F.) for 15 minutes.

Slice 2 quarts large juicy ripe strawberries into a bowl. Add 1 cup sugar. Spread sugared berries on each buttered layer, topping the second layer with whipped cream. Serves 6.

✱ *Strawberries, until comparatively recently, grew wild in sunny fields, small and distinctly sweet. The Indians introduced the white men of the Plymouth Colony to them. The first strawberry shortcake was probably made of cornmeal.*

New Hampshire Soda Biscuits

- 2 cups flour
- ½ teaspoon soda
- 1 teaspoon cream of tartar
- ½ teaspoon salt
- ¼ cup lard
- 1 cup milk (about)

Sift flour once, measure, add soda, cream of tartar, and salt, and sift again. Cut in shortening quickly and lightly until well mixed. Add milk until a soft dough is formed. Turn out on lightly floured board and knead with as few strokes as possible, working dough rapidly. Pat ½-inch thick, cut with floured biscuit cutter. Bake on ungreased baking sheet in hot oven (450° F.) 12 to 15 minutes. Makes 12 biscuits, marvels of lightness and sweetness. Soda biscuits still retain their flavor when they are warmed over in the oven. Old-fashioned New Hampshire cooks invariably prefer this recipe to all other biscuit recipes.

Hasty Pudding

[*Today it is more often called Cornmeal Mush*]

- 6 cups boiling water
- 1 teaspoon salt
- 1 cup yellow cornmeal

Bring water to a rapid boil in top of double boiler; add salt. Slowly sift in cornmeal, stirring constantly until mixture is smooth and boils. Set over hot water and steam for 30 minutes or longer. Serve hot with molasses or milk, or sugar and butter with nutmeg. Serves 8.

* *If mush is to be fried, mix 4 tablespoons flour with cornmeal. This makes it easier to slice. Empty baking powder tins or drinking glasses make excellent molds. Rinse with cold water before pouring in the mush. When ready to use, slice and lightly flour the slices before frying on a hot greased griddle. New Orleans molasses was the preferred old-time accompaniment. Butter and maple syrup are more often served with fried mush today.*

Hasty Pudding was given its name because it could be made and served in so short a time. Since it could be eaten as a vegetable, a dessert, the main dish for lunch or supper, or served for breakfast, it saved the day for many a housewife in an emergency.

Spider Corn Bread

- 1 cup cornmeal
- ⅓ cup flour
- 2 tablespoons sugar
- 1 teaspoon salt
- 2 teaspoons baking powder
- 1 egg
- 1¾ cups milk and water (half of each)
- 1 tablespoon butter

Mix and sift dry ingredients. Beat the egg and add 1 cup of the milk and water mixture. Stir in dry ingredients. Turn into an iron spider (about 8 inches in diameter) in which butter has been melted. Pour the rest of the milk and water over the top, but do not stir. Bake in a moderately hot oven (375° F.) 25 to 30 minutes. Cut into 8 pie-shaped pieces.

* *A spider is a black frying pan that once had legs and sat on the hearth. Spider bread should have a line of creamy custard through the center. It is sliced as a pie. A large piece of butter is placed on top of each slice and it is eaten with a fork.*

Vermont Bannock

1 cup cornmeal
½ teaspoon salt
boiling water, almost 2 cups
2 tablespoons soft butter

Combine cornmeal and salt. Pour on boiling water to make cornmeal the consistency of thick cream. Add butter. Spread thin in large well-buttered pan and bake in a moderate oven (350° F.) about 60 minutes. Serve with butter and maple syrup or with milk. Cut into 8 large squares.

❋ *Bannock is crisp, like a cracker. It is an acquired taste. The best that can be said for it is that it is filling. It was a great favorite with early Yankees.*

Ripe Olive Fondue

1 cup pitted ripe olives
2 cups soft bread crumbs
1 cup grated cheese
2 eggs, beaten
½ teaspoon salt
2 teaspoons onion, minced
1 tin (14 oz.) evaporated milk
½ teaspoon dry mustard
1 teaspoon Worcestershire sauce

Quarter olives; arrange bread crumbs, cheese, and olives in layers in greased 1-quart casserole. Stir eggs into undiluted milk, add onion and seasonings and pour over bread-olive-cheese mixture. Bake in a pan of hot water in 350° F. oven 45 to 50 minutes. Serves 4.

Cornmeal Soufflé

[A variation of an old recipe]

- ⅓ cup Rhode Island white or yellow cornmeal
- 1 tablespoon butter
- 2 cups milk, scalded
- 4 tablespoons grated cheese
- 1 teaspoon salt
- ¼ teaspoon paprika
- few grains cayenne
- 3 egg yolks, well beaten
- 3 egg whites, stiffly beaten

Place cornmeal and butter in a kettle, pour on milk. Cook until the consistency of mush. Add cheese, seasonings, and egg yolks, cook slowly 1 minute longer. Cool. Fold in egg whites. Bake in an ungreased baking dish in a moderate oven (350° F.) about 25 minutes. Serve with green salad and ham, bacon, or sausage for luncheon or supper. Serves 4.

Boston Brown Bread

- 1 cup rye flour
- 1 cup yellow corn
- 1 cup graham flour
- ¾ tablespoon soda
- 1 teaspoon salt
- ¾ cup molasses
- 2 cups sour milk or 1¾ cups sweet milk or water
- 1 cup raisins or dates (if desired)

Mix and sift dry ingredients, add molasses and milk; stir until well mixed, turn into a well-buttered mold, and steam 3½ hours. The cover should be buttered before being placed on the mold, and then tied down with string; otherwise the bread in rising may force off the cover. Mold should never be filled more than ⅔ full. A melon-mold or one-pound baking-powder tins make the most attractive shaped loaves, but a 5-pound lard pail answers the purpose. For steaming, place mold on a trivet in kettle containing boiling water, allowing water to come halfway up around mold, cover closely, and steam, adding more boiling water as needed. 1 cup of raisins or dates may be added if desired.

Cheese Strata

[*Dorrice Barr, Sandwich, Mass.*]

- 6 slices bread
- butter or margarine
- ¼ pound American cheese
- ¼ teaspoon salt
- ¼ teaspoon paprika
- 4 eggs, beaten
- 2 cups milk

Remove crusts of bread; butter each slice and place in buttered baking dish in layers. Grate cheese or cut in thin slices and spread evenly between slices. Beat eggs, mix well with milk, and pour over bread and cheese layers, sprinkling each layer with salt and paprika. Let stand in refrigerator overnight. Bake in pan of water at 325° F. for 1¼ hours. Serve hot. Serves 4.

Yankee Toast

[*A country breakfast dish*]

Slice lengthwise, but do not peel, about twice the number of McIntoshes you think your family should eat for breakfast, and fry them (the apples, not the family) in butter with 3 tablespoons water and ¼ cup sugar for every 5 apples. Serve on French or German toast with broiled bacon.

Sour Milk Cheese

[*Called also Dutch, Curd, Cottage Cheese, and Connecticut Pot Cheese*]

- 1 quart thick sour milk
- 1 tablespoon soft butter
- ½ teaspoon salt
- pepper
- 1 tablespoon cream

Place the milk in a pan on the back of the stove or over hot water until curd has separated from the whey. Spread a cheesecloth over a strainer, pour in the milk, lift the edges of the cloth and draw them together; drain or squeeze quite dry. There will be about ⅔ cup of curd. Add the butter, salt, pepper, and cream. A little minced onion or chopped parsley or chives may also be added.

Indians, Ancestors and Herbs

by

Harriet Grindrod Beckwith

I remember, as a little girl, how delightful it was to be wrapped up in a huge apron and allowed to "help" cook. Our big farm kitchen was a wonderful place for a little girl with bowls and spoons to lick, delicious smelling things to stir, and all sorts of good things to sample. I'm not sure I was much help, but I loved it when I was allowed to try.

My mother was the family baker and her pies, cakes, and pastries were the most delicious in the whole world. Her Apple Roll was a special family favorite, and one day she let me make it all by myself. My grandfather, I must admit, did help me a little by peeling the apples. As he peeled the skin would unwind in one long continuous strip. It was the prettiest spiral, almost like a Christmas tree ornament. When dessert time came that evening, I brought in my Apple Roll and served it myself. My father finished his portion in no time and announced he just couldn't stand the sight of my Apple Roll! You can imagine how badly I felt. Then my father grinned and said the reason he couldn't stand it in his sight was because it was the most delicious Apple Roll he had ever eaten. He then proceeded to eat every bit left on the serving dish. I was the proudest cook you can possibly imagine and the Apple Roll became my specialty.

My aunt was the jam, jelly, and molasses taffy expert. Our

taffy pulls usually dissolved into gales of laughter as one of us would get hopelessly tangled in the sticky taffy and stand there giggling until Auntie rushed to the rescue, buttered wooden paddle in hand, to scrape off the globs of taffy and put it into our mouths. We didn't get much taffy pulled as we ate most of it.

My grandfather was the family storyteller. I could listen to his stories by the hour, especially the one about my grandmother and the Indians. This is how he told it: "When your grandmother was a tiny baby there were still tribes of Indians living right here. One day, one of these Indian tribes swooped down on your grandmother's house with loud warwhoops, burning the house to the ground, and killing all of the family except your grandmother for some unexplained reason. They took her back with them to their village. She grew up with the Indian children of the tribe, learning their games and their language. When she was six years old, the Indians and the white settlers stopped fighting and peace was declared.

"About this time, some of your ancestors heard about the little white girl of the Wappinger tribe. They checked the dates of the massacre of your family and decided the little girl must indeed be your 'lost' grandmother. The Indians had become so fond of her that it took the family much time, and many pow-wows, before the Indian chief could be persuaded to let her go back to her own people. Your grandmother was so unhappy about leaving her Indian adopted mother that the family took the squaw and her son along, too. They lived in a little house on the property and your grandmother lived in the big house. I lived nearby and became a close friend of the Indian boy. We went fishing and he taught me to catch fish the Indian way with a snare and we built small animal traps from branches and vines. One of my Indian friend's chores was collecting roots and herbs for his mother and the medicine man. He took me along on many of these collecting trips and I learned which plants and roots were good to eat, which ones were bitter and made good medicine, and which ones were poisonous. We took your grandmother along with us sometimes but she didn't like to see animals in our traps and would leave us to run back to the house as fast as she could."

I never tired of this story and now I delight in telling it to my grandson and granddaughter when, wrapped in aprons many sizes too big for them, they "help" me in the kitchen.

Pudding, Pies, Cakes, and Cookies

Original Injun' Puddin'

[*One of the oldest of New England's desserts*]

5 cups milk
⅔ cup dark molasses
⅓ cup granulated sugar
½ cup yellow cornmeal
¾ teaspoon cinnamon
⅜ teaspoon nutmeg
1 teaspoon salt
4 tablespoons butter

Heat 4 cups of the milk and add molasses, sugar, cornmeal, salt, spice and butter to it. Cook 20 minutes or until mixture thickens. Pour into baking dish, add remaining cold milk. Do not stir. Put into slow oven (300° F.) and bake for 3 hours without stirring. Serve warm with cream or Hard Sauce (page 196), or vanilla ice cream. Serves 8. This pudding is also called Whitpot (also Whitspot) Pudding.

* *The famous Durgin-Park recipe that follows calls for an egg and a pinch of baking powder; tapioca is sometimes added, also a few tablespoons of white flour to increase the whey. Some cooks add seeded raisins, and spices vary slightly according to individual preference. One of the most delicious of all variations calls for the addition of 1 pint of sliced sweet apples or home-grown pears. These translucent sweet slices rise to the top and form delicious islands in a sea of red brown juice. Serve in a soup plate with thick, yellow sweet cream.*

Baked Indian Pudding

[*Durgin-Park, 30 North Market St., Boston, Mass.*]

3 cups milk
¼ cup black molasses
2 tablespoons sugar
2 tablespoons butter
¼ teaspoon salt
⅛ teaspoon baking powder
1 egg
½ cup yellow cornmeal

Mix all the ingredients thoroughly with one-half of the milk and bake in a hot oven (450° F.) until mixture boils. Stir in remaining half of hot milk and bake in a slow oven (300° F.) for 5 to 7 hours. Bake in a stone crock well greased inside. Serve warm with whipped cream or vanilla ice cream. Serves 6.

Sixty-Minute Baked Indian Pudding

1 quart milk, scalded
5 tablespoons yellow cornmeal
2 tablespoons butter
1 cup dark molasses
1 teaspoon salt
¾ teaspoon cinnamon
½ teaspoon ginger
2 eggs
1 cup cold milk

Put milk in double boiler, add meal slowly, stirring constantly. Cook 15 minutes, then add butter, molasses, seasonings, and eggs, beaten well. Turn into buttered dish and pour cold milk over mixture, but do not stir. Bake 60 minutes in a moderate oven (350° F.). Serve with cream, vanilla ice cream, or Hard Sauce (page 196). Serves 8.

Apple Pandowdy

[*From a cook book published in 1880*]

"Fill a heavy pot heaping full of pleasant apples, sliced. Add 1 cup molasses, 1 cup sugar, 1 cup water, 1 teaspoon cloves, 1 teaspoon cinnamon. Cover with baking powder biscuit crust, sloping it over the sides. Bake overnight. In the morning cut the hard crust into the apple. Eat with yellow cream or plain."

* *Modern recipes for pandowdy call for 5 apples, sliced; 3 tablespoons sugar, 3 tablespoons molasses, ¼ teaspoon nutmeg, cinnamon, and salt. Bake in casserole until apples*

are soft. Prepare a rich soft biscuit dough. Turn out over apples and bake 15 minutes longer in a hot oven. Serve with Hard Sauce (page 196), Lemon Sauce (page 194), Nutmeg Sauce (page 174), or cream. Serves 6. Pandowdy is also called "Apple Jonathan" and "Apple Pot-Pie."

Maine apple pandowdy is something else again. "Try out 3 slices of home-raised salt fat pork in a dinner kettle which already has in it enough water to more than cover 8 or more tart apples sliced and ⅔ cup molasses. Make a dozen dumplings as for soup and drop in, cook 20 minutes, being careful that the mixture does not 'catch on.' Serve hot."

Apple Brown Betty is made according to the modern recipe for pandowdy. In place of the biscuit crust 1½ cups bread crumbs combined with ½ cup sugar are sprinkled in layers on top of the sweetened apples. Dot crumbs with bits of butter. Bake in a moderate oven (350° F.), 45 minutes.

Apple Dumplings

[*A Massachusetts recipe*]

2 cups flour, sifted
2½ teaspoons baking powder
½ teaspoon salt
½ cup shortening
¾ cup milk
8 small apples, pared and cored
butter, cinnamon, sugar

Sift flour, baking powder, and salt; cut in shortening. Add milk, stirring until a soft dough is formed. Knead on slightly floured board and roll ⅛-inch thick. Divide into 8 parts. Place apple on each part. Fill each hollow with 1 tablespoon sugar and 1 teaspoon butter. Fold dough up over apple, pressing edges together. Place apples on pan, sprinkle with cinnamon and sugar and dot with ¼ teaspoon butter. Bake in moderately hot oven (375° F.) 30 to 40 minutes. Serve with cream or Hard Sauce (page 196). Serves 8.

* *Left over apple jelly may be used in addition to sugar to fill centers of apples. Grandmother's recipe reads: "Tie dumplings in loose cloths which have been dipped in water and floured on the inside. Boil steadily in plenty of water 1 hour." Dumplings may be steamed, too, but modern Yankee cooks usually prefer theirs baked.*

Apple Crumb

- 4 cups apples, sliced
- ¼ cup hot water
- ½ cup butter
- ½ cup flour
- ½ cup sugar

Butter baking dish and cover with sliced apples; pour water over apples. Work butter, sugar, and flour together until mixture is like crumbs. Spread over apples. Bake in hot oven (450° F.) 10 minutes. Reduce heat to moderate (350° F.) and bake 30 minutes longer. Serve with cream. Serves 4.

Preacher's Apple Crisp

- 4 or 5 good-sized apples
- 1 cup flour
- 1 cup sugar
- 1 teaspoon baking powder
- 1 egg
- ⅓ cup butter, melted

Peel, core, and slice the apples thin. Arrange them on the bottom of a large greased baking dish or pan. Mix flour, sugar, and baking powder. Break the egg over this mixture and stir until crumbly. Place the mixture as a topping over the apples and dust on the cinnamon. Pour the melted butter evenly over the topping.

Bake at 325° F. 45 minutes. Serve warm with vanilla ice cream or Hard Sauce.

* *Mrs. Julius E. Kelley of East Sandwich, Mass., who contributed this recipe, serves it with hard sauce flavored with cherry brandy. One cup of powdered sugar and ½ cup of butter creamed until smooth and brandy added to flavor and color is her recipe.*

Yankee Apple John

6 tart apples, thinly sliced
¾ cup sugar
¾ teaspoon cinnamon
½ teaspoon nutmeg
⅛ teaspoon salt
2 cups flour, sifted
3 teaspoons baking powder
pinch salt
½ cup shortening
⅔ cup milk (about)

Grease shallow baking dish and fill with sliced apples. Mix sugar, spices, and salt and sprinkle over apples. Sift flour with baking powder and salt. Cut in shortening until mixture is fine. Add milk, mixing until a soft dough is formed. Knead lightly on floured board, roll to fit over pan; brush with milk, bake in a hot oven (450° F.) about 25 minutes, or until apples are tender. Serve with Nutmeg Sauce. Serves 5.

NUTMEG SAUCE

1 cup sugar
¼ teaspoon nutmeg
2 tablespoons flour
dash salt
2 cups boiling water
1 tablespoon butter
1 tablespoon vinegar

Mix sugar, nutmeg, flour, and salt in saucepan. Add boiling water, stirring constantly until blended. Add butter and boil 5 minutes. Remove from fire, add vinegar.

Apple Seventh Heaven

6 apples
2 tablespoons sugar
⅛ teaspoon salt
¼ teaspoon cinnamon
½ cup brown sugar
½ cup butter
1 cup finely chopped or shaved nuts

Spread bottom and sides of oblong cake pan 8″ x 12″ generously with butter. Peel apples, cut into 8 equal parts and place in parallel rows closely in pan. Mix sugar, salt, and cinnamon and sprinkle over apples. Cream brown sugar and butter; add nuts. Spread over and between apples, then pat to make a smooth surface. Bake for ½ hour in quick oven (450° F.) or until apples are tender. Serve with thick cream. Serves 6.

My Grandmother's Apple Turnover

Bake a rich biscuit shortcake; split, butter, and fill in between and on top with hot applesauce, seasoned with nutmeg and sweetened to taste with sugar and dotted lightly with butter. Serve cut in squares with Butter Sauce.

BUTTER SAUCE

½ cup butter
1½ tablespoons flour
2 cups boiling water

Blend butter and flour, stir in hot water gradually and cook until it thickens. No sugar is added. Makes 2 cups sauce.

Apple Tapioca

¼ cup pearl tapioca	5 medium apples, peeled and quartered
2 cups water	½ cup sugar
¼ teaspoon salt	

Soak tapioca in water overnight or for several hours. Then place over direct heat to cook for 20 minutes or until tapioca is transparent. Add salt. Pour tapioca over apples and sugar in baking dish. Bake in a moderate oven (350° F.) until apples are tender, about 45 minutes. Serves 6.

"Freshman's Tears"

[*A cream tapioca pudding popular in western Massachusetts*]

3 tablespoons pearl tapioca	3½ cups milk, scalded
1 cup water	1 tablespoon cornstarch
⅛ teaspoon salt	½ cup sugar
3 eggs, separated	1 teaspoon vanilla

Soak the tapioca several hours, add the water and salt, and cook in the top of a double boiler about 2 hours, or until the tapioca is transparent. Beat the yolks of the eggs, add the milk, and combine with the tapioca. Mix the cornstarch and sugar and add. Return to the double boiler and cook until thick and creamy, about 15 minutes. Just before serving, fold in the whites of the eggs, beaten stiff, and vanilla. Serve cold. Serves 8.

* *If quick-cooking tapioca is used in place of pearl, soaking and advance cooking is not necessary.*

Apple Snow

Peel and grate a large sour apple, sprinkling ¾ cup powdered sugar over it. Break into this the whites of 2 eggs and beat all constantly until pudding is light and frothy. Take care to make in a large bowl as it beats very stiff and light. Heap into a glass dish and pour a custard around it and serve cold. Serves 4.

* *Easy to make with an electric beater; otherwise, long and tedious. A very delicate dessert.*

Brandy Gelatin

1 cup cold water
3 envelopes unflavored gelatin
2 cups boiling water
1 cup sherry
1 cup brandy

Sprinkle gelatin on cold water to soften, letting it soak 5 minutes or longer; add boiling water and stir until sugar is dissolved. Add the sherry and brandy, strain, turn into 1 large or 8 small molds and allow to jell. Serve with whipped cream. Serves 6.

Mrs. Haynes' Apple Dessert

2 apples, peeled and chopped fine
½ cup nuts, chopped
1 egg, beaten
1 cup sugar
2 tablespoons flour
1 teaspoon baking powder
⅛ teaspoon salt

Combine all the ingredients and mix. Bake in a shallow greased pan in a moderate oven (350° F.) about 25 minutes or until a macaroon-like crust forms on top. Remove from pan while warm. Place in sherbet glasses. Serve cold with whipped cream. Serves 4.

Blueberry Slump

2 cups blueberries, washed
½ cup sugar
1 cup water
1 cup flour, sifted
2 teaspoons baking powder
¼ teaspoon salt
½ cup milk (about)

Stew blueberries, sugar, and water. Mix and sift flour, baking powder and salt; add milk, stirring quickly to make a dumpling dough that will drop from the end of a spoon. Drop into the boiling sauce. Cook 10 minutes with the cover off and 10 minutes with cover on. Serve with plain or whipped cream. Serves 4. On Cape Cod they call this pudding Blueberry Grunt. A steamed berry pudding is also known as a Grunt.

Apple Slump is made in the same way, substituting apples for blueberries. Stew 6 well-flavored apples with ¼ cup molasses, ¼ cup sugar, and ½ cup water and proceed as above.

Blueberry Upside-Down Cake

[*A delicious Maine recipe*]

2 tablespoons butter
1 cup brown sugar
½ cup blueberry syrup
1 medium-sized tin of blueberries, drained
3 egg yolks, beaten
1 cup sugar
5 tablespoons blueberry syrup
1 cup flour, sifted
1 teaspoon baking powder
1 teaspoon salt
3 egg whites, beaten stiff
whipped cream

Cook together butter, sugar, and ½ cup blueberry syrup from a tin of blueberries until sugar is dissolved. Cover the bottom of a 10-inch baking dish with all the blueberries. Pour the cooked syrup over berries. Make a batter by beating together egg yolks, sugar, and the 5 tablespoons blueberry syrup. Sift flour, baking powder, and salt and add. Fold in egg whites. Pour mixture over the blueberries and bake in a moderate oven (350° F.) 45 minutes. Serve upside down, topped with sweetened whipped cream or Berry Sauce (page 204). Serves 5.

Cranberry Upside-Down Cake

- 3 tablespoons butter
- 1 cup brown sugar
- 1 can cranberry sauce
- 1 small (number 2) tin apricots
- ½ cup sugar
- ¼ cup shortening
- ½ teaspoon vanilla
- 1 egg, well beaten
- 1¼ cups flour, sifted
- 2 teaspoons baking powder
- ½ teaspoon salt
- ½ cup milk

Melt butter in skillet or upside-down cake pan. Add brown sugar; cook slowly 2 or 3 minutes; add cranberry sauce and apricots. To make batter: cream sugar and shortening; add vanilla and egg, sift flour with baking powder and salt. Add alternately with milk. Pour batter over fruit in skillet. Bake in a moderate oven (350° F.) about 25 minutes. Turn out onto large plate so that fruit is on top. Serve with whipped cream. Serves 6.

New Hampshire "Plate Cake"

Fill a pie tin with any fresh fruit, such as berries, sliced apples, or peaches. Sprinkle with sugar. Cover with a biscuit crust rolled ½-inch thick. Bake in a hot oven (450° F.) until crust is brown and fruit soft, about 15 to 20 minutes. Loosen the crust around the edge, invert the dish and serve upside down with the cooked fruit on top. Cover with sweetened whipped cream. Especially good made with blueberries, raspberries, or wild strawberries.

Mother's Blueberry Bread and Butter Pudding

8 thin slices white bread
¼ cup butter
1 quart blueberries
1 cup sugar
pinch of salt
¾ cup cream, whipped

Remove crusts of bread. Butter each slice. Stew berries, sugar, and salt for 15 minutes. Butter a deep baking dish. Alternate slices of bread and stewed berries until all are used. Bake in a moderate oven (350° F.) for 15 to 20 minutes. Serve very cold with whipped cream. Serves 6.

Molly's Pleasant Pudding

A layer of bits of butter
One of grated bread
One of applesauce
One of sugar

Repeat the layers until a medium-sized buttered baking dish is filled. Make a custard of 3 eggs, 2 cups milk, ¼ teaspoon salt. Pour over. Bake in a moderate oven for half an hour. Serves 4 to 6.

Caramel Bread Pudding

1 cup brown sugar
5 slices of bread
3 cups of milk
⅛ teaspoon salt
2 eggs, beaten
1 teaspoon vanilla

Place sugar in bottom of a buttered casserole or baking dish. Butter bread, remove crusts, cut slices into quarters, and place on top of sugar. Mix the milk, salt, eggs, and vanilla and pour over the bread. Bake in moderate oven (350° F.) about 40 minutes or until a knife inserted in the middle does not adhere. Serve with top milk, cream, or ice cream. Serves 4.

* *This recipe comes from an old Portsmouth, N. H., family where it was served almost every Sunday for dessert. From Helen Kane, 256 Danforth St., Portland, Me., who suggests that it be brought to the table directly from the oven while it is still puffy.*

Brown Bread Brewis

Take hard crusts from brown bread, put in a pan with a little salt and cold water. Cover pan and set over low fire to simmer. Add a small piece of butter and a little cream or rich milk. Cook until mixture is the consistency of thick mush. Serve with cold meats, or as a pudding with milk or syrup. New England Hard-Scrabble is another name for this dish.

Gooseberry Fool

1 quart ripe gooseberries
2 cups water
1 tablespoon butter
1 cup sugar
dash of salt
4 egg yolks
4 egg whites
2 tablespoons powdered sugar

Top and stem the gooseberries, stew in water until tender. Press through a colander to remove skins. Add butter, sugar, salt and egg yolks beaten together until light. Pour into a glass bowl. Beat egg whites, stiff, add powdered sugar. Heap on berries. Serve cold without sauce. Serves 6 to 8.

Maple Hickory Nut Whip

- ¾ cup maple syrup
- 2 egg yolks, well beaten
- 1 tablespoon gelatin
- ¼ cup cold water
- 1 cup heavy cream
- 2 egg whites
- 2 tablespoons powdered sugar
- ½ cup hickory nuts, broken
- ½ teaspoon salt

Cook maple syrup and beaten egg yolks in double boiler until slightly thickened, about 5 minutes. Soak gelatin in cold water for 5 minutes, dissolve over hot water, and add to custard. Remove from fire and cool. Whip cream until stiff. Beat egg whites until stiff but not dry, fold in powdered sugar; fold cream and eggs into the cooled custard as soon as it begins to thicken. Add nuts and salt. Serve in sherbet glasses. Serves 6.

Down East Sizzlers

- 1 cup flour, sifted
- 1 tablespoon sugar
- 1 teaspoon baking powder
- ½ teaspoon salt
- 2 tablespoons butter
- ½ cup milk
- 1 egg, beaten
- canned blueberries, drained

Sift flour, sugar, baking powder, and salt. Cut in butter until mixture is consistency of coarse cornmeal. Combine egg and milk and stir into dry ingredients. Roll thin on a floured board and cut about the size of a saucer. Place 1 tablespoon blueberries on each pastry and seal edges with water. Fry in hot deep fat (370° F.) until a golden brown. Serve hot. Makes 20 sizzlers.

PLUM DUFF

- ½ cup brown sugar
- ¼ cup melted butter
- 1 egg, well beaten
- 1 cup cooked, seeded unsweetened prunes
- ½ cup pastry flour, sifted
- ¼ teaspoon soda
- ¼ teaspoon baking powder
- ¼ teaspoon salt
- 1 tablespoon milk

Add sugar to melted butter, cool slightly and stir in the egg. Cut prunes into small pieces. Mash and measure. Mix and sift dry ingredients. Add fruit pulp to first mixture, sift in dry ingredients, and add the milk. Bake in well-greased muffin tins filled ⅔ full in a moderate oven (350° F.) about 25 minutes. Serve warm with Foamy Sauce (page 189). Serves 4.

✱ *The original Plum Duff (i.e., plum dough), named by seamen, was a stiff flour pudding with raisins or currants, boiled in a bag. This one has a lighter flavor and will be welcomed by landlubbers, too.*

UNCOOKED SNOW CREAM

[*A child's delight; some children call it "Snow Mush"*]

Fill a tall glass with light new clean snow. Pour in rich milk. Add a tablespoon of sugar, a few drops of red (vegetable) coloring, 2 or 3 drops of vanilla to taste. Beat mixture with longhandled silver spoon and serve immediately.

Queen of Puddings

[*Eve Leland, Round Pond, Me.*]

2 cups fine dry bread crumbs
4 cups milk
2 tablespoons butter
1 cup sugar
4 egg yolks, well beaten
grated rind 1 lemon
jam, jelly, or raspberries
4 egg whites, beaten stiff
¾ cup sugar
juice of ½ lemon

Soak crumbs in milk 5 minutes. Cream butter, stir in sugar, and add egg yolks and lemon rind. Stir into soaked crumbs. Turn into greased casserole, place in a pan of hot water and bake in a moderate oven (350° F.) until firm, about 1 hour. Spread a layer of jam or jelly or fresh raspberries on top of the pudding. Add sugar and lemon juice to egg whites, spread on pudding, and replace in oven until meringue is lightly browned. Serve without sauce. Serves 6.

Bird's Nest Pudding

8 tart apples, peeled and sliced
¾ cup sugar
½ teaspoon cinnamon
baking powder biscuit dough (recipe page 159)

Fill deep buttered dish with tart apples to within 2 inches of top. Add sugar mixed with cinnamon. Roll biscuit crust 1-inch thick and cover. Bake in a moderate oven (350° F.) for 40 minutes. Serve with Sour Sauce. Serves 6.

SOUR SAUCE

½ cup sugar
1 tablespoon flour
¾ cup water
2 tablespoons butter
2 or 3 tablespoons vinegar

Cook sugar, flour, water, and butter until smooth and thick. Remove from fire; add vinegar. If vinegar is strong, 2 tablespoons will be enough.

* *Yankees differ widely as to what a Bird's Nest Pudding should taste like. The only ingredient on which all agree is apples. In Connecticut they pour a baked custard mixture over apples and bake 1 hour. In Vermont, where maple sugar is widely used, they serve a sour sauce over the pudding. In Massachusetts, where there are comparatively few maple trees, they serve it with shaved maple sugar.*

Honeycomb Pudding

[*A Tamworth, N. H., recipe*]

3 tablespoons butter
2 tablespoons milk
3 eggs, separated
1 cup molasses
1 tablespoon lemon juice
1 cup flour
⅛ teaspoon salt
½ teaspoon cinnamon

Melt shortening, add milk, beaten yolks of eggs, molasses, and lemon juice. Sift together flour, salt, and cinnamon and add. Fold in stiffly beaten whites. Pour into a greased casserole and bake in a very slow oven (250° F.) for 1 hour. Serve with whipped cream or Hot Lemon Sauce (page 194).

Poverty Pudding

[*Marion Fitch, Hartwell Farm, Littleton, Mass.*]

1 quart cornflakes
1 quart milk
2 eggs
¼ cup molasses
¼ cup sugar
1 teaspoon ginger
1 teaspoon salt
1 teaspoon cinnamon

Put cornflakes in greased pudding dish, mix remaining ingredients, and pour them over the cornflakes. Set pudding dish in a pan of hot water and bake in a moderate oven (350° F.) 30 minutes. Serves 4.

Creamy Rice Pudding

[*Family recipe from Mrs. Harriet Grindrod Beckwith, Oxford, Conn.*]

½ cup uncooked rice
3 cups hot milk
½ cup sugar
¾ teaspoon salt
1 tablespoon flour
2 egg yolks
2 egg whites
1 whole egg
1 teaspoon confectioners' sugar
¼ teaspoon vanilla flavoring

Put rice in cold water, bring to boil, stirring occasionally; pour off water. Add hot milk to rice, put in top of double boiler, and cook till soft (30 minutes). Mix sugar, salt, flour, 2 egg yolks slightly beaten, 1 whole egg slightly beaten. Stir gently into rice and cook till whole thickens. Pour into buttered dish and cool. Make a meringue of 2 egg whites, confectioners' sugar, and vanilla flavoring. Dot meringue over top of pudding, put under broiler until meringue is light brown. If desired, add white or dark raisins (which have been soaked in hot water to plump). The tablespoon of flour prevents the pudding from curdling. Do not use quick-cooking rice. Long-grain rice makes the best pudding. Serves 4.

Vermont Rice Pudding

¼ cup long-grain rice
¼ teaspoon salt
2 cups milk
½ cup sugar
½ cup heavy cream
maple syrup

Place rice, salt, and milk in the top of a double boiler and cook over water for 3 hours. Stir in the sugar, cool. Whip the cream and fold in the cold rice. Serve with a small pitcher of hot maple syrup. Serves 4.

Steamed Blueberry Pudding

2 cups flour, sifted
4 teaspoons baking powder
½ teaspoon salt
2 tablespoons sugar
2 tablespoons butter
2 tablespoons molasses
⅞ cup milk
1 cup blueberries, floured

Mix and sift dry ingredients; cut in butter, combine molasses and milk, and add gradually; add blueberries and turn into a greased mold. Steam 1½ hours. Serve with Colonial Pudding Sauce (page 205) or Hard Sauce (page 196). Serves 5. On Cape Cod this pudding is called Blueberry Grunt.

For Steamed Blackberry Pudding substitute blackberries for blueberries.

* *Pudding bags were made of muslin or knit out of cotton yarn. Those that were knit looked like a man's stocking top.*

Before the bags were used, they were dipped into boiling water, floured, and filled while hot. Apples and raisins were favored in the puddings. Half the room in the bag was allowed for the pudding to swell. Whether or not you allowed room, the pudding did swell, just the same!

Puddings were either steamed on top of the vegetables

in the great black iron kettles or dropped into rapidly boiling water. Pudding dishes were called Twifflers.

Some cooks made a new bag each time they made a pudding; others used the same bag. It was indeed a chore to clean a pudding bag!

Blackberry Flummery

1 pint blackberries
2 cups water
3½ tablespoons cornstarch
¼ cup cold water
½ cup sugar

Simmer the blackberries and the 2 cups water; do not stir. The berries should be tender in 10 minutes. Dissolve cornstarch in ¼ cup water and stir carefully into berries. Simmer for 5 minutes, add sugar, and when cold, pour into a glass dish. Serve very cold with sugar and cream. Serves 4.

Lemon Sponge Pudding

1 cup sugar
1 tablespoon flour
2 tablespoons butter
2 egg yolks
pinch of salt
rind and juice of 1 lemon
1 cup milk
2 egg whites, stiffly beaten

Sift the sugar, flour, and salt and blend with the beaten egg yolks. Add the milk, lemon juice, and rind, beating thoroughly. Melt butter and add. Fold in the stiffly beaten egg whites and bake with pudding dish set in a pan of hot water for ¾ hour in a moderate oven (350° F.). The pudding has a layer of lemon jelly, a topping of cake-like consistency, and nice brown crust. Serve cold. Serves 6.

Steamed Cranberry Pudding

[*A Cape Cod recipe*]

1 cup flour, sifted
1 teaspoon baking powder
½ teaspoon salt
⅓ cup brown sugar
½ cup bread crumbs
⅔ cup suet, chopped
1 cup cranberries, washed and picked over
1 egg
⅓ cup water

Mix ingredients, turn into a greased mold. Steam 2 hours. Serve with Hard Sauce (page 196) or Foamy Sauce (page 189). Serves 6.

Cracker Pudding

7 large common crackers, rolled
4 eggs, slightly beaten
1 cup raisins
¼ cup butter
7 cups milk

Mix these ingredients, pour into a steamer or the top of a double boiler, and steam for about 2 hours. Serve with Foamy Sauce. Serves 8 to 10.

FOAMY SAUCE

½ cup sugar
½ cup butter
2 teaspoons water
1 egg, beaten
½ teaspoon vanilla

Stir the sugar, butter, and water together in a saucepan over low heat until well blended. Keep warm. Just before serving, stir in the beaten egg and vanilla. To serve with plum pudding, add ¼ cup brandy or ½ cup rum.

Oatmeal Pudding

✱ *The following recipe was taken from* In the Kitchen, *written by Elizabeth S. Miller, Geneva, N. Y., in 1875 and dedicated to the Cooking Class of the Young Ladies' Saturday Morning Club of Boston, Mass.*

- 4 cups milk
- 2 cups oatmeal
- 3 eggs
- ½ pound suet, chopped fine
- ¼ pound seedless raisins
- ¼ pound currants
- 1 teaspoon salt
- ½ cup sugar
- 1 teaspoon nutmeg

Scald the milk at night and pour it over the oatmeal. Stir, cover, and let remain overnight. Next day beat the eggs, stir in the other ingredients, and pour into the overnight mixture, mixing well. If you are old-fashioned lay a pudding cloth in a bowl and pour the pudding into it, tying it tight but leaving room to swell, and plunge it into boiling water, cover tight, and boil for 2 hours. If you are not old-fashioned, steam it in the top of a double-boiler. In any event, serve it with Maple Sugar Sauce. Serves 8.

MAPLE SUGAR SAUCE

- ½ pound maple sugar
- 4 tablespoons hot water
- ¼ pound butter

Crack the sugar in small bits, add hot water and let simmer a few minutes until clear. Take from fire and stir in the butter.

Snow Balls

[*A Rhode Island recipe*]

- 2 cups flour, sifted
- ½ teaspoon salt
- 2 teaspoons baking powder
- ½ cup butter
- 1 cup sugar
- ¾ cup milk
- 4 egg whites, beaten stiffly

Sift the flour, salt, and baking powder. Cream the butter, stir in the sugar gradually. Stir in the dry ingredients alternately with the milk. Fold in the beaten egg whites. Fill buttered custard cups ⅔ full; fasten waxed paper over the top and tie securely. Steam 50 minutes. Unmold and serve with sliced peaches, crushed strawberries, or Raspberry Sauce. Serves 6 to 8.

RASPBERRY SAUCE

1 cup canned or fresh raspberries
¼ cup sugar

Crush berries, strain to remove seeds. Add sugar and cook to a heavy syrup.

Rhubarb Roly Poly

[*Easier to take than the usual sulphur and molasses spring tonic*]

2 cups flour, sifted
2 teaspoons baking powder
1 teaspoon salt
2 tablespoons sugar
4 tablespoons shortening
¾ cup milk
2 cups rhubarb, cut in pieces
1 cup sugar
butter

Sift flour, baking powder, salt, and sugar. Cut in shortening. Add milk to make a soft dough. Knead on slightly floured board and roll ⅛-inch thick. Spread with rhubarb, dot generously with butter, sprinkle with sugar and roll like a jelly roll. Bake in a moderate oven (350° F.) 30 to 40 minutes. Serve with cream or Hard Sauce (page 196). Serves 6.

Grandmother's Apple Roll

[*Mrs. James Grindrod, Meriden, Conn.*]

biscuit dough (see preceding recipe)
butter
4 tart apples, peeled and chopped
½ cup brown sugar
honey
1 teaspoon cinnamon
1 teaspoon nutmeg
¼ teaspoon salt

Roll dough ½ inch thick. Put small dots of butter over surface. Add brown sugar and a drizzling of honey, nutmeg, cinnamon, and salt to apples and cover biscuit dough with them. Roll into a log, wrap in wax paper, and refrigerate for ½ hour. Remove and cut in 1-inch slices. Bake in moderate oven (350° F.) for about 30 minutes. Delicious as is, or when served with a hot, tart lemon sauce. Makes 1 roll.

Huckleberry Pudding

2 cups flour, sifted
4 teaspoons baking powder
2 teaspoons sugar
½ teaspoon salt
⅔ cup milk
1 cup huckleberries
¾ cup sugar

Sift dry ingredients, add milk; pat dough into a square about ½-inch thick. In the center of the dough place huckleberries, washed and sugared. Roll or fold dough, keeping the berries in the center until berries are entirely surrounded by dough. Tie or sew in a white cloth or bag, allowing room for swelling. Plunge bag in boiling water and steam 1 hour. Serve hot on a large platter with Pudding Sauce or Berry Sauce (page 204). Serves 5.

PUDDING SAUCE

¾ cup sugar
⅛ teaspoon salt
1 tablespoon cornstarch
1 cup boiling water
1 tablespoon butter
¼ teaspoon vanilla

Mix sugar, salt, and cornstarch. Cook in boiling water until clear. Add butter and vanilla. Serve hot.

✻ *Apple Pudding is made in the same way, substituting apples for huckleberries.*

Apple Puffets

- 2 cups flour, sifted
- 1½ teaspoons baking powder
- ½ teaspoon salt
- 2 eggs, beaten
- 1 cup milk
- 2 cups chopped apples

Sift dry ingredients, add eggs and milk and beat until smooth. Fill baking cups alternately with a layer of batter and then of chopped apples until cups are ⅔ filled. Steam 1 hour. Serve hot with sweetened and flavored cream. Other fruits may be substituted for the apple. Serves 4.

Steamed Fig Pudding

- 1 pound chopped figs
- 1 cup suet, chopped
- 1 cup molasses
- ¾ cup milk
- ½ cup sugar
- 2 eggs
- 1 teaspoon soda
- 3 cups pastry flour, sifted
- ¼ teaspoon salt

Mix ingredients, turn into greased mold or covered baking dish and steam 5 hours. Serve with Hot Lemon Sauce or whipped cream sweetened and flavored with rum or brandy. Serves 6 to 8.

HOT LEMON SAUCE

½ cup sugar
1 tablespoon cornstarch
⅛ teaspoon salt
1 cup boiling water
1 teaspoon grated lemon rind
3 tablespoons lemon juice
3 tablespoons butter

Mix sugar, cornstarch, and salt; stir in hot water, gradually; bring to a boil and cook 15 minutes, stirring until thick and clear. Remove from fire, stir in lemon rind, juice, and butter. Makes 1¼ cups sauce.

Harriet's Suet Pudding

1 cup soft bread crumbs
½ cup chopped suet
½ cup seeded raisins
1 cup sugar
2 cups flour, sifted
½ cup molasses
½ cup shredded citron
2 apples, chopped fine
3 eggs, beaten
1 teaspoon soda
1 teaspoon allspice
1 teaspoon cinnamon
1 teaspoon salt

Combine ingredients, mixing well. Fill well-greased mold half full. Steam 3 hours. Serve with Hard Sauce (page 196), or Foamy Sauce (page 189). Serves 8.

Desire's Baked Plum Pudding

1 quart milk, heated
3 tablespoons butter
3 cups bread crumbs
½ teaspoon salt
3 eggs, beaten
1 cup brown sugar
¾ cup molasses
1 pound raisins
½ pound currants
½ teaspoon mace
½ teaspoon cinnamon
⅔ teaspoon clove

Pour hot milk in which butter is melted over bread crumbs, add remaining ingredients and bake 3 to 4 hours in a moderately slow oven (325° F.). Stir once or twice before the crust forms. Serve with Hard Sauce (page 196, or Foamy Sauce (page 189). Serves 8.

Deacon Porter's Hat

[*Recipe from the Office of the Steward, Mount Holyoke College, South Hadley, Mass.*]

1 cup ground suet
1 cup molasses
1 cup raisins
1 cup currants
3 cups flour, sifted
2 teaspoons baking powder
½ teaspoon salt
1 teaspoon cloves
1 teaspoon cinnamon
1½ cups milk
¾ cup chopped nuts (optional)

Combine suet, molasses, raisins, and currants. Mix and sift dry ingredients. Add to suet mixture alternately with milk, beating until smooth after each addition. Turn into a greased 2-quart mold, cover tightly, and steam 3 hours. Serve hot with hard sauce. Send to the table whole. Serves 10 to 12.

* *This dessert is well known to students of Mount Holyoke College. Deacon Porter, an early trustee of the college, wore a stovepipe hat, style 1837. This pudding, when it came to the table whole, was given this epithet by some college wag. A light-colored steamed pudding, made in a similar mold, was called Deacon Porter's Summer Hat. Mount Holyoke College, when it was Mount Holyoke Seminary, used to be called "The Minister's Rib Factory" because it turned out so many wives for ministers and missionaries.*

Yankee Christmas Pudding

- 1 loaf day-old bread, with crusts discarded
- ¼ pound citron, cut in small pieces
- ¾ pound suet, chopped
- 1 pound currants
- 1 pound raisins
- grated rind of 1 lemon
- ¼ teaspoon cloves
- 1½ cups sugar
- 1 teaspoon salt
- 3 apples, chopped fine
- 1 wineglass brandy
- 6 eggs, beaten

Crumb the bread; mix all ingredients in the order given. Turn into greased 1½-quart mold, cover and steam 6 hours (or steam 4 hours if placed in 2 molds). Serve with Hard Sauce or Foamy Sauce (page 189). Serves 12.

HARD SAUCE

- 4 tablespoons butter
- 1 cup confectioners' sugar
- ⅛ teaspoon salt
- 1 tablespoon heavy cream
- 1 teaspoon vanilla, rum, whisky, or brandy

Cream butter thoroughly, add sugar gradually and cream together until fluffy. Add cream and vanilla, beating well. Makes about ¾ cup.

Chocolate Mint Cream

- 1 cup milk
- 1½ squares cooking chocolate
- 4 cream mints
- 1 tablespoon gelatin
- 2 tablespoons cold water
- ½ cup sugar
- ¼ teaspoon salt
- 1 cup heavy cream

Scald the milk; in it, dissolve the chocolate and the mints. When dissolved, beat with egg beater to blend the mixture. Add gelatin, previously softened in cold water; then sugar and salt. Cool. Add the cream. Chill until the mixture begins to harden. Whip until the mixture holds its shape. Serve with whipped cream. Serves 4.

Maine Chocolate Pudding

1 square chocolate, cut in pieces
2 cups milk, scalded
2 tablespoons cornstarch or
    4 tablespoons flour
⅓ cup sugar
⅛ teaspoon salt
¼ cup cold milk
½ teaspoon vanilla

Combine chocolate and scalded milk in top of double boiler until chocolate has melted. Beat with rotary egg beater until well blended. Mix cornstarch (or flour), sugar, and salt; stir in the cold milk to make a smooth paste. Stir into the scalded chocolate milk and continue to stir over boiling water until mixture has thickened. Cover, cook 15 or 20 minutes, remove from stove; add vanilla. Serve cold with thick cream poured gently over the top of the pudding so that delicate scum will not be broken. Serves 4.

Littleton Pudding

2 cups milk
2 tablespoons cornstarch
¼ cup cold water
½ cup sugar
¼ teaspoon salt
1 egg white, stiffly beaten
⅓ cup shredded coconut
1 square chocolate
1 cup cream, whipped

Heat milk in double boiler; add cornstarch dissolved in cold water, sugar, and salt; cook until thick. Remove from stove, add beaten egg white. Divide mixture into 2 parts. To one add coconut, to the other the melted chocolate. Fill sherbet glasses half full of the coconut mixture, top with chocolate mixture. Before serving add sweetened whipped cream. Serves 4.

Vermont Baked Custard

[*In France they call it Crême Brûlée*]

2 cups heavy cream
3 tablespoons maple sugar, shaved
4 eggs
⅛ teaspoon salt
¼ cup maple sugar, shaved

Put the cream into a saucepan and bring to the boiling point. Beat the eggs slightly with the 3 tablespoons of sugar and salt. Pour the hot cream slowly over this mixture, stirring constantly. Then put in a double boiler over hot water and cook for 5 minutes, beating all the time with an egg beater. Pour into a pudding dish and cool. When ready to serve cover the top, gently, with ¼ cup finely shaved maple sugar and place under the broiler until the sugar melts and becomes smooth and glossy and forms a thin hard crust over the soft custard. Serve without sauce. Serves 4 to 6.

Pumpkin Custard

2 cups milk
1 teaspoon butter
3 eggs, beaten
½ cup light brown sugar
¾ teaspoon salt
¾ teaspoon cinnamon
1 cup pumpkin, strained

Scald milk, add butter, eggs, sugar, salt, cinnamon, and pumpkin. Pour into baking dish or individual molds and set in a pan of hot water. Bake in a moderate oven (350° F.) about 40 minutes or until blade of a knife inserted in center does not adhere. Serve warm or chilled.

SALEM CUSTARD SOUFFLÉ

2 tablespoons butter	3 tablespoons sugar
2 tablespoons flour	½ teaspoon vanilla
1 cup milk	¼ teaspoon almond extract
4 eggs, separated	⅛ teaspoon salt

Cream the butter and the flour; heat the milk and pour it gradually over the butter and flour. Cook 8 minutes in a double boiler, stirring often. Beat egg yolks well; add suger, flavoring, and salt and stir in. Fold in egg whites stiffly beaten. Turn into greased baking dish and place in a pan of hot water. Bake in a moderate oven (350° F.) 50 to 60 minutes or until firm. Serve at once from baking dish with sweetened whipped cream, flavored with sherry, strawberry sauce, or soft maple sugar. Serves 6.

QUAKING CUSTARD

[*A 125-year-old recipe from Westfield, Mass. Also called Spanish Cream*]

1 tablespoon gelatin	2 egg yolks, slightly beaten
2 tablespoons cold water	2 cups milk, scalded
⅓ cup sugar	2 egg whites, stiffly beaten
½ teaspoon salt	1 teaspoon vanilla

Soak gelatin in cold water for 5 minutes. Mix sugar and salt and egg yolks and pour the scalded milk over this mixture. Return to top of double boiler, stir over hot water until mixture coats spoon. Pour over gelatin and stir until gelatin is dissolved. Chill until slightly thickened, then fold in egg whites and vanilla. Turn into mold. Cool until firm. Unmold. Serve with cream. Serves 6.

Add ½ cup of macaroon crumbs to the cooked custard and pour over macaroons for a variation. Replace vanilla with ¼ teaspoon almond extract.

Maple Custard

3 eggs, beaten
½ cup maple syrup
2 cups milk
dash of salt

Combine eggs, syrup, milk, and salt. Pour into individual molds. Set molds in a pan of hot water. Bake in a moderate oven (350° F.) about 40 minutes, or until blade of a knife inserted in center does not adhere. Serve warm or chilled. Serves 4.

✻ *Although not popular today, a favorite dessert several generations ago was Minute Pudding. Scald 3 cups milk and pour over mixture of 1 cup cold milk blended with ¾ cup flour and 1 teaspoon salt. Return to double boiler for 20 minutes. Serve with maple syrup or honey. Serves 6 to 8.*

Sea Moss Blanc Mange

½ cup sea moss
3 cups milk
⅛ teaspoon vanilla or lemon

Soak moss 15 minutes in cold water; pick out discolored pieces. Add moss to milk and cook in double boiler 25 minutes. Strain. Add salt and flavoring. Turn into individual molds. Chill, unmold, and serve with crushed, sweetened berries or sliced bananas and cream. Serves 5.

Tipsy Parson

Arrange slices of sponge cake on individual plates. Moisten each piece with 2 tablespoons sherry. Pour chilled custard sauce over each serving.

Maple Charlotte

1 tablespoon gelatin
½ cup cold water
2 cups maple syrup
2 cups heavy cream, whipped

Dissolve gelatin in cold water. Heat maple syrup and add gelatin. Let stand until the mixture begins to thicken. Fold in whipped cream. Pour into individual serving glasses. Sprinkle with chopped butternuts, if desired, and serve ice cold. Serves 6.

Syllabub

1 pint heavy cream, beaten stiff
½ cup confectioners' sugar
whites 2 eggs, beaten stiff
1 glass white wine (sweet Madeira or Sauterne)

Fold in half the sugar with the cream, the remainder with the eggs. Mix well, add the wine slowly. Serve over Trifle, lady fingers, macaroons, sponge cake, or sliced bananas.

Trifle

Put slices of sponge cake together, sandwich fashion, with strawberry jam. Cover with a soft custard, delicately flavored with almond extract. Serve with Syllabub. Trifle is also made with macaroons softened with custard and served with Syllabub.

Cider Jelly

2 tablespoons gelatin
½ cup cold water
2 cups boiling sweet cider
¾ cup sugar
⅓ cup lemon juice

Dissolve gelatin in cold water for 5 minutes. Add remaining ingredients in order given. Pour in a mold and chill. Unmold and serve with whipped cream. Sprinkle with nutmeg. Serves 4.

Maple Mousse

- 2 eggs, separated
- ⅛ teaspoon salt
- ½ cup maple syrup
- ½ pint cream, whipped

Beat yolks of eggs until lemon-colored; add salt, add maple syrup, and cook in top of double boiler until mixture thickens. Cool. Beat egg whites until stiff. Combine maple syrup mixture, egg whites, and cream. Freeze in ice cube tray, stirring frequently so that crystals do not form.

Coffee Mousse

- 1 cup strong coffee
- 1 cup milk
- 1 cup sugar
- ⅛ teaspoon salt
- ½ tablespoon flour
- 4 eggs, separated
- 1 pint cream, whipped

Use 4 tablespoons of coffee to 1 cup water in making coffee so that it will be very strong. Add milk to coffee and heat. Combine sugar, salt, and flour and stir into coffee mixture. Cook, stirring constantly, until it reaches the boiling point. Pour over the well-beaten yolks of the eggs and cook in the top of double boiler until mixture thickens. Cool. Add egg whites, beaten stiff, and cream. Freeze in ice cube tray, stirring frequently so that crystals do not form.

Rhubarb Ice Cream

[*Parker House, Boston, Mass.*]

- 2 cups water
- 2½ pounds rhubarb, cut in pieces
- 2⅓ cups sugar
- 4 cups heavy cream, whipped

Add water to rhubarb and boil 5 to 10 minutes. Add sugar; cool and add cream. Pack in freezer in finely chopped ice and rock salt and freeze. Makes about 2 quarts ice cream.

Concord Grape Ice Cream

[*Parker House, Boston, Mass.*]

- 1 pound Concord grapes
- ½ pound Malaga grapes
- ½ pound seedless grapes
- ½ pound Tokay grapes
- 2⅓ cups sugar
- 4 cups heavy cream, whipped

Pick grapes from stems; wash. Heat the grapes but do not boil; press the mixture through a sieve. Combine grape juice and sugar; cool and add cream. Pack in freezer in finely chopped ice and rock salt and freeze. Makes about 2 quarts.

Orange Pineapple Ice Cream

- 1 cup crushed pineapple
- 1 cup orange juice
- 1½ cups sugar
- 1 cup milk
- ½ pint cream, whipped

Mix pineapple, orange juice, and sugar and let stand overnight. Add milk and cream. Pack in freezer in finely chopped ice and rock salt and freeze. Serves 6.

Currant-Raspberry or Cranberry Ice

2 cups currant juice (whole berries put through blender and strained to yield clear juice) or 1 cup currant juice and 1 cup raspberry juice or 2 cups cranberry juice
2 cups water
2 cups sugar
3 egg whites

Heat juice, water, and sugar to boiling point. Pour over stiffly beaten whites of eggs and whip mixture thoroughly. Freeze when cool in ice cube tray, stirring frequently so that crystals do not form. Serves 6.

Lemon Sherbet

[*Mrs. Silas Snow, Williamsburg, Mass.*]

2 cups sugar
½ teaspoon lemon extract
juice 2 lemons
4 cups milk
2 egg whites, beaten stiff

Mix sugar, extract, and juice. Add milk and egg whites. Pack at once in freezer in finely chopped ice and rock salt and freeze. Serves 8.

BERRY SAUCE

[*Miss Lillian V. Dearborn, 55 Beach Ave., Melrose, Mass.*]

1 cup sugar
¼ cup soft butter
1 egg white
1 cup mashed berries (strawberries, raspberries, blueberries)

Beat sugar and butter to a cream; add egg white beaten to a froth. Stir in mashed berries. Makes 2 cups sauce.

MAPLE SAUCE FOR VANILLA ICE CREAM

[*Mrs. Silas Snow, Williamsburg, Mass.*]

Boil maple syrup to 227° F. or until it spins a fine short thread when dropped from spoon. Cool slightly and pour over ice cream.

COLONIAL PUDDING SAUCE

[*To eat on Deep Dish Apple Pie or Steamed Blueberry or Apple Pudding or Bean Pot Apples*]

3 cups rich heavy cream
⅔ cups soft maple sugar

Stir cream and maple sugar and thoroughly blend. Flavor with grated nutmeg.

Pies

Yankee Pie Crust

[*For 1 two-crust (9-inch) pie*]

2½ cups flour, sifted
¾ teaspoon salt
¾ cup shortening
¼ cup ice water (about)

Mix and sift flour and salt; cut in shortening until the size of a pea. Add water gradually, blending with a fork. Use only enough water to hold dough together, putting to one side pieces of dough as soon as formed. Shape into a ball and chill thoroughly, first wrapping dough in waxed paper. Roll on lightly floured board, using as little flour as possible. Roll the dough in one direction only and do not stretch the dough. Prick bottom crust and sides with fork and cut several small gashes in top crust to allow steam to escape. Pie crust may be made in advance and kept in a cool place.

Do not grease the pan. Remember the old saying, "A good pie crust greases its own tin."

* *A pastry blender keeps crust flaky. Excess water toughens the crust; too little makes it crumbly. Use only enough to dampen the dough in order to roll it. Yankee cooks prefer lard to butter or margarine because it makes a more tender crust.*

To Make A Pye with Pippins

[The Compleat Cook's Guide—*1683*]

"Pare your pippins, and cut out the cores, then make your coffin of crust. Take a good handful of quinces sliced and lay at the bottom, then lay your pippins on top, and fill the holes where the core was taken out with syrup of quinces, and put into every pippin a piece of orangado, then pour on top the syrup of quinces, then put in sugar, and so close it up, let it be very well baked, for it will ask much soaking, especially the quinces."

Maple Apple Pie

1½ quarts apples, peeled and sliced thin
1 cup soft maple sugar
¼ teaspoon salt
¼ teaspoon cinnamon
1 tablespoon flour
2 tablespoons butter
cream

Have pie pan lined with pastry. Put in sliced tart apples. Spread over them maple sugar, salt, cinnamon, and flour; dot with butter. Cover with perforated top crust, brush with cream, and bake in a hot oven (450° F.) for 10 minutes; then reduce heat to moderate (350° F.) and bake 40 to 50 minutes longer. Makes 1 two-crust (9-inch) pie.

Prize New England Apple Pie

⅔ cup lard
2 cups all-purpose flour, not sifted
1½ teaspoons salt
¼ cup cold water
6 to 8 tart apples
1 cup sugar
cinnamon and nutmeg
2 tablespoons butter
2 tablespoons heavy cream

Mix lard, flour, and salt, leaving a few lumps the size of a pea in order to make crust flaky. Pour water over mixture gradually, working it in with a fork. With hands shape mixture into a ball. Divide into two parts for upper and lower crust. Pare, core, and slice apples, fill pan to slightly rounding. Pour sugar on top of apples. Add a shaking of both cinnamon and nutmeg. Cut butter into small pieces and dot the top. Shake a little additional salt over all. (If apples are juicy a sift or two of flour and a little additional sugar on lower crust should be added before apples are placed in pie.) Moisten edges of crust and put top crust in place. Press and crimp edges. Gloss crust with heavy cream. Bake in a hot oven (450° F.) 15 to 20 minutes. Reduce heat to (350° F.) and bake 30 to 40 minutes longer.

Maine Crab Apple Pie

3 cups unpeeled crab apples, cored and quartered
1½ cups sugar
¼ teaspoon salt
¼ cup cold water

Have a pie pan lined with pastry. Put in apples. Sprinkle sugar and salt and water over them. Cover with top crust and bake in a hot oven (450° F.) for 10 minutes; then reduce heat to moderate (350° F.) and bake 40 to 50 minutes longer. Makes 1 two-crust (8-inch) pie. The flavor is delicious and the color a lovely pink.

Pork Apple Pie

[*Mrs. Wm. Dodge, Hannah Dustin Drive, Canterbury, N. H.*]

- 8 to 10 tart apples, peeled, cored and sliced
- 20 pieces of fat salt pork, cut the size of peas
- ¾ cup sugar (maple sugar preferred)
- ½ teaspoon cinnamon
- ¼ teaspoon nutmeg
- ¼ teaspoon salt

Fill a deep dish with apples. Mix salt pork, sugar, spices, and salt and sprinkle the mixture over the apples. Cover with pie crust. Cut slits for steam to escape. Bake in a hot oven (450° F.) for 10 minutes; then reduce heat to moderate (350° F.) and bake 30 to 35 minutes longer. If crust becomes brown, cover with brown paper so that it will remain a golden brown. While pie is baking, blend a package of cream cheese with 1 tablespoon thick cream and allow to become firm in refrigerator. Serve pie warm with slice of cheese.

✱ *Old-time New Englanders used salt pork from soup to dessert. This recipe is said to have been made first by an old fisherman who used dried apples, salt pork, and molasses. His wife improved upon it, using fresh apples and maple sugar. It became a popular dish, often served in Vermont homes for the Sunday evening meal. Calvin Coolidge, in the White House, extolled its goodness. Pork Pie has a more succulent flavor than ordinary apple pie.*

No Crust Apple Pie

- 8 to 10 tart apples, peeled, cored and sliced
- 1½ cups brown sugar
- juice ½ lemon
- 2 tablespoons brandy
- ⅛ teaspoon cinnamon
- ¼ pound butter
- 1 cup flour
- pinch salt

Add to the apples half the brown sugar, lemon juice, brandy, and cinnamon. Let stand 15 minutes. Butter an 8-inch pie plate. Mix with fingers butter, flour, salt, and balance of brown sugar. Sprinkle mixture on top of apples, pressing down firmly around edges. Bake in a 350° F. oven for 1 hour.

Vermont Fried Apple Pies

[*Mrs. A. A. Durham, 200 Fern St., W. Hartford, Conn.*]

½ teaspoon salt	3 tablespoons butter
2 cups flour	½ cup milk (about)

Add salt to flour, cut in shortening; add milk to make a dough a little softer than pie crust. Roll thin and cut in rounds about the size of a saucer. In the center of each place a spoonful of thick spiced applesauce. Fold over, wet edges with milk and seal with fork. Fry in hot deep fat (370° F.) until golden brown. Drain. May be dusted with powdered sugar and served hot with maple syrup or cream; may also be stored in a jar and warmed over when needed. Makes 4 turnovers.

* *These pies were often made with dried apples. Early in the fall apples were peeled, sliced in eighths, strung on twine, and hung on the clothesline in the sun or laid on the oven after the heat was turned off. Or, sometimes a sheet was spread on a piazza roof and the apples were placed on the sheet for 4 days, but always taken in at*

night, in case of rain. Some of the old recipes call for the addition of 1 egg and 1 teaspoon baking powder to the milk. Doughnut dough is also used by many old-time cooks.

Mince Pie

Use 2 cups mincemeat. Bake between 2 crusts.

✱ *In Colonial days New England housewives often baked as many as 100 pies at a time, stacked them in big jars, and stored them in a shed where they'd freeze. When a pie was wanted it was placed in the pie cupboard in the fireplace chimney and thawed out.*

Mincemeat

- 3 pounds lean beef, chopped fine
- 2 pounds suet, chopped fine
- 3 quarts apples finely chopped
- 3 pounds seeded raisins, chopped
- 2 pounds currants
- 1 pound citron, cut in small pieces
- ½ cup candied orange peel, chopped
- ½ cup candied lemon peel, chopped
- ½ cup lemon juice
- ¼ cup orange juice
- 2 tablespoons salt
- 4 cups sugar
- 1 cup coffee
- 2 cups cider (not too new)
- 1 teaspoon cloves
- 1 teaspoon allspice
- 2 teaspoons cinnamon
- 3 cups brandy (1 bottle about ¼ size)
- 1 cup sherry
- 1 cup currant jelly

Mix all ingredients except brandy and sherry, and cook 2 hours; when cool, not cold, add liquor; let stand in crock a week before using. This makes about 12 quarts and will keep indefinitely in a cool place. This recipe came from Maine and is very old.

Cranberry Mince Pie

[*A modern Cape Cod recipe*]

Stir contents 1 can cranberry sauce until it is broken into pieces. Combine with 1 cup mincemeat. Fill an 8-inch unbaked pastry shell and criss-cross the top with strips of pastry making a lattice-work upper crust. Bake in a hot oven (450° F.) 10 minutes; then reduce heat to moderate (350° F.) and bake 25 minutes longer. Makes 1 two-crust (8-inch) pie.

Coolidge Mincemeat

½ peck apples
½ pound currants
2 pounds seeded raisins
½ pound citron, diced small
2 pounds sugar
2½ quarts cider
1 pound boiled beef, diced
1 pound suet, cut small
½ teaspoon salt

Pare, core, and chop the apples fine. Chop together the currants, raisins, and citron; add the apples, sugar, and cider and boil about 4 minutes. Add meat and suet and simmer about 1 hour, stirring frequently to prevent burning. Add salt last. Season to taste with cinnamon, cloves, and nutmeg. A little jelly or fruit juice will improve the flavor. Use 2 cups for a 9-inch pie. Makes about 5 quarts.

Cranberry Raisin Pie

[*A Cape Cod recipe, sometimes called Mock Cherry Pie*]

1 cup cranberries, coarsely chopped
1 cup raisins, coarsely chopped
1 cup sugar
1 tablespoon flour
¼ cup boiling water
⅛ teaspoon salt
¼ teaspoon vanilla

Line pie plate with pastry. Mix sugar, flour, and salt; add water and vanilla, then raisins. Beat smoothly and add cranberries and turn into pastry-lined plate. Top with a lattice of pastry strips. Bake in a hot oven (450° F.) 10 minutes; reduce heat to moderate (350° F.) and bake 30 to 40 minutes longer. Makes 1 two-crust (8-inch) pie.

Mock Mince Pie

[*A 100-year-old recipe*]

1 cup rolled cracker crumbs
1 cup vinegar
1 cup water
1 cup raisins
1 cup molasses
½ cup butter
1 teaspoon cinnamon
1 teaspoon cloves
¼ teaspoon salt
⅔ cup sugar

Cook slowly a few minutes until it is the consistency of mincemeat. Bake between 2 crusts, following directions for baking mince pie.

Green Tomato Mincemeat

8 quarts green tomatoes
3 pounds brown sugar
1 cup vinegar
1 teaspoon salt
1 pint boiled cider
2 pounds seeded raisins
1 tablespoon clove
1 tablespoon cinnamon
1 tablespoon nutmeg
1 tablespoon allspice

Cook all together about 2¼ hours. Put in jars and seal. Makes 5 quart jars.

Uncooked Blueberry Pie

1 pastry shell previously baked
1 cup whipped cream
2 cups berries, washed and drained
½ cup powdered sugar

When ready to serve, fill shell with berries, sprinkle with the powdered sugar, cover with the whipped cream.

Blueberry Pie

4 cups blueberries, washed and drained
⅛ teaspoon salt
1½ cups sugar
1½ tablespoons flour
1 tablespoon butter
milk

Mix all ingredients thoroughly. Line plate with pastry, fill with blueberries and dot with butter; adjust top crust, brush with milk and bake in a hot oven (450° F.) 10 minutes; then reduce heat to moderate (350° F.) and bake 25 minutes longer. Makes 1 two-crust (9-inch) pie.

Deep Blueberry Pie

4 cups blueberries
¼ teaspoon salt
1½ cups sugar

Combine berries, salt, and sugar in a deep baking dish with no under crust. Put an inverted cup in the middle. This serves to keep the crust up so that it will not be soaked with the juices. Put on top crust. Bake in a hot oven (450° F.) 10 minutes; then reduce the heat to moderate (350° F.) and bake 35 minutes longer. Serve hot with cottage cheese. Makes 1 deep dish (9-inch) pie.

Cherry Pie

[*A Vermont recipe*]

- 3 cups cherries
- ⅔ to 1¼ cups sugar (according to the acidity of the fruit)
- 1 tablespoon butter
- 1 tablespoon quick cooking tapioca
- ¼ teaspoon salt

Place the cherries in an unbaked pie shell. Sprinkle over them a mixture of sugar, tapioca, and salt and stir quickly until they are well coated. Dot with butter. Cover with a top crust or lattice crust. Bake in a hot oven (450° F.) for 10 minutes; then reduce heat to medium (350° F.) and bake 25 minutes longer. Makes 1 two-crust pie.

Rhubarb, Gooseberry, Blueberry, and Strawberry may be made following this same recipe. For Rhubarb Pie use peeled, diced rhubarb.

Mock Cherry Pie

- 1 cup cranberries, washed and looked over
- ¾ cup raisins
- 1 cup sugar
- 2 teaspoons flour
- ⅛ teaspoon salt
- 1 tablespoon butter

Cut cranberries in halves; mix together cranberries, raisins, and dry ingredients and turn into an unbaked pastry shell; dot with butter and adjust top crust or criss-cross lattice crust. Bake in a hot oven (450° F.) 10 minutes; then reduce heat to moderate (350° F.) and bake 25 minutes longer. Makes 1 two-crust (7-inch) pie.

Cape Cod Cranberry Pie

3½ cups cranberries, washed and looked over
1½ cups sugar
1½ tablespoons flour
¼ teaspoon salt
3 tablespoons water
2 tablespoons melted butter

Chop cranberries and mix with remaining ingredients. Fill an unbaked pie crust with the mixture and arrange strips of pie crust criss-cross over the top. Bake in a hot oven (450° F.) 10 minutes; then reduce heat to moderate (350° F.) and bake 40 minutes longer. Makes one (9-inch) pie.

✱ *A cranberry pie wouldn't taste right to a Cape Codder unless it was covered with a criss-cross lattice crust.*

Prune and Apricot Pie

1½ cups cooked prunes
½ cup cooked apricots
½ cup sugar
1 tablespoon flour
1 teaspoon lemon juice
2 tablespoons prune juice
2 tablespoons apricot juice
1 tablespoon butter

Cut prunes and apricots in small pieces, add sugar. Place in an unbaked pie shell, sprinkled with flour. Combine lemon juice, prune juice, and apricot juice and pour over fruit. Dot with butter. Place top crust on pie and bake in a hot oven (450° F.) 10 minutes, then reduce heat to moderate (350° F.) and bake 20 to 25 minutes longer. Makes 1 two-crust (7-inch) pie. If fruit is sweetened, omit the sugar.

Peach Pie

Line a deep pie dish with unbaked pastry. Peel ripe, juicy peaches; do not remove the pits. Fill pie dish with the peaches. Sprinkle ½ cup sugar over peaches. Lay the upper crust on very gently. Do not press it to the lower crust on the edge. When the pie is baked lift the upper crust carefully and pour in a filling.

FILLING

- 2 egg whites, stiffly beaten
- ¾ cup rich milk, scalded
- 1 tablespoon sugar
- ½ teaspoon cornstarch
- 2 tablespoons milk

Stir the egg whites into the milk, add the sugar and the cornstarch dissolved in the 2 tablespoons milk. Cook in the top of a double boiler 5 minutes. Cool. This filling should be cold when poured over hot pie. Replace the crust, allow pie to cool, eat while slightly warm.

✱ *Apple pies are often baked in a similar manner. The apples are sliced and placed in the pie without sugar or spices. The top crust is removed, sugar, cinnamon, and nutmeg are added and the top crust replaced. The uncooked sugar gives a fresher flavor to the apples and there is no juice to cook out. Honey is sometimes used in place of sugar.*

Concord Grape Pie

- 1 cup sugar
- 2 tablespoons flour
- ¼ teaspoon salt
- 1 egg, beaten
- 2 cups Concord grapes, cut and seeded but not skinned
- 2 tablespoons butter

Combine sugar, flour, and salt; add egg and mix with grapes. Place in an unbaked pie shell and dot with butter. Add upper crust. Bake in a hot oven (450° F.) for 10 minutes. Reduce heat to moderate (350° F.) and bake 20 minutes longer. Makes 1 two-crust (7-inch) pie.

Strawberry Chiffon Pie

[*Toll House, Whitman, Mass.*]

- 1 tablespoon gelatin
- ¼ cup water
- 4 eggs, separated
- ½ cup sugar
- 1 tablespoon lemon juice
- ½ teaspoon salt
- 1 cup strawberry pulp and juice
- ¼ cup sugar
- whipped cream
- garnish of strawberries

Soak gelatin in water for 5 minutes. Beat egg yolks slightly; add ¼ cup sugar, lemon juice, and salt. Cook over boiling water until of custard consistency. Add softened gelatin, stirring thoroughly. Then add strawberry pulp. (A little red coloring gives a pleasing color to the pie.) Cool, and when mixture begins to congeal fold in the stiffly beaten whites of the eggs to which has been added the ¼ cup sugar. Fill baked pie shell and chill. Before serving spread a thin layer of whipped cream over pie and garnish with strawberries. Makes 1 one-crust (9-inch) pie.

Rhubarb Pie

[*A Rhode Island recipe*]

- 1 tablespoon butter
- 1¼ cups sugar
- 2 cups rhubarb cut in ½-inch pieces but not peeled
- 2 eggs, separated
- 1 tablespoon flour
- 4 tablespoons sugar

Melt the butter, add 1 cup of the sugar and rhubarb, cook until the rhubarb is slightly softened and the sugar melted. Add the egg yolks, beaten slightly. Mix the remaining ¼ cup sugar with the flour and add. Cook until rhubarb is of a jelly-like consistency. Pour into baked pie shell and top with meringue made by gradually beating sugar into beaten egg whites. Brown in a slow oven (300° F.) about 15 minutes. Makes 1 one-crust (8-inch) pie.

For Strawberry Rhubarb Pie substitute 1 cup strawberries for 1 cup of the rhubarb.

Green Currant Pie

1 scant quart mixed green and half-ripe currants	1½ cups sugar
	2 tablespoons flour

Wash and stem currants. Mix sugar and flour and sprinkle over currants. Line a pie plate with pastry; fill with fruit and adjust top crust, sealing edges carefully, as this pie is very juicy. Bake in a hot oven (450° F.) 10 minutes; then reduce heat to moderate (350° F.) and bake 25 to 30 minutes longer. Makes 1 two-crust (9-inch) pie.

Prize-Winning Date Pie

1 pound pitted dates	¼ teaspoon salt
3 cups milk	1 tablespoon sugar
2 eggs, slightly beaten	

Cook dates in 2 cups of the milk in the top of a double boiler until tender. Press through a sieve. Add remaining cup of milk, eggs, salt, and sugar. Pour into an unbaked pie shell. Bake in a hot oven (450° F.) 10 minutes; then reduce heat to moderate

(350° F.) and bake 25 minutes longer, or until knife comes out clean when inserted in custard. Cool. Makes 1 one-crust large (10-inch) pie.

* *Some cooks cover this pie with meringue; others with whipped cream. Many prefer it plain.*

Apple Custard Pie

1½ cups applesauce
½ cup sugar
½ teaspoon cinnamon
3 eggs, beaten
¼ teaspoon salt
1½ cups milk

Mix applesauce, sugar, cinnamon, eggs, salt, and milk. Line a pie plate with pastry. Pour apple custard mixture into crust and bake in a hot oven (450° F.) 10 minutes. Then reduce heat to moderate (350° F.) and bake 25 to 30 minutes longer or until knife inserted comes out clean. Makes 1 one-crust (9-inch) pie.

Custard Pie

2 whole eggs and 2 egg yolks, slightly beaten
½ cup sugar
¼ teaspoon salt
⅛ teaspoon nutmeg
½ teaspoon vanilla
2 cups milk, scalded

Combine eggs with sugar and salt. Flavor with nutmeg and vanilla, add hot milk. Line pie plate with pastry; brush with egg white and allow to dry in refrigerator. Pour in custard filling; bake in a hot oven (450° F.) for 10 minutes, then reduce heat to moderate (350° F.) and continue baking 30 minutes longer or until knife inserted comes out clean. Cool. Makes 1 one-crust (9-inch) pie.

Maple Custard Pie

1 cup maple sugar, packed
2 tablespoons butter
1½ cups milk, scalded
1 tablespoon cornstarch
½ cup milk
3 eggs, slightly beaten
½ teaspoon salt
sprinkling of nutmeg

Have pie pan lined with pastry with fluted edge. Fill with custard prepared thus: heat maple sugar and butter until they bubble, add scalded milk, and stir until sugar is dissolved. Add cornstarch which has been dissolved in cold milk, eggs, and salt. Pour into unbaked pastry shell. Sprinkle nutmeg over top. Bake 10 minutes in a hot oven (450° F.), then reduce heat and finish baking in moderate oven (350° F.) for about 25 minutes, or until knife inserted comes out clean. (Grandmother used to test this pie with a broom straw.) Makes 1 one-crust 8-inch pie.

The "Mason Girls" Rose Custard Pie

[*A New Hampshire recipe*]

4 egg yolks
2 egg whites
1 cup sugar
1½ teaspoons flour
¼ teaspoon ginger
¼ teaspoon salt
3 cups milk, scalded
½ teaspoon rose flavoring
2 egg whites, beaten stiff
2 tablespoons sugar

Line a 9-inch pie plate with unbaked pastry. Combine yolks and 2 egg whites and beat; mix sugar, flour, ginger, and salt and add the eggs; stir in milk gradually. Add flavoring. Pour into pastry and bake in a hot oven (450° F.) 10 minutes; then reduce heat to moderate (350° F.) and bake 25 to 30 minutes longer or until knife inserted comes out clean. Cool, frost with meringue made by adding sugar to beaten egg whites. Brown in oven (300° F.). Makes 1 one-crust (9-inch) pie.

Coolidge Lemon Custard Pie

2 eggs, separated
juice and grated rind
 1 lemon
1 cup sugar
⅛ teaspoon salt
4 teaspoons flour
1 teaspoon melted butter
1 cup milk

Beat the egg yolks until thick and lemon colored. Add the lemon juice and rind, sugar, salt, flour, butter, and milk. Fold in the egg whites, beaten stiff. Pour into an unbaked pastry shell (with the edges fluted) and bake in a hot oven (450° F.) 10 minutes; reduce heat to moderate (350° F.) and bake 20 mintes longer. Makes 1 (7-inch) pie.

Lemon Meringue Pie

[*Parker House, Boston, Mass.*]

¾ cup sugar
⅛ teaspoon salt
3 tablespoons cornstarch
1 cup boiling water
⅓ cup lemon juice
2 egg yolks, slightly beaten
1 teaspoon butter
meringue

Mix the sugar, cornstarch, and salt; stir in the boiling water gradually, pour the mixture into a saucepan and stir until it thickens. Beat the egg yolks slightly; add the lemon juice, stir the mixture into the saucepan; cook one minute. Remove from the stove; stir in the melted butter. Cool slightly, pour into baked shell; cover with meringue. Makes filling for one (7-inch) pie.

MERINGUE

2 egg whites
⅛ teaspoon salt
3 tablespoons confectioners' sugar
or
2 tablespoons fine granulated sugar

Beat the egg whites until peaks will form when beater is lifted from the bowl. Add the salt and 1 tablespoon of the sugar; beat; continue until all the sugar is used. Pile the meringue lightly on the lemon filling. Bake in a slow oven (300° F.) for 15 to 20 minutes or until delicately browned.

Pumpkin Pie

1 cup steamed, strained pumpkin
⅔ cup brown sugar
½ teaspoon ginger
1 teaspoon cinnamon
3 eggs, well beaten
2 cups cream (rich milk will do)
½ teaspoon salt

Mix all together. Pour into an unbaked pastry shell and bake in a hot oven (450° F.) 10 minutes; then reduce heat to moderate (350° F.) and bake 20 to 25 minutes longer, or until knife comes out clean when inserted in custard. Makes 1 one-crust (9-inch) pie.

✻ *One secret of good pumpkin pie is to include at least ½ teaspoon ginger among the spices. Some cooks substitute nutmeg (½ teaspoon) for the cinnamon. A delightful variation is to add 1½ teaspoons ground coriander seeds to the recipe, or ½ cup finely cut butternut meats.*

Squash Pie

Substitute squash for pumpkin. Vermonters will tell you the proper sweetening for squash or pumpkin is 1 cup of maple syrup instead of brown sugar.

✻ *Cooks of Concord, Mass., fail to agree as to whether spice or rose water is the more suitable flavoring for squash pie.*

Advocates of spice find rose water insipid. Rose water champions find spice lacking in subtlety. This argument is one of long-standing in the town and never fails to bring on heated discussions at club suppers and church luncheons.

Chocolate Cream Pie

[*A Rhode Island recipe*]

- 1 square chocolate
- 1½ cups milk, scalded
- 4 tablespoons flour
- ⅓ cup milk
- 1 egg yolk
- ¼ cup sugar
- ⅛ teaspoon salt
- 1 tablespoon butter
- ¼ teaspoon vanilla extract
- whipped cream or meringue

Add chocolate to milk in top of double boiler and melt. Mix flour and ⅓ cup milk to a smooth paste and stir into hot mixture. Cook until thickened, stirring constantly. Cover and let cook about 10 minutes. Mix egg yolk with sugar and salt, combine this with the hot mixture, and cook 2 minutes longer; add butter and flavoring. Allow mixture to cool. Turn into a baked pie shell. Top with whipped cream or meringue. Makes 1 one-crust (9-inch) pie.

* *Alternate layers of sliced bananas and cooled filling (with a topping of bananas) makes Chocolate Banana Cream Pie. Omit chocolate and increase flour to 5 tablespoons for Banana Cream Pie. For Coconut Pie omit chocolate, add ⅔ cup shredded coconut to the filling. Sprinkle ⅓ cup plain or toasted coconut over the top.*

Vinegar Pie

- 2 egg yolks
- 2 cups water
- ½ cup vinegar
- 1 tablespoon melted butter
- 1½ cups sugar
- 4 tablespoons flour
- ½ teaspoon lemon extract

Line a pie plate with pastry. Combine egg yolks, water, vinegar, and melted butter. Add flour to sugar and combine with vinegar mixture. Add flavoring and pour into pastry-lined pie plate and bake in a hot oven (450° F.) 10 minutes; then reduce heat to moderate (350° F.) and bake 20 to 30 minutes longer. Cool. Makes 1 one-crust (8-inch) pie.

Boiled Cider Pie

[*A recipe as old as New England Boiled Dinner*]

- 1 cup sugar
- ¼ cup water
- 2 tablespoons butter
- 7 tablespoons boiled cider
- 2 eggs, separated
- few gratings nutmeg

Combine sugar, water, butter, and thick boiled cider and simmer about 10 minutes. Cool. Add egg yolks, well beaten. Fold in egg whites, beaten stiff.

Line a plate with unbaked pie crust. Pour in filling. Dust with nutmeg. Add a top crust and bake in a hot oven (450° F.) for 10 minutes; then reduce the heat to moderate (350° F.) and bake for 25 to 30 minutes. Makes 1 (8-inch) pie.

✱ *Plain cider will not do. Use old-fashioned boiled cider made in the fall from sweet cider boiled until it is thick and dark and rich. Cider pie will be "runny." It does not "set" like other pies.*

Old-Fashioned Cream Pie

[*This recipe originally appeared in* Godey's Lady's Book]

Line a deep pie plate with unbaked pastry. Over it spread a layer of butter the thickness of a nickel. Over this sprinkle a layer of sugar, the same thickness. Next another layer of butter the same thickness. Next, a layer of flour also the thickness of a nickel. Pour 1 pint of cream flavored with ½ teaspoon vanilla and ⅛ teaspoon nutmeg over all. Bake in a hot oven (450° F.) 10 minutes; then reduce the heat to moderate (350° F.) and bake for 40 minutes or until knife inserted comes out clean. The butter bubbles up through the layer spread above it, making the pie a delicious confection.

✱ *Don't make it if you are dieting.*

Maple Cream Pie

- 1 pint milk, scalded
- 1 cup maple sugar, packed
- 3 tablespoons cornstarch
- ¼ cup milk
- 2 eggs, beaten
- ½ teaspoon salt
- 1 tablespoon butter
- 1 teaspoon vanilla
- whipped cream

Heat milk and maple sugar in double boiler until sugar is dissolved. Add cornstarch dissolved in cold milk. Let cook ½ hour, stirring occasionally. Add to beaten eggs, return to double boiler, and cook 1 minute. Remove from fire; add salt, butter, and vanilla. Cool. Pour into baked pastry shell. Cover with whipped cream before serving.

✱ *Some Vermonters add a speck of black pepper to this filling before pouring it into the pastry shell. Others bake it in 2 crusts and omit the whipped cream.*

White Navy Bean Pie

- 2 cups navy bean pulp
- 1 cup evaporated milk (undiluted)
- 2 tablespoons cornstarch
- ¼ cup water
- ½ teaspoon nutmeg
- ½ teaspoon cinnamon
- ¾ cups sugar
- 3 egg yolks
- 3 egg whites

Cook the beans until very soft. Put them through a sieve to have 2 cups of pulp. Mix cornstarch with water; add spices to sugar. Mix with the bean and milk mixture. Add beaten egg yolks. Put in an unbaked pie shell and bake in a hot oven (450° F.) for 10 minutes; then reduce heat to moderate (350° F.) and bake 25 minutes longer or until "set." Remove from the oven and top with egg whites beaten stiff with 3 tablespoons sugar; then return to oven until delicately brown. Makes 1 one-crust (9-inch) pie.

Butterscotch Pie

[*A Massachusetts recipe*]

- 2 tablespoons butter
- ¾ cup brown sugar, firmly packed
- 1½ cups milk
- 4 tablespoons flour
- ¼ teaspoon salt
- 2 egg yolks or 1 egg, beaten slightly
- whipped cream or meringue

Put butter, sugar, and 1 cup milk in the top of double boiler; heat until milk is scalded. Mix flour and salt and stir in ½ cup cold milk. Stir into mixture in double boiler. Stir constantly until mixture thickens; cover and cook 10 minutes. Stir a little of the hot mixture into the eggs, pour into the double boiler; cook 2 minutes. Cool, fill baked pie crust (8-inch) with the mixture. Top with whipped cream or meringue.

Maple Butternut Chiffon Pie

- ¾ cup maple syrup
- 2 egg yolks, beaten
- ½ teaspoon salt
- 2 teaspoons gelatin
- ¼ cup cold water
- 2 egg whites, beaten
- 3 tablespoons sugar
- ½ cup whipped cream
- ½ cup butternut meats, broken

Heat maple syrup in double boiler, add to egg yolks, return to double boiler, and cook until mixture thickens. Add salt. Soak gelatin in cold water 5 minutes, set over hot water until it dissolves, then add to first mixture. Cool. Beat egg whites until frothy, add sugar gradually, and beat until stiff but not dry. Fold in whipped cream. When first mixture begins to set, fold in egg and cream mixture. Pour into (7-inch) baked pie shell. Sprinkle butternut meats over top.

Sour Milk Pie

[*Mrs. Priscilla L. Jones, Wrentham, Mass.*]

- 1 egg, slightly beaten
- 1 cup sour milk (or cream)
- 1 cup sugar
- 1 tablespoon vinegar
- 1 teaspoon cinnamon
- ½ teaspoon cloves
- ½ teaspoon allspice
- 1 cup seedless raisins
- ⅛ teaspoon salt

Combine all the ingredients, stirring until thoroughly mixed. Let stand 45 minutes so that the raisins will absorb some of the liquid. Turn into an unbaked pie shell. Cover with another crust, or not, as desired. Bake in a hot oven (450° F.) 10 minutes, then reduce heat to moderate and bake 25 to 30 minutes longer. Cool. Makes 1 (7-inch) pie.

Ice Cream Pie

[*Toll House, Whitman, Mass.*]

3 egg whites, beaten
½ cup sugar
1 teaspoon vanilla
1 pint ice cream

Cover an inverted pie plate with pastry, bringing pastry well onto the sides and trimming off at edges of plate. Prick pastry several times on bottom and sides of plate and bake at 450° F. for 20 minutes or until brown. Cool crust. Beat egg whites until stiff, add sugar, slowly beating all the time. Lastly add vanilla. Fill pastry shell with ice cream (chocolate or coffee is delicious) cover with meringue and brown under broiler until meringue is "set" and a golden brown color. Pastry shells may be made by covering inverted muffin tins if desired. These make individual pies. One pint of ice cream will fill 6 muffin tin shells.

Maine Molasses Pie

3 cups molasses
1 cup sugar
3 eggs, beaten
1 tablespoon melted butter
juice 1 lemon
½ teaspoon nutmeg
¼ teaspoon salt

Beat all ingredients together and turn into unbaked pastry shell. Bake in a hot oven (450° F.) 10 minutes; then reduce heat to moderate (350° F.) and bake 30 minutes longer, or until knife inserted comes out clean. Makes 1 one-crust (9-inch) pie.

Cakes and Cookies

One-Egg Cake

2 cups cake flour, sifted
3 teaspoons baking powder
¼ teaspoon salt
1 cup sugar
4 tablespoons butter or other shortening
1 egg
¾ cup milk
1 teaspoon vanilla

Sift together 3 times flour, baking powder, and salt. Cream butter, add sugar gradually, and cream together. Add unbeaten egg and beat thoroughly. Add flour alternately with the milk, beating after each addition until smooth. Add vanilla. Bake in 2 well-greased (8-inch) layer tins in a moderate oven (350° F.) about 25 minutes. Frost with any desired frosting. Makes 2 (8-inch) square layer cakes or 18 cup cakes.

Boston Cream Pie

Spread Cream Filling between the layers of One-Egg Cake. Sift powdered sugar over top. Cut in pie-shaped wedges.

CREAM FILLING

½ cup sugar
½ cup flour
¼ teaspoon salt
2 cups milk, scalded
2 eggs (or 4 egg yolks), slightly beaten
½ teaspoon vanilla
1 tablespoon butter

Combine sugar, flour, and salt and mix with egg yolks; stir in hot milk slowly, to form a smooth paste. Cook over boiling water 10 minutes, stirring constantly the first 5 minutes. Cool and add vanilla. Add butter last.

Parker House Chocolate Cream Pie

Frost Boston Cream Pie with chocolate icing and cut in pie-shaped wedges.

Old Maine Lobster Cake

[*Old-fashioned marble cake*]

- 3 cups flour, sifted
- ¾ teaspoon cream of tartar
- ½ teaspoon soda
- ¼ teaspoon salt
- 1 cup butter
- 2 cups sugar
- 1 cup milk
- 4 eggs, beaten

Sift flour, cream of tartar, soda, and salt together 3 times. Cream butter thoroughly. Add sugar gradually and cream together well. Add eggs one at a time and beat well. Add flour alternately with milk, beating until smooth. Divide mixture into 2 bowls. To one part add ½ cup molasses, ½ teaspoon cloves, ¼ teaspoon nutmeg. To the other part add ½ cup chopped raisins, ½ cup chopped citron. Put by tablespoons into greased loaf pan (15 x 9 x 2 inches) alternating light and dark mixture. Bake in moderate oven (350° F.) about 1 hour. Frost or not, as desired.

One-Egg Mocha Cake

[*Mrs. L. G. Young, 58 Preston St., Windsor, Conn.*]

- 2 tablespoons butter
- 1 cup sugar
- 1 egg, separated
- ¾ cup milk
- 1 cup flour, sifted
- ¼ teaspoon salt
- 1½ teaspoons baking powder
- ½ teaspoon vanilla
- 2 squares chocolate, melted

Cream butter, add sugar and cream together. Add egg yolk and beat; add milk alternately with remaining dry ingredients, sifted together. Beat in chocolate and vanilla then fold in egg white beaten stiff. Turn into 2 greased layer pans and bake in moderate oven (350° F.) about 25 minutes. Makes 2 thin (8-inch) layers. Put Chocolate Filling between layers and Mocha Frosting on top.

CHOCOLATE FILLING

- ¾ cup water
- 1 tablespoon cornstarch
- ½ cup sugar
- ½ teaspoon butter
- 1 square chocolate
- ½ teaspoon vanilla
- ⅛ teaspoon salt

Place all the ingredients except vanilla into a saucepan over boiling water. Cook over low heat, stirring constantly until thick and smooth. Cook 10 minutes longer. Cool, add vanilla.

MOCHA FROSTING

- ¼ cup butter
- 1½ cups confectioners' sugar
- 1 teaspoon vanilla
- ⅛ teaspoon salt
- 2 tablespoons hot, strong coffee (about)
- 2 teaspoons cocoa

Cream butter until soft; gradually stir in the cocoa and half the sugar, then add vanilla and salt. Add remaining sugar alternately with coffee, beating until smooth after each addition and adding enough coffee for proper consistency to spread.

Angel Sponge Cake

[*Mrs. Annie E. Bumpus, 466 Main St., Brockton, Mass.*]

- 4 eggs, separated
- 1¼ cups sugar
- ¾ cup water
- 1 teaspoon baking powder
- 1½ cups cake flour, sifted 3 times
- ¼ teaspoon salt
- 1 teaspoon vanilla

Beat the egg yolks in a large bowl until lemon-colored. Add sugar, beat again, add water and beat thoroughly. Sift flour, baking powder, and salt and add to the egg mixture and beat with a spoon until smooth. Add vanilla and fold in stiffly beaten egg whites. Turn into ungreased cake pan and bake in a moderate oven (350° F.) about 1 hour. Invert pan 1 hour, or until cold.

Johanna Cake

[*Marion Smith, Tamworth, N. H.*]

- 1⅔ cups flour, sifted
- 1 teaspoon cream of tartar
- ¼ teaspoon salt
- ½ teaspoon soda
- ½ cup butter
- 1¼ cups sugar
- 3 eggs, separated
- ½ cup milk
- ½ cup thinly sliced citron
- ½ teaspoon vanilla

Sift together flour, cream of tartar, salt, and soda. Cream butter, add sugar, and cream thoroughly. Add egg yolks and beat; add flour alternately with milk, a small amount at a time. Stir in citron, add vanilla and fold in stiffly beaten egg whites. Bake in 2 greased (8-inch) layer pans in a moderate oven (350° F.) about 25 minutes. Spread with any desired frosting.

Coconut Cream Layer Cake

- 3 cups cake flour, sifted
- 3 teaspoons baking powder
- ¼ teaspoon salt
- 1 cup butter
- 3½ cups confectioners' sugar
- 4 eggs, separated
- 1 cup milk
- 1 teaspoon vanilla
- 1 cup shredded coconut

Sift flour, baking powder, and salt together 3 times. Cream butter, add sugar gradually, and cream together thoroughly. Add egg yolks and beat well. Add flour alternately with milk, a little at a time, beating until smooth. Add vanilla and coconut. Fold in stiffly beaten egg whites. Bake in 3 greased (9-inch square) layer pans in a moderate oven (350° F.) about 30 minutes. Frost with 7-minute icing or boiled icing and sprinkle 1½ cups coconut between layers and over the cake while frosting is soft. With the addition of the coconut, both the 7-minute icing and the boiled icing given below make enough frosting for this 3-layer cake if used sparingly between the layers.

SEVEN-MINUTE ICING

- 2 egg whites, unbeaten
- 1½ cups sugar
- 5 tablespoons water
- 1½ teaspoons light corn syrup
- ¼ teaspoon salt
- 1 teaspoon vanilla

Combine egg whites, sugar, water, corn syrup, and salt in the top of a double boiler. Place over rapidly boiling water, beat constantly with rotary egg beater, and cook 7 minutes or until frosting will stand in peaks. Remove from boiling water, add flavoring, and beat until the right consistency to spread. Makes frosting to cover top and sides of a 2-layer (9-inch) cake or 2 dozen cup cakes.

BOILED ICING

- 1½ cups sugar
- ½ teaspoon light corn syrup
- ⅔ cup water
- ¼ teaspoon salt
- 2 egg whites, beaten stiff
- 1 teaspoon vanilla

Combine sugar, corn syrup, water, and salt. Bring to a boil, stirring only until sugar is dissolved. Boil rapidly until syrup spins a long thread when dropped from top of spoon (240° F.). Pour syrup slowly over egg whites, beating constantly. Add vanilla. Continue beating until frosting is the right consistency to spread. Makes enough frosting to cover top and sides of a 2-layer (9-inch) cake or 2 dozen cup cakes.

1-2-3-4 Cake

1 cup butter
2 cups sugar
3 cups flour, sifted
4 eggs
1 cup water or milk
3 teaspoons baking powder
¼ teaspoon salt
1 teaspoon vanilla

Cream the butter, add the sugar, and cream thoroughly. Add the eggs one at a time and beat well. Sift the remaining dry ingredients twice, and add alternately with the water or milk. Beat well, add the vanilla. Turn into greased pan or pans and bake in a moderate oven (350° F.) 25 minutes (in layers) to 1 hour (in 1 square pan). Makes 1 large loaf cake or 2 (9-inch) layers.

Connecticut Raised Loaf Cake

[*Also called Election Cake, March Meeting Cake, and Dough Cake*]

2 cups milk, scalded
½ cup brown sugar, tightly packed
½ teaspoon salt
1 compressed yeast cake
5 cups flour, sifted
1½ cups sugar
¾ cup shortening
2 eggs
1½ cups raisins
¼ pound citron sliced thin (optional)
½ teaspoon nutmeg
½ teaspoon mace

Place milk, brown sugar, and salt in a mixing bowl. When lukewarm add crumbled yeast cake and 4½ cups of the flour; beat thoroughly and let rise overnight. In the morning cream the sugar and shortening and add. Stir in the eggs, raisins, citron, nutmeg, mace, and remaining ½ cup flour. Mix thoroughly, using hands if necessary. Place in greased bread tins lined with waxed paper and again greased. Rise until double in bulk. Bake in a moderately hot oven (375° F.) until brown, about 50 minutes. Makes 2 loaves.

Pork Cake

1 pound fat salt pork
2 cups boiling water
8 cups flour, sifted
2 teaspoons soda
¼ teaspoon salt
2 teaspoons cinnamon
2 teaspoons cloves
2 teaspoons allspice
2 teaspoons nutmeg
2 cups raisins, chopped
4 eggs
2 cups sugar
2 cups molasses

Put pork through food chopper, using finest knife; pour boiling water over pork and let stand 15 minutes. Mix and sift flour, soda, salt, and spices and mix with raisins. Combine eggs, sugar, and molasses and add the pork mixture; gradually stir in flour-fruit mixture and mix thoroughly. Turn into 4 greased deep loaf pans, lined with waxed paper and again greased. Bake in slow oven (300° F.) for 1¼ hours. Makes 4 loaves. Recipe can be easily halved or quartered.

✱ *This cake conserves the more expensive shortenings and uses salt pork of which the supply was plentiful. It is a delicious cake and keeps fresh for months if carefully wrapped and placed in a stone crock. In fact it improves in flavor if kept for some time.*

Aunt May's Spice Cake

- ½ cup butter and lard, mixed
- 1 cup sugar
- 1 egg, beaten
- 2 cups cake flour, sifted
- 1 teaspoon soda
- ¼ teaspoon salt
- 1 teaspoon cloves
- 1 teaspoon cinnamon
- 1 teaspoon nutmeg
- 1 cup sour milk
- 1 teaspoon vanilla extract
- 1 teaspoon lemon extract
- ½ cup seedless raisins

Cream shortening and sugar; beat in egg. Mix and sift flour, soda, salt, and spices. Add to sugar mixture alternately with the sour milk. Add lemon and vanilla and raisins. Bake in moderate oven (350° F.) for 50 minutes or until done. Makes 1 loaf.

My Grandmother's Sour Cream Spice Cake

[*Mrs. Arthur Graves, 40 Adrian Ave., W. Springfield, Mass.*]

- 1 egg
- ⅞ cup sour cream (about)
- 1 cup sugar
- 2 cups flour, sifted
- 1 teaspoon soda
- ¼ teaspoon salt
- ½ teaspoon cinnamon
- ½ teaspoon nutmeg
- ¼ teaspoon cloves
- ½ cup raisins

Break the egg into a cup and fill cup with sour cream. Pour into a bowl and beat thoroughly with Dover egg beater. Add sugar and beat. Sift remaining dry ingredients twice; add raisins; combine with first mixture. Pour into a greased baking sheet; bake in a moderate oven (350° F.) 45 minutes. Makes 1 (8-inch) square cake. Or pour into muffin tins and make into cup cakes. Makes 12 cup cakes. Stewed prunes, cut into pieces, may be added, and ¼ cup prune juice substituted for ¼ cup of the sour cream. Nuts may also be substituted for the raisins. Serve with a big pitcher of creamy milk.

Black Cake

[*A delicious spice cake*]

4 cups flour, sifted
1 teaspoon soda
½ teaspoon salt
1 teaspoon cream of tartar
1 teaspoon cloves
1 teaspoon nutmeg
1 cup seedless raisins, chopped
1 cup butter
1½ cups sugar
½ cup molasses
1 cup milk
3 eggs

Mix and sift flour, soda, salt, cream of tartar, cloves, and nutmeg; mix ½ cup with raisins. Cream butter until soft, add sugar, creaming until fluffy, and beat in thoroughly one egg at a time. Add flour mixture alternately with combined molasses and milk, beating until smooth after each addition, then beat in raisins. Turn into greased square pan and bake in moderate oven (350° F.) about 45 minutes. Makes 2 loaf cakes.

UNCOOKED ICING

When cake has cooled, frost with an icing made by beating whites of 2 eggs until stiff; gradually beat in 2 cups sugar, 1 teaspoon cream, 1 tablespoon grated orange rind. Beat vigorously until smooth. If frosting becomes too thick, add a little orange juice.

Hot Water Cake

[*A spice cake without eggs*]

½ cup shortening
½ cup sugar
1 cup molasses
2½ cups flour, sifted
1½ teaspoons soda
½ teaspoon salt
½ teaspoon cinnamon
½ teaspoon allspice
½ teaspoon cloves
1 cup boiling water

Cream shortening, add sugar, and cream again. Add molasses and remaining dry ingredients sifted together. Last of all add boiling water. Bake in a moderate oven (350° F.) about 35 minutes. Makes 1 (10-inch) square cake.

Betty Allen's Wedding Cake

4 cups pastry flour, sifted
1½ teaspoons baking powder
½ teaspoon salt
1 teaspoon cinnamon
1 teaspoon nutmeg
½ teaspoon cloves
½ pound butter
3½ cups sugar
6 eggs, beaten
2 pounds seeded raisins (cut)
1 pound currants
½ pound citron, finely cut
1 cup orange juice or other fruit juice
½ pound walnut meats, chopped

Mix and sift flour, baking powder, salt, and spices. Cream butter, add sugar gradually, creaming until fluffy. Add eggs, beating thoroughly, then put in fruits, fruit juices, and nuts. Add dry ingredients gradually, beating well after each addition. Turn into greased bread tins (lined with heavy paper) and again greased; bake in very slow oven (275° F.) about 2 hours. Makes 3 loaves.

Vermont Scripture Cake

1 cup butter	Judges 5:25
2 cups sugar	Jeremiah 6:20
3½ cups flour	I Kings 4:22
2 cups raisins	I Samuel 30:12
2 cups figs	I Samuel 30:12
1 cup almonds	Genesis 43:11
1 cup water	Genesis 24:20
6 eggs	Isaiah 10:14
a little salt	Leviticus 2:13
1 tablespoon honey	Exodus 16:31
spice to taste	I Kings 10:2

Follow Solomon's advice for making good boys (Prov. 23:14).

Wellesley Fudge Cake

- 2 cups cake flour, sifted
- 2 teaspoons baking powder
- ½ teaspoon soda
- ¼ teaspoon salt
- ½ cup butter
- 1¼ cups firmly packed brown sugar
- 1 egg, well beaten
- 2½ squares chocolate, melted
- ¾ cup milk
- 1 teaspoon vanilla
- ½ cup walnuts, chopped

Sift flour, baking powder, soda, and salt 3 times. Cream butter, add sugar, and cream thoroughly. Add egg and chocolate and beat well. Add flour alternately with milk, beating well. Add vanilla. Turn into 2 layer pans (8 x 8 inches) and bake in a moderate oven (350° F.) about 25 minutes. Cool and frost with Fudge Frosting between layers and on top and sides of cake. Sprinkle chopped nutmeats on top.

FUDGE FROSTING

1½ cups sugar
¾ cup water
1 tablespoon light corn syrup
⅛ teaspoon salt
3 squares chocolate
3 tablespoons butter
1 teaspoon vanilla

Combine sugar, water, corn syrup, and salt. Boil without stirring, until mixture forms a very soft ball in cold water (235° F.). Remove from stove, add chocolate (it is not necessary to cut it fine) and cool to lukewarm. Add butter and vanilla. Beat until frosting is the right consistency to spread. Makes enough frosting to cover tops and sides of an 8-inch layer cake.

Chocolate "Weary Willie" Cake

[*A Vermont inn called "The Weathervane" originated this recipe*]

1 cup flour, sifted
1½ teaspoons baking powder
¼ teaspoon salt
1 cup sugar
1 egg
⅞ cup milk (about)
2 squares chocolate
2 tablespoons butter
1 teaspoon vanilla

Sift the flour, baking powder, salt, and sugar into a mixing bowl. Break egg into a measuring cup and fill cup with milk; add the flour and beat well. Add chocolate, melted with the butter, and beat again. Add vanilla. Pour into greased 8-inch pan lined with waxed paper and bake in a moderate oven (350° F.) for about 35 minutes. Makes 1 (8-inch) square cake. Frost with Marshmallow Icing.

MARSHMALLOW ICING

2 tablespoons milk
1 cup confectioners' sugar
2 tablespoons marshmallow fluff
1 square chocolate
1 teaspoon butter
½ teaspoon vanilla

Add milk to sugar and stir until smooth. Add marshmallow fluff and beat. Then add the chocolate and butter which have been melted together and mix thoroughly. Spread on cake.

Apple Sauce Cake

1 cup sugar
½ cup shortening
1 cup apple sauce (warm)
1 teaspoon soda
1⅔ cups flour, sifted
1 teaspoon cinnamon
½ teaspoon cloves
¼ teaspoon nutmeg
¼ teaspoon salt
1 cup raisins, floured

Cream sugar and shortening; add apple sauce in which soda has been dissolved; add flour and spices and salt sifted together and lastly floured raisins. Turn into a greased loaf tin and bake in a moderately slow oven (325° F.) about 45 minutes. Makes 1 loaf. Keeps moist a week if stored in closely covered cake box.

Date Cake

2 cups flour, sifted
1 teaspoon soda
¼ teaspoon salt
½ teaspoon cloves
⅛ teaspoon nutmeg
½ cup butter
1 cup sugar
1 cup sour milk
½ pound dates or prunes, cut up fine

Sift together flour, soda, salt, and spices. Cream butter, add sugar, and cream again thoroughly. Add flour to creamed mixture, alternately with the sour milk, beating well. Add dates or prunes. Turn into a well-greased loaf pan and bake in a moderate oven (350° F.) about 1 hour. Makes 1 loaf (8 x 4 inches).

Cider Cake

- 6 cups flour, sifted
- 1 teaspoon soda
- ½ teaspoon salt
- 1 grated nutmeg
- 1 cup butter
- 3 cups sugar
- 4 eggs beaten
- 1 cup cider

Mix and sift flour, soda, salt, and nutmeg; cream butter well, add sugar gradually, creaming until fluffy, then eggs, and beat thoroughly. Add flour mixture alternately with cider, beating until smooth after each addition. Turn into greased loaf pan (4 x 9½ x 9½) and bake in a moderate oven (350° F.) about 1 hour. Keep moist in a glass jar with apples.

* *This cake will keep for a year. It is not unlike pound cake. Nuts, cherries, figs or citron may be added. This recipe is over 100 years old.*

Jelly Roll

[*An old Rhode Island recipe*]

- ¾ cup cake flour, sifted
- 1 teaspoon baking powder
- ¼ teaspoon salt
- 4 eggs, separated
- ¾ cup sugar, sifted
- 1 tablespoon lemon juice
- 1 cup jelly

Mix and sift flour, baking powder, and salt. Beat egg yolks until thick and lemon-colored; gradually beat in sugar and lemon juice. Fold in 2 of the stiffly beaten egg whites; gradually fold in flour, a few tablespoons at a time, then fold in the remaining egg whites. Turn into pan (15 x 10 inches) which has been greased and lined with waxed paper and again greased. Bake in moderately hot oven (375° F.) about 15 minutes. Quickly turn from pan on paper sprinkled with powdered sugar. Cut off crisp edges and remove wax paper; spread with jelly (beaten enough to spread easily) and roll lengthwise. Wrap in cloth and cool on rack. Makes 1 roll.

Maple Butternut Tea Cakes

[*A Vermont recipe*]

- 2½ cups flour, sifted
- 2 teaspoons baking powder
- ½ teaspoon baking soda
- ½ teaspoon salt
- ½ cup butter
- ½ cup sugar
- 2 eggs
- ½ cup hot water
- 1 cup maple syrup
- ½ teaspoon vanilla
- 1 cup butternut meats, finely cut

Sift together flour, baking powder, soda, and salt. Cream butter, add sugar, and cream thoroughly. Add eggs and beat well. Combine maple syrup and water and add alternately with the flour, beating well after each addition. Add vanilla and butternut meats. Bake in greased cup-cake pan in a moderate oven (350° F.) about 20 minutes. Makes 16 to 20 cakes. Frost or not, as desired.

MAPLE FROSTING

- 2 cups maple syrup
- 2 egg whites, stiffly beaten

Boil syrup without stirring until it spins a long thread (240° F.). Pour syrup slowly over egg whites and beat until stiff enough to spread. Makes enough frosting for 24 cup cakes or tops and sides of a 2-layer (8-inch) cake.

* *In olden days maple sugar was about the consistency and color of brown sugar today and was the only sugar used by the early settlers.*

Pie, Jam, and Cake Tart

Line muffin pans with pie crust. Add one heaping tablespoon of jam or jelly. Fill remaining space with the following cake mixture:

½ cup shortening
1 cup sugar
2 eggs, separated
¾ cup milk
2 cups flour
2 teaspoons baking powder
¼ teaspoon salt
1 teaspoon vanilla

Cream shortening and sugar. Add egg yolks; beat. Sift flour, baking powder, and salt. Add alternately with milk to creamed mixture. Add vanilla and stiffly beaten egg whites. Bake in a moderate oven (350° F.) about 25 minutes. Makes 12 cakes.

Lace Molasses Wafers

[*Marjorie Mills, Boston, Mass.*]

½ cup molasses
½ cup sugar
½ cup butter
1 cup flour
½ teaspoon baking powder
¼ teaspoon soda

Slowly heat molasses, sugar, and butter to boiling point. Boil 1 minute and remove from fire. Add flour, baking powder, and soda, which have been sifted together. Stir well. Set pan in vessel of hot water to keep batter from hardening. On buttered baking sheets or inverted dripping pans drop quarter teaspoons of batter 3 inches apart. Bake in moderate oven (350° F.), until brown, about 10 minutes. Cool slightly, then lift carefully with thin knife. If desired, roll around the handle of a spoon to shape while still warm. Makes about 4 to 5 dozen cookies.

Brandy Snaps

½ cup molasses
½ cup butter
⅔ cup powdered sugar
1 cup flour
1 teaspoon lemon juice
½ teaspoon grated lemon rind

Heat the molasses, butter, and sugar together. Add the flour, juice, rind, and mix well. Drop the mixture from the tip of a small spoon in patties about 3 inches apart to allow for spreading. Bake in a hot oven (400° F.), 10 to 15 minutes. If desired, they can be rolled while still hot about a greased spoon or knife handle. Serve plain or filled with whipped cream. Makes about 3 dozen snaps.

Ginger Snaps

1 cup granulated sugar
¾ cup shortening
¼ cup molasses
1 egg
2 cups flour, sifted
1½ teaspoons soda
½ teaspoon salt
1 teaspoon cinnamon
½ teaspoon cloves
¼ teaspoon nutmeg
1½ teaspoons ginger
½ cup sugar

Cream sugar and shortening together until light and fluffy. Add molasses and beaten egg. Beat thoroughly. Sift flour with soda, salt, and spices. Add to cream mixture. Blend together carefully. Roll small portions of dough into small balls, about the size of small walnut. Roll balls in granulated sugar. Place 2 inches apart on greased cooky sheet. Bake in 375° F. oven for 15 minutes. The cookies flatten out as they bake. When they are baked, remove at once from cooky sheet and cool on wire cake rack. Makes about 5 dozen cookies.

Soft Ginger Cookies

[*Mrs. L. G. Young, 58 Preston St., Windsor, Conn.*]

- 1 cup sugar
- ½ cup butter
- ½ cup lard
- 1 egg
- 1 cup molasses
- 1 cup sour milk
- 2 teaspoons soda
- 1 teaspoon cinnamon
- 1 teaspoon ginger
- ¼ teaspoon each cloves, allspice, nutmeg
- 1 teaspoon salt
- 5 cups flour, sifted (about)

Cream sugar and shortening; add egg and beat well. Add molasses, then milk, then remaining ingredients, adding flour until dough is just stiff enough to roll. Chill thoroughly. Roll ⅛-inch thick and cut in desired shape. Bake on greased baking sheet in a moderately hot oven (375° F.) about 12 minutes. Makes about 12 dozen cookies. Store in covered cooky jar.

Maple Ginger Snaps

[*A Vermont recipe*]

- 2 cups soft maple sugar
- 1 cup butter
- 2 eggs, beaten
- ¼ teaspoon salt
- 4 cups flour (about)
- 1 tablespoon ginger
- 1 teaspoon soda
- 1 cup sour cream

Cream the maple sugar and butter and add the eggs. Sift the salt, flour, and the ginger together. Add the soda to the cream. Add the flour and ginger to the first mixture alternately with the cream. Roll thin and bake in a moderately hot oven (375° F.) about 8 minutes. Makes about 5 dozen cookies.

Calais Cookies

- 1 cup lard
- 1 cup sugar
- 1 egg
- ½ cup molasses
- ½ cup cold water
- 4 cups flour
- 1 teaspoon ginger
- 1 teaspoon salt
- 1 teaspoon soda

Cream the lard and sugar. Drop in egg and beat well. Stir in molasses. Add cold water. Add flour sifted 3 times with ginger, salt, and soda. Mix to a soft dough, kneading as little as possible. Roll out ½-inch thickness for soft cookies, ¼-inch thickness for medium crisp, and ⅛-inch for very crisp. With a 2½-inch cutter, the rule makes 6 dozen medium crisp cookies. Bake in moderately hot oven (375° F.) about 10 minutes. If stored as soon as cool, crisp cookies remain crisp and soft cookies soft.

Peanut Butter Cookies

- ½ cup butter
- ½ cup peanut butter
- ½ cup sugar
- ½ cup brown sugar
- 1 egg, well beaten
- 1¼ cups flour, sifted
- ¼ teaspoon salt
- ½ teaspoon baking powder
- ¼ teaspoon soda

Cream butter and peanut butter; add sugar gradually, add egg, and combine with peanut butter mixture. Sift together flour, salt, baking powder, and soda and add. Mix well. Chill dough. Roll out cookies and bake 10 to 15 minutes in a moderate oven (350° F.). Makes 24 cookies.

Chocolate Cookies

[A Massachusetts recipe]

- ½ cup butter
- 1 cup sugar
- 1 egg, beaten
- 3 squares chocolate, melted
- ⅛ teaspoon soda
- ¼ cup milk
- 2 cups flour, sifted
- 2 teaspoons baking powder
- ½ teaspoon salt

Cream the butter, add sugar, egg and chocolate, soda (dissolved in the milk), flour, baking powder, and salt. Chill dough, then roll to ⅛-inch thickness. Cut in desired shape and bake on a greased baking sheet in a moderately hot oven (375° F.) about 8 minutes. Makes about 3 dozen cookies.

Chocolate Raisin Drop Cookies

[A Rhode Island recipe]

- 1 cup cake flour, sifted
- 1 teaspoon baking powder
- ¼ teaspoon salt
- 4 tablespoons butter or other shortening
- ⅔ cup sugar
- 1 egg, well beaten
- 2 squares unsweetened chocolate, melted
- ½ cup finely cut raisins
- ½ cup chopped walnut meats
- ¼ cup heavy sour cream
- 1 teaspoon vanilla

Sift flour once, measure, add baking powder and salt, and sift again. Cream butter thoroughly, add sugar gradually, and cream well. Add egg and beat thoroughly; add chocolate and blend; then raisins and nuts, and mix well. Add flour, alternately with cream, beating well after each addition. Add vanilla. Drop from teaspoon on ungreased baking sheet and bake in moderate oven (350° F.) 15 minutes, or until done. Makes 30 cookies.

Caraway Cookies

1 cup butter
2 cups sugar
2 eggs, beaten slightly
1 cup sour cream
1 teaspoon soda
½ teaspoon salt
flour to roll as soft as possible (about 4 cups)
¾ teaspoon caraway seed

Cream butter and sugar, add eggs, cream (in which soda is dissolved), and salt. Sift flour and add gradually. The less flour used, the more tender the cooky. Add caraway seed and chill. Roll to ⅛-inch thickness. Bake in a moderately hot oven (375° F.) about 8 minutes. Makes about 8 dozen cookies.

New Meadows Inn Cookies

½ cup butter
1 cup sugar
1 egg
⅓ cup milk
2½ cups flour
1 teaspoon cream of tartar
½ teaspoon soda
½ teaspoon salt
½ teaspoon nutmeg
¼ teaspoon mace

Cream shortening, add sugar, egg, and milk. Mix and sift dry ingredients and add. Let stand overnight. Roll very thin and bake in a moderately hot oven (375° F.). Makes 10 dozen 3-inch cookies.

Mother's Sugar Cookies

1 cup shortening
1 teaspoon salt
1 teaspoon vanilla
¼ teaspoon soda
2 cups sugar
1 egg, well beaten
5 cups flour, sifted
4 teaspoons baking powder
1 cup milk

Combine shortening, salt, vanilla, and soda. Add sugar gradually and cream well. Add beaten egg and mix thoroughly. Sift flour with baking powder. Add to creamed mixture alternately with milk, mixing well. Drop from teaspoon on baking sheet. Let stand a few minutes then flatten cookies. Bake in moderately hot oven (375° F.) 12 to 15 minutes. Makes about 8 dozen cookies.

Oatmeal Cookies

- 2 cups flour, sifted
- ½ teaspoon salt
- ½ teaspoon soda
- 1 teaspoon baking powder
- ½ teaspoon cinnamon
- ¼ teaspoon cloves
- ¼ teaspoon nutmeg
- 1 cup quick-cooking oatmeal
- ⅔ cup walnuts, chopped fine
- ¾ cup butter or other shortening
- 1 cup brown sugar, firmly packed
- 2 eggs
- 3 tablespoons molasses
- 2 tablespoons hot water

Add salt, soda, baking powder, and spices to flour and sift again. Mix in the oatmeal and the chopped walnuts. Cream the shortening. Add sugar gradually, creaming well together. Beat in eggs one at a time. Add molasses and hot water. Gradually mix in the dry ingredients. Drop by teaspoon onto greased baking sheet, about an inch apart. Bake in a moderately hot oven (375° F.) 8 to 10 minutes. Makes about 36 cookies.

Filled Cookies

[*Mrs. Harold S. Bowker, 201 June Street, Worcester, Mass.*]

- ½ cup butter (or lard)
- 1 cup sugar
- 1 egg, beaten
- 1 teaspoon vanilla
- 2 teaspoons cream of tartar
- 1 teaspoon soda
- 3 cups flour, sifted (about)
- ½ teaspoon salt
- ½ cup milk

Cream butter, add sugar, egg, and vanilla. Mix and sift dry ingredients and add to the first mixture alternately with the milk. The dough should be stiff enough to roll out thin. Cut with a cooky cutter. Place filling on one cooky and then place another cooky on top of filling. Press down edges. Bake in a moderate oven (350° F.) about 12 minutes. Makes about 20 cookies.

FILLING

½ cup sugar
2 tablespoons cornstarch
1 cup raisins
½ cup water

Combine sugar and cornstarch, add water and raisins. Cook in top of double boiler until thick.

Brambles

pastry
1 cup seeded raisins, chopped fine
1 cup sugar
1 egg, beaten
juice and grated rind 1 lemon

Roll pastry ⅛-inch thick; cut in 4-inch oblongs. Combine raisins, sugar, egg, and lemon juice and rind. Cook slowly over low heat until thick; place a heaping teaspoonful on each oblong. Wet edges with cold water and fold over. Press edges together with floured fork, prick top and bake in a hot oven (450° F.) about 15 minutes. Makes about 20 brambles.

Brownies

½ cup flour, sifted
½ teaspoon baking powder
¼ teaspoon salt
2 squares chocolate
⅓ cup butter, melted
1 cup sugar
2 eggs, beaten
2 tablespoons milk
1 teaspoon vanilla
1 cup walnuts, broken

Sift flour, baking powder, and salt. Melt chocolate and add butter. Add sugar to eggs, then add chocolate mixture and beat well. Stir in flour, milk, vanilla, and nuts, spread on greased pan 8 x 8 inches. Bake in a slow oven (300° F.) 50 minutes. Cool. Cut in strips and remove from pan. Makes 16 brownies.

Maple Nut Cookies

[*A Vermont recipe*]

- 3 cups flour, sifted
- 1 teaspoon baking powder
- ½ teaspoon salt
- 1½ cups soft maple sugar
- 3 eggs, beaten
- 1 teaspoon soda
- ½ cup hot water
- 1 cup walnut meats, chopped
- 1½ cups dates, cut in pieces

Mix and sift flour, baking powder, salt. Beat maple sugar into eggs, stir in dry ingredients; add soda dissolved in hot water, nuts, and dates. Drop from a teaspoon on baking sheet and bake in a moderately hot oven (375° F.) about 12 minutes. Makes about 5 dozen cookies.

Snickerdoodles

- 2 cups confectioners' sugar, sifted
- 2 eggs, well beaten
- 4 tablespoons butter
- 4 cups flour
- 4 teaspoons baking powder
- 1 teaspoon salt
- 1 cup chopped raisins
- 1 cup milk
- 1 tablespoon vanilla
- sugar and cinnamon

Add sugar to eggs, then stir in butter which has been softened but not melted. Mix and sift dry ingredients; add raisins and add to first mixture alternately with the milk. Beat well, add vanilla. Drop by teaspoonfuls on greased cooky sheet. Sprinkle cookies generously with sugar and cinnamon mixed together. Bake 20 minutes in a moderate oven (350° F.). Do not place snickerdoodles close together on cooky sheet as they spread. Makes 36 cookies.

Butterscotch Cookies

- 4 cups flour, sifted (about)
- 1 teaspoon soda
- 1 teaspoon cream of tartar
- ½ teaspoon salt
- 1 cup shortening (butter and lard)
- 2 cups brown sugar
- 2 eggs
- 1 teaspoon vanilla
- 1 cup nutmeats (optional)

Mix and sift dry ingredients; cream shortening until soft; beat in sugar, eggs, vanilla and nuts. Stir in dry ingredients and knead into two rolls. Chill several hours or overnight in refrigerator. Slice paper-thin and bake in a moderately hot oven (375° F.) for 8 minutes. Makes about 8 dozen cookies.

Lemon Wafers

- ½ cup flour, sifted
- ¼ cup butter
- ¼ cup sifted powdered sugar
- ½ teaspoon grated lemon rind
- 1 teaspoon lemon juice
- 2 tablespoons milk

Sift flour once, measure, and sift again. Cream butter and sugar, add lemon rind and juice, and blend. Add flour alternately with milk, mixing well. Drop ¼ teaspoon on an ungreased baking sheet, placing about 2 inches apart. Bake in moderate oven (375° F.) about 5 minutes. Make about 3 dozen wafers.

Rocks

3 eggs
1½ cups brown sugar
⅓ cup lard, melted
⅓ cup butter, melted
½ cup raisins
½ teaspoon salt
2 cups flour, sifted
1 teaspoon baking powder
1 teaspoon cinnamon

Beat the eggs, add the sugar, and beat. Add melted shortening, raisins, and dry ingredients sifted together. Mix thoroughly. Drop from teaspoon on greased baking sheet and bake in moderately hot oven (375° F.) about 12 minutes. Makes about 3 dozen cookies.

Sauces, Preserves, Pickles, Jellies, and Jams

Vermont Boiled-Cider Apple Sauce

[*An original old recipe*]

"Boil yr. cider on the stove till it's down to a thick mush. This will require lots of replenishing. It takes a terrible lot of cider. Either use this in mincemeat, so, or mix it with straight apple sauce to eat."

Boiled Cider Apple Sauce

[*A later recipe*]

2 quarts sweet apples, cored and pared
1 quart sweet cider reduced by boiling one-half

Put apples in a kettle, add cider, simmer 3 or 4 hours. If cider is sour add maple sugar or brown sugar to taste.

Apple Butter

2 gallons cider
8 quarts apples, pared and quartered
6 cups sugar
2 tablespoons cinnamon
1 teaspoon cloves
1 teaspoon allspice

Let cider boil until it cooks down to half its original volume. Add apples, a quart or two at a time; cook over low fire 4 or 5 hours. Add sugar and spices, stirring frequently lest apple butter "catch on." Makes about 6 quarts.

* *All jars should be hot when mixture is poured in to prevent breakage. They should also be sterile, filled to the top and sealed at once.*

Sweet Pickled Apples

Select tart, well-flavored apples. Cut in halves and remove core but do not peel. Put 3 cloves in each half. Make a syrup of equal parts sugar and water, using 1 pound sugar to 2 pounds apples. Simmer apples in syrup until tender. Store in a stone crock.

Baked Apples

Choose firm apples; core and cut ½-inch band of skin about their equators before baking. Place in baking dish. Add boiling water to ¼ the depth of the apples. Bake covered or uncovered in a hot, medium, or slow oven until apples are tender. If uncovered, baste occasionally with the water in the pan. Remove apples, boil syrup until thick, and pour over apples. Apples may have many different fillings to give variety—brown sugar and butter, raisins, nuts or cranberry jelly. Serve with cream.

Christmas Apples

12 apples
3 cups sugar
2 cups water
1 cup quince jelly
½ cup brandy

Pare and core perfect apples. Simmer (in a syrup made from the sugar and water) until firm but tender. Place apples in a shallow serving dish, taking care to keep them whole and unbroken. Fill the centers with quince jelly. Boil down the syrup in which the apples were cooked until thick. Pour over the apples. Just before serving, pour the brandy over the apples, light, and bring to table. Serves 8 to 10.

Apple Ball Sauce

Pare apples and shape into 3 cups of balls, using vegetable cutter. Make a syrup by boiling 2 cups sugar, 1½ cups water, 10 cloves, and 4 shavings of lemon rind for 7 minutes. Remove rinds and cloves, add ⅓ of the balls and cook until soft. Repeat twice. Cook syrup until reduced ½ and pour over balls. Serves 6.

Blushing Apples

[*To serve with roast pork or fowl—or as a salad or dessert*]

½ cup red cinnamon candies
½ cup sugar
1 cup water
6 firm cooking apples, pared and cored

Dissolve sugar and candies in water. Put apples in a casserole with cover. Pour syrup over, cover, and bake slowly in an oven 300° F. for 1 to 1½ hours, basting frequently. Lacking the candies, substitute 2 sticks cinnamon, a few drops red vegetable coloring, and 1 cup sugar.

Bean Pot Apple Sauce

Peel, quarter, and core apples. Place in a bean pot, sprinkle layers with sugar and cinnamon (½ cup sugar and ½ teaspoon cinnamon to 8 apples is a good proportion). Cover with sweet cider and bake in a slow oven (250° F.) 2 to 3 hours or until fruit is tender but has not lost its shape.

✻ *Yankees call it apple sass. If it is to be eaten hot stir in a big piece of butter; if it is to be served cold with pork it may be seasoned with a spoonful or two of horseradish.*

Baked Prunes

Wash 20 to 30 large prunes and put in a bean pot, barely covering them with hot water. Add sugar to taste, 3 cloves, and the rind of ½ lemon. Bake slowly with cover on jar until prunes have almost candied, about 1 hour. Serve cold with whipped cream, thick cream, or rich milk. Serves 4.

Baked Pears

Fill an earthen bean pot with Sheldon or Seckel pears, left whole and unpeeled. Add to each quart of fruit—

½ cup brown sugar
½ cup maple sugar
½ cup hot water
¼ teaspoon ginger

Bake slowly (300° F.) for 1½ hours, replacing water as needed in order to keep the pears from burning and to make a syrup in the bottom of the bean pot.

Ten-Minute Cranberry Sauce

½ cup sugar
2 cups water
4 cups cranberries

Boil sugar and water 5 minutes. Add cranberries and boil without stirring until the skins pop open (5 minutes is usually sufficient). Remove from fire and allow the sauce to remain in the vessel until cool. Makes 4 cups.

Grandmother's Catsup

[*Avis Williams, Brunswick Rd., Gardiner, Me.*]

1 peck ripe tomatoes (about)
2 cups sharp vinegar
6 tablespoons salt
4 tablespoons allspice
2 tablespoons mustard
1 tablespoon powdered cloves
1 teaspoon black pepper
¼ teaspoon red pepper

Cook and rub tomatoes through a sieve into a kettle until there is 1 gallon of liquid, free from seeds. Mix the vinegar and spices, and stir them into the tomato juice. Simmer until mixture thickens (about 3 hours), stirring constantly. Remove kettle from fire and allow to stand until cold. Stir and pour into small-necked bottles. Makes about 8 pints.

Tomato Catsup

[*A Massachusetts recipe*]

1 gallon tomato stock
½ pint vinegar
3½ teaspoons cinnamon
⅛ teaspoon cayenne pepper
⅓ cup salt
2 cups sugar

Cook 1 peck washed ripe tomatoes until soft without removing peel. (There should be about one gallon of stock.) Let stand for a few days in a crock. Force through wire sieve. Add the other ingredients. Simmer with tomato stock until proper thickness, adding sugar when nearly ready to bottle (in order to prevent burning). Bottle and keep in a cool place.

✻ *This recipe was used about 100 years ago by Joshua Davenport who manufactured and sold vinegar, catsup, and many kinds of pickles.*

Grape Catsup

[*Mrs. P. John Finnan, 80 Elmwood Ave., Waterbury, Conn.*]

5 pounds grapes, cleaned and stemmed
2 pounds sugar
1 pint vinegar
1 tablespoon cloves
1 tablespoon cinnamon
1 tablespoon allspice
1 teaspoon pepper
1 teaspoon salt

Boil grapes in enough water to keep from burning. When soft, strain through a sieve. Add remaining ingredients. Boil until catsup thickens. Makes about 6 pints.

Currant Catsup

[*Mrs. Russell G. Cameron, 5 Seeall St., Gloucester, Mass.*]

5 pounds currants
3 pounds sugar
½ pint vinegar
1 teaspoon cloves
1 teaspoon cinnamon
1 teaspoon salt
1 teaspoon allspice
½ teaspoon black pepper
dash red pepper

Boil all ingredients about 1½ hours or until thick. Bottle. Makes 2 bottles.

Bread and Butter Pickles

4 quarts cucumbers
8 small white onions, thinly sliced
2 green peppers, shredded
½ cup salt
5 cups sugar
1 teaspoon tumeric powder
½ teaspoon cloves
2 tablespoons mustard seed
1 teaspoon celery seed
5 cups mild vinegar

Select small, crisp cucumbers. Wash and slice (do not peel) in paper-thin slices. Add onions, peppers and salt; cover with a weighted lid and let stand overnight. Then make a pickling syrup of the sugar and spices. Add the vinegar and pour over sliced pickles. Place over low heat and stir occasionally. Heat the mixture to scalding point but do not boil. Pour into hot sterilized jars and seal. Makes about 6 quart jars.

One quart of cracked ice added to the vegetables and salt before adding the pickling syrup makes a crisper pickle.

Brine for Cucumber Pickles

Wash small pickling cucumbers as soon as picked. Place in a crock and cover with a brine of 1 cup salt to each 4 quarts water. Let stand 2 days completely covered with brine. Then make into sweet or sour pickles.

Sour Cucumber Pickles

Place cucumbers that have stood in brine (see above) in mixture 1 part vinegar to 3 parts water, covering pickles completely. Simmer 3 minutes, pack in jars, add 6 whole cloves, and fill jars with boiling vinegar and seal at once. Or pack fresh from vines into jars and add hot vinegar and spice mixture. Seal at once. Longer method gives crisper pickles.

Sweet Cucumber Pickles

Prepare cucumbers that have stood in brine (see above) in mixture 1 quart vinegar, 1 cup sugar, 1 stick cinnamon, 12 whole cloves. Heat to boiling, boil 3 minutes, turn into jars and seal. This mixture is the amount for 10 medium-sized cucumbers and will approximately fill 1 quart jar.

Oil Cucumber Pickles

[*Mary A. Martin, 24 John St., Springfield, Mass.*]

24 small (6-inch) cucumbers
2 quarts boiling water
1½ cups salt
1 cup olive oil
¼ pound white mustard seed
¼ pound black mustard seed
6 cups vinegar

Wash, dry, and slice cucumbers in very thin slices without paring. Cover with a brine made of water and salt and let stand overnight. Drain thoroughly, place in a crock. Mix olive oil, mustard seed, and vinegar and pour over cucumbers. Stir frequently. Makes 4 pint jars.

Maine Sweet Mixed Pickles

[*Mrs. Roland B. McConnell, Adams Ave., Saugus, Mass.*]

2 quarts green tomatoes
2 quarts cauliflower
2 quarts firm cucumbers
2 quarts onions
1½ quarts vinegar
2½ pounds brown sugar
2 tablespoons mixed pickling spice

Wash, trim, and cut in pieces but do not slice the vegetables. Soak overnight in 4 quarts water and 1 cup salt. Drain. Heat to the boiling point in 2 parts water and 1 part vinegar to cover. Drain again. Make a syrup of the 1½ quarts vinegar, brown sugar, and pickling spice. Boil 5 minutes, add well-drained vegetables, and cook until well heated through or until desired tenderness is reached. (Cucumbers will look white when done.) Seal in jars. Makes about 8 quarts.

Quince Pickles

8 pounds quinces
8 cups sugar
2 cups vinegar
½ ounce cloves
½ ounce cinnamon
¼ ounce allspice

Barely cover quinces with water and boil for 20 minutes. Boil sugar, vinegar, and spices for 8 minutes. Drain quinces and add to syrup. Boil another 8 minutes. Put into jars, seal after cold. Makes about 6 quarts.

Chow Chow

[*Mrs. Vinie Watts, Machiasport, Me.*]

4 peppers
12 ripe cucumbers
4 pounds cabbage
1 bunch celery
1 quart onions
½ cup salt
1 cup flour
2 tablespoons mustard
1 teaspoon turmeric
3 quarts vinegar

Chop vegetables fine, sprinkle with salt, and let stand overnight. Drain well. Make a paste of the flour, mustard, turmeric, and about 1 cup of the vinegar. Add to remaining vinegar. Cook in double boiler until mixture thickens. Pour over chopped vegetables. Cook 10 minutes. Pour into sterilized jars and seal. Makes about 5 quart jars.

Mustard Pickles

[*Mrs. L. G. Young, 58 Preston St., Windsor, Conn.*]

2 quarts green tomatoes
1 large cauliflower
6 red peppers
1 cup salt
1 quart small white pickling onions
1 dozen small sweet gherkins

Dressing:

3 tablespoons flour
3 tablespoons mustard
½ tablespoon turmeric
1 cup water
2 cups sugar
1 quart vinegar

Cut tomatoes, cauliflower, and peppers in small pieces. Add onions whole, add salt, cover with water, and let stand overnight. In the morning bring to a boil and cook 3 minutes. Drain. Make mustard dressing by mixing the flour, mustard, and turmeric to a paste with the water. Add the vinegar and sugar and bring to boiling point. Add vegetables and gherkins and simmer 5 minutes. Pack in sterilized jars and seal. Makes about 7 pints.

Pickled Eggs

1 dozen eggs
1 quart vinegar
½ ounce black pepper
½ ounce ginger

Boil eggs 12 minutes. Remove shell. Mix vinegar with the pepper and ginger and simmer 10 minutes. Place eggs in a stone jar, pour on the seasoned vinegar boiling hot. Keep in stone jar in cool place.

* *Attractive garnish for cold platters and excellent for picnics. Popular in England in country pubs.*

Lemon Pickle

small lemons	vinegar
pickling spices	salt

Wash and wipe lemons, then cut off the rind as thinly as possible.

Place lemons in a jar and cover with fine salt. Leave them about 10 days or until they feel soft. Wipe off a little of the salt and place lemons in clean jar.

Allow 1 ounce of pickling spice to each quart of boiling vinegar. Put the spice in a small muslin bag and boil with the vinegar for 10 minutes. Pour boiling vinegar over lemons. It must completely cover them.

Put the bag of spice in the jar. Cover the pickle and make it as air-tight as possible. The lemons will be ready for use in 3 months. They are delicious served with veal or poultry.

Pickled Onions

[*Celia M. Mooney, Georgetown, Mass.*]

1 quart small silver-skinned pickling onions	1 tablespoon salt
	2 cups vinegar

Peel onions and cover with water to which salt is added. Let stand overnight. Scald in this brine to keep onions white. Pack in jars, cover with hot vinegar. Makes about 4 half-pint jars.

Piccalilli

- 1 peck green tomatoes, sliced
- 3 pounds onions, sliced
- 3 large green peppers, cut into strips
- 3 red peppers, cut into strips
- 1 cup salt
- 2 cups sugar
- 1½ quarts vinegar
- 1 cup whole mixed pickling spice
- 2 cups water

Put vegetables into a kettle in layers with salt sprinkled between the layers. Let stand overnight. Drain. Rinse with cold water and drain again. Cook vegetables with sugar, vinegar, pickling spice, and water until mixture has thickened slightly. Turn into sterilized jars and seal. Makes about 7 quart jars.

Rummage Pickles

- 2 quarts green tomatoes
- 1 quart ripe tomatoes
- 3 sweet green or red peppers
- 6 onions
- 1 small cabbage
- 1 bunch celery
- 1 cauliflower
- 2 pounds sugar
- 1 quart vinegar
- ½ cup salt
- 1 teaspoon pepper
- 1 teaspoon mustard

Put all vegetables through food chopper, add salt, let stand overnight, and drain. Heat sugar, vinegar, and spices to boiling; add vegetables. Simmer 5 minutes and seal. Makes about 5 quart jars.

Green Sliced Tomato Pickle

[*To accompany baked beans*]

1 peck green tomatoes
1 cup salt
1 dozen large onions
1 cup sugar
6 red sweet peppers
2 tablespoons celery seed
1 tablespoon ground allspice
1 tablespoon cinnamon
1 teaspoon clove
1 tablespoon mustard
vinegar

Slice tomatoes, sprinkle with the salt, and leave overnight. In the morning drain off the liquor, slice the onions; combine tomatoes, onions, and other ingredients. Place in kettle, cover with cider vinegar, and simmer until tender, about 20 minutes. Pour into clean hot jars and seal at once. Makes 8 quart jars.

Chili Sauce

[*Mrs. Chester A. Knowlton, 129 Laurel Gardens, Saugus, Mass.*]

18 ripe tomatoes, chopped
6 onions, chopped
3 green peppers, chopped
1 cup sugar
2 teaspoons salt
1 teaspoon cinnamon, allspice, and nutmeg
½ teaspoon cloves
2½ cups sharp vinegar

Cook chopped vegetables until tender then add sugar, salt, spices, and vinegar. Simmer until thick. Then place in sterilized jars, and seal. Makes about 3 pints.

Rhode Island Relish

- 20 large ripe tomatoes, cut in small pieces
- 6 tart apples, pared and cut in small pieces
- 6 large pears, pared and cut in small pieces
- 6 large onions, chopped fine
- 6 large peaches, cut in small pieces
- 3 large green peppers, chopped fine
- 4 cups white corn, cut from the cob
- 2 tablespoons salt
- 1 quart vinegar
- 2½ tablespoons mixed spice, put in a bag

Put tomatoes on to cook; simmer 15 minutes. Add remaining ingredients and simmer together about 2 hours; seal in jars. Makes about 6 quart jars.

* *The first local peaches were put on the market in Boston in 1828 for such as were able to pay 3 cents a dozen.*

Pepper Relish

[*A Vermont recipe*]

- 24 sweet peppers
- 2 hot peppers
- 18 large onions
- 3 cups sugar
- 2 tablespoons salt
- 1 quart vinegar
- 2 tablespoons celery seed

Seed peppers and chop with onions. Cover with boiling water and let stand 10 minutes. Drain, put in a kettle, add sugar, salt, vinegar, and celery seed. Simmer 30 minutes. Bottle in small bottles. Makes approximately 6 half-pint bottles.

Potsfield Pickles

- 3 pints chopped green tomatoes
- 3 pints chopped red tomatoes
- 3 pints chopped cabbage
- 3 pints chopped onions
- 6 red peppers
- 2 bunches celery
- ½ cup horseradish
- ½ cup salt
- 2 quarts vinegar
- 3 cups sugar
- ½ teaspoon cinnamon
- ½ teaspoon cloves
- ½ cup white mustard seed

Combine vegetables and cover with salt. Let stand overnight. Drain and add vinegar, sugar, and spices. Cook 20 minutes and seal in jars. Makes about 6 quarts.

Aunt Melissa's Yellow Tomato Conserve

- 2 quarts small yellow tomatoes
- 1 lemon, cut in thin slices
- ½ pound candied ginger, chopped (optional)
- 8 cups sugar
- 1 cup water

Do not peel or slice the tomatoes. Combine all ingredients and cook until thick. Seal while hot in sterilized glasses. Makes about 8 pints.

* *The yellow tomatoes used for this preserve are no bigger than crab apples and look like drops of sunshine. Delicious in winter with hot biscuits.*

Ripe Tomato Pickle

- 1 quart tomatoes, skinned and quartered
- 2 cups granulated sugar
- ¾ cup cider vinegar
- ½ teaspoon salt
- spice bag
- 2-inch stick cinnamon
- ½ piece whole mace
- 12 whole cloves

Place ingredients in kettle and boil slowly until tomatoes are transparent and juice the consistency of 30 percent cream. Pour into jars and seal. If pickle is to be used immediately, place in crocks and place in refrigerator until time for serving.

Tomatoes should be firm and not too ripe. Allow ¼ pound waste for every pound of tomatoes as purchased. Makes about 2 pint jars.

Reed Family Tomato Relish

- 3½ pounds sugar
- 1 pint vinegar
- 7 pounds tomatoes
- 1 tablespoon whole cloves, ground in food chopper
- 1 tablespoon allspice
- 1 stick cinnamon, ground in food chopper
- 3 large or 4 small red peppers, cut in strips

Boil sugar, vinegar, and tomatoes. As soon as skins break, take out tomatoes and let drain 3 days; then put them back into syrup and boil several hours. Add spices in a spice bag; also add red peppers. Boil until thick and dark red colored. Seal in jars. Makes 6 pint jars. Pieces of ginger added to this make it taste similar to chutney.

Spiced Cranberries

5 pounds cranberries
7 cups brown sugar
2 cups vinegar
1 tablespoon ground cinnamon
1 tablespoon ground allspice
1 tablespoon ground cloves
½ tablespoon ground ginger

Boil sugar, vinegar, and spices for 20 minutes. Then add cranberries and boil slowly for 2 hours. Seal in jars.

Winter Chili Sauce

2 onions
2 peppers (no seeds)
1 large can tomatoes
1 cup vinegar
1 tablespoon salt
½ teaspoon cinnamon
½ teaspoon allspice
¼ teaspoon clove
½ cup brown sugar
1 teaspoon pepper

Chop or grind onions and peppers. Combine all and simmer 2 hours. Makes approximately 3 cups chili sauce.

Mint Chutney

Mint leaves
seeded raisins
½ teaspoon salt
3 tablespoons vinegar
pinch red pepper

Wash mint thoroughly and shake off all water. Remove leaves. Put 3 handfuls of leaves and 3 of raisins into a food chopper. Add salt, red pepper, and vinegar. Chop until almost smooth. Put in sterilized jars. Keep in refrigerator.

Chutney Sauce

- 2 red or green peppers
- 6 green tomatoes
- 4 small onions
- 2 cups brown sugar
- 1 cup raisins
- 1 quart vinegar
- 2 tablespoons salt
- 2 tablespoons celery seed
- 2 tablespoons mustard
- 12 large sour apples

Remove seeds from peppers. Cut vegetables in fine pieces, add raisins, cook slowly 1 hour with vinegar, sugar and spices. Add apples, cored and quartered. Cook slowly until soft and thick. Bottle and seal. Makes about 4 pint jars.

Rhubarb Chutney

- 4 pounds rhubarb
- 2 cups sugar
- 6 onions, finely chopped
- 2 ounces curry powder
- 3 tablespoons salt
- ½ pound raisins
- 2 cups vinegar

Cut up rhubarb into 1-inch chunks and boil with sugar till soft. Add onions and other ingredients. Stir until mixture thickens and chutney is soft. Seal in jars.

Uncooked Saccharine Pickles

[*Mrs. Charles L. Keene, West Poland, Me.*]

Wash and dry cucumbers (large ones may be split lengthwise and small ones left whole). Pack into dry, clean jars and fill to overflowing with the following *uncooked* syrup:

- 2 quarts vinegar
- ¼ cup salt
- 1½ teaspoons cinnamon
- ½ teaspoon cloves
- ½ teaspoon allspice
- 3 tablespoons mustard
- 2 teaspoons powdered alum
- 1 teaspoon saccharin
- ½ cup prepared horseradish

Syrup to make 4 quarts; pickles may be used in 2 weeks.

Pickled Nasturtium Seeds

Gather nasturtium seeds when they are small and green, before the inner kernel has become hard. Remove the stems and let stand in salted water overnight. Freshen in cold water, pack in small bottles, cover with boiling vinegar. Use as substitute for capers. Some cooks sweeten and spice the vinegar.

String Bean Pickle

- 1 peck butter beans or string beans, cut fine
- 1 dozen onions, chopped
- 2 bunches celery, chopped
- 2 quarts vinegar
- 3 pounds brown sugar
- 1 cup mustard
- 1 cup flour
- 2 tablespoons turmeric
- 2 tablespoons celery seed

Boil vegetables together in lightly salted water, to cover, about 30 minutes, then drain. Bring to a boil in a separate kettle vinegar and brown sugar; mix the mustard, flour, and turmeric with a little cold water and add gradually to hot mixture as in making gravy. Add celery seed and simmer all together 20 minutes, stirring constantly. Then add vegetables and simmer 10 minutes. Fill jars to overflowing and seal at once. Makes about 14 quart jars.

Mint Relish

- ½ cup mint leaves
- 1 pound tart apples
- ¾ pound raisins
- 1 dozen ripe tomatoes
- 2 red peppers
- 6 small onions
- 1 ounce white mustard seed
- ½ cup salt
- 2 cups sugar
- 1½ quarts vinegar

Put mint leaves, apples, raisins, tomatoes, peppers, and onions through a food chopper. Add sugar, salt, and mustard seed. Boil and cool vinegar, mix with other ingredients. Put in a crock for 10 days, stirring daily. Pour into sterilized bottles and seal. Makes 3 quart jars.

Corn Relish

- 18 large ears corn
- 4 large onions, chopped
- 2 green peppers, seeded and chopped
- 1 red pepper, seeded and chopped
- 1¼ pounds light brown sugar
- ¼ cup salt
- 3 tablespoons celery seed
- 3¼ tablespoons dry mustard
- 2 quarts vinegar

Cut corn from cob but do not scrape the ear, mix with onions and peppers, and add remaining ingredients. Cook slowly 15 to 20 minutes. Turn into sterilized jars and seal. Makes about 5 pint jars.

Red Cabbage Relish

1 large red cabbage
½ cup salt
1 quart sharp vinegar
2 tablespoons whole cloves
¼ teaspoon pepper
1 teaspoon allspice

Quarter the cabbage, cutting out the hard core; shred finely and place in a wooden or earthen bowl with ½ cup salt. Place in a cool place for 24 hours, stirring occasionally. Rinse in cold water and drain through a colander. Add vinegar; also cloves, pepper, and allspice, tied in a piece of muslin. Bring to a boil, add cabbage. Simmer 10 to 12 minutes, then allow to cool with cover on kettle. Will be ready to use in 2 or 3 days. Keep in a covered crock in a cold cellar. Will keep several weeks. Makes about 2 quarts.

Celery Sauce

15 small ripe tomatoes
1 small green pepper
2 onions
2 large celery heads
1½ tablespoons salt
¾ cup sugar
2 cups vinegar

Chop all the vegetables. Mix with the salt, sugar, and vinegar. Boil until thick. Bottle. Makes about 2 half-pint jars.

Horseradish Jelly

½ cup horseradish
3¼ cups sugar
½ cup vinegar
½ cup liquid pectin

Mix horseradish, sugar, and vinegar until the sugar is dissolved. Bring to a boil, then at once add the pectin, stirring constantly. Let come to a full rolling boil and boil for ½ minute. Remove from the fire, skim, and pour quickly into small jelly molds. When firm, unmold as a garnish for beef pot roast. Makes 5 small molds.

Dedham Rhubarb Relish

1 quart rhubarb, diced
1 pint vinegar
1 quart onions, chopped fine
2 pounds brown sugar
1 teaspoon salt
1 teaspoon pepper
1 teaspoon cinnamon
1 teaspoon cloves
1 teaspoon celery salt

Cook rhubarb and vinegar 20 minutes; add the remaining ingredients and cook slowly about 1 hour. Seal. Makes about 4 pint jars.

Sweet Pickled Gooseberries

6 pounds gooseberries
1 pint vinegar
6 pounds sugar

Remove the little blossom end of the gooseberries. Add vinegar and ½ of the sugar. Cook 20 minutes. Add remaining sugar and cook 20 minutes longer. Seal in glass jars. Makes about 6 pint jars.

Carrot Marmalade

1½ pounds carrots
2 lemons
sugar

Wash and scrape carrots, boil till soft, then grind through a food chopper.

Cook the grated rinds and strained juice of the lemons for 5 minutes. Measure the carrots, add an equal amount of sugar to the lemons, and cook for 10 minutes. Seal in jelly glasses.

Peach Marmalade

Pare, stone, and weigh the fruit. Boil one-half the peach kernels in enough water to cover them well. Quarter the peaches and add to the water, after straining it. Heat slowly, stirring often with a wooden spoon. Boil gently for 45 minutes. Add ¾ pound of sugar to each pound of fruit, boil for 5 minutes, skim, and add the juice of 1 lemon to every 3 pounds of fruit. Boil a few minutes, stewing to a smooth paste. When nearly cold, put in sterilized glass jars and seal.

Cranberry Marmalade

cranberries
sugar
baking soda

To every quart of fruit add 2 cups water. Cook slowly for 1 hour, stirring occasionally. Put the pan to one side and add ½ teaspoon soda for every quart of cranberries. Stir well and remove all scum as it rises. Rub through a fine sieve and to every cupful of the purée add 1 cup sugar.

Return to pan and cook gently for 30 minutes. Divide into jars and seal.

Amber Marmalade

[*A Martha's Vineyard recipe*]

1 grapefruit
3 oranges
3 lemons
water
sugar

Cut fruit into pieces and remove seeds. Measure, add 3 times as much water as fruit. Let stand overnight. Drain, reserving water.

Cut fruit in very thin shreds, return to water, boil 10 minutes, and let stand overnight. The second morning add 1 cup sugar for each cup of fruit and juice and boil until it sheets from the spoon. Makes about 10 glasses.

New England Apple Marmalade

2½ pounds sugar
1¼ cups water
2½ pounds tart apples, peeled
1 orange
1 lemon

Heat the sugar and water until the sugar is dissolved. Slice and core the apples; add the juice of the orange and lemon and the peel sliced very thin. Simmer until mixture is thickened, about 1¼ hours. Turn into glasses and when cold cover with paraffin. Makes about 6 large glasses.

Rose Honey

5 pounds white sugar
6 cups water
lump of alum, size of a cherry
petals of 8 double fragrant roses
12 red clover blossoms
20 white clover blossoms

Boil the sugar and water until thick and clear (232° F.). Add the alum and boil 4 minutes longer. Remove from fire. Add the petals and blossoms. Let stand 10 minutes; strain and pour into sterilized jars while hot. Makes about 6 jars. Delicious with soda biscuits and gems.

Rose Petal Jam

2 cups rose petals
2 cups warm water
2¾ cups sugar
2 tablespoons strained honey
1 teaspoon lemon juice
pink coloring

Cut the rose petals into strips with kitchen shears, discarding the tough white base. Pack tightly in measuring cup but do not bruise. Add warm water and cook about 10 minutes, or until tender. Lift the petals carefully, allowing them to drain. Measure 1 cup rose petal liquid; add sugar and honey and cook until sugar spins a fine short thread (220° F.). Add the drained petals and cook very slowly about 40 minutes. Add lemon juice and simmer until thick. Add a suggestion of pink coloring and seal at once. Makes 3 or 4 small glasses.

Coolidge Tomato Marmalade

[*A Plymouth, N. H., recipe*]

4 quarts tomatoes (measure them whole)
3 oranges
2 lemons
½ ounce cinnamon stick
¼ ounce whole cloves

Blanch the tomatoes with boiling water and pare them. Slice into a shallow kettle. Slice the oranges and lemons very thin and quarter the slices. Pour off half the juice from the tomatoes. Weigh the sliced tomatoes and add an equal weight of granulated sugar. Stir until the sugar is dissolved. Now add the oranges, lemons, cinnamon stick, and whole cloves.

No more than 4 quarts of tomatoes (dry measure) should be boiled at one time. In order to preserve the beautiful color, a large shallow kettle should be used over high temperature so that the marmalade will reach boiling point quickly. Stir often and reduce the heat somewhat after the marmalade has begun to boil. Test by cooling a teaspoon in a saucer. When the mixture shows the crinkling signs of jellying it is ready for the jars. Makes about 6 pint jars.

Apple Jelly

Wipe apples, remove stem and blossom ends, cut in quarters and put in large kettle; add cold water until apples are nearly covered. Cover and cook slowly about 25 minutes, or until apples are soft; turn into a jelly bag of canton flannel or several thicknesses of cheesecloth and allow juice to drain. (Do not squeeze, as squeezing makes a cloudy juice.) Measure juice; boil 5 minutes; add ¾ cup sugar for every cup of juice; continue boiling until jelly sheets from the spoon (220° F.). Skim and turn into glasses, cover until jelly has set; then cover jelly with a layer of hot melted paraffin. Porter apples make a sweet jelly; Gravensteins a spicy jelly. Two pounds apples makes about 4 glasses of jelly. For best results cook only 4 or 5 cupfuls of juice at a time. Some cooks heat the sugar before adding; others do not.

Combination Apple Jellies

Equal parts of apple and cherry, apple and rhubarb, apple and strawberry, apple and cranberry make delicious jellies. Three parts apple to one part barberries or quince also makes a satisfactory jelly.

Mint Jelly

Follow recipe for apple jelly. Before removing jelly from the fire bruise the leaves of a bunch of fresh mint and add. Add a small amount of green coloring. Remove leaves when desired strength of mint flavor is obtained.

Quince Chips

Pare, quarter, and core ripe quinces; cut each quarter into thin slices, weigh, and to each pound allow 1 pound of sugar. Put the quince slices into a pan, cover with boiling water, and boil quickly for 10 minutes. Drain.

Put the chips back into pan with sugar, add 1 cup water, put pan over slow burner so sugar will melt slowly; cook quinces until they are dark red and transparent.

Lift each piece with a slotted spoon, in order to remove excess syrup, and put on waxed paper to dry. When dry, roll in granulated sugar and pack in boxes with waxed paper between layers.

Quince Jelly

Wash and quarter quinces. Remove the seeds. Follow the recipe for Apple Jelly.

Currant Jelly

Wash currants, but do not stem. Place in a kettle. Add ¼ as much water as fruit. Cook until currants are soft and colorless. Drain through a jelly bag. For each cup of juice allow ¾ cup sugar. Follow recipe for Apple Jelly.

Mock Guava Jelly

1 pound dried apples
water
5 cups sugar (about)
¾ cups lemon juice

Wash apples and soak overnight in cold water to cover well. Cook apples in the same water until soft; strain through a jelly bag. Measure. There should be about 5 cups of juice. Add an equal quantity of sugar that has been heated, and lemon juice. Boil until jelly sheets from edge of spoon. Pour into glasses and cover with paraffin when cool. Makes about 12 glasses.

Paradise Jelly

20 cooking apples
3 quarts cranberries
12 quinces
sugar

Cut the apples and quinces in quarters, but do not peel. Add the cranberries. Cover with water, boil until soft. Strain through a jelly bag. Measure juice and add 1 cup of sugar for each cup of juice. Boil until jelly sheets from spoon. Pour into glasses and when cold cover with paraffin. Makes 12 to 16 glasses.

Grape Jelly

Select Concord grapes that are not fully ripe. Wash and drain, place in a preserving kettle, mash well, and heat until the juice flows freely. Strain through a jelly bag and add to the juice ¾ cup sugar for each cup juice. Boil until sugar sheets from edge of spoon, about 10 to 20 minutes. Pour into sterilized glasses. When cool, cover with hot melted paraffin. Two pounds of grapes make 3 to 4 glasses of jelly.

Beach Plum Jelly

Wash beach plums that are red (not ripe), pick over and place in a kettle. Cover with water, heat to scalding. Pour off and discard this water and start all over again! Pour on fresh hot water so that it can be seen among the fruit but does not cover it. Cook until fruit is soft. Strain liquid through jelly bag. Measure. Add 1 cup sugar for each cup of juice. Proceed as for Apple Jelly.

✻ *Attached to a very old recipe for beach plum jelly is this note: "Never make this jelly on a damp day."*

Beach Plum Jam

Follow recipe for Beach Plum Jelly. When fruit is soft, press through sieve. Measure fruit, add 1 cup sugar for each cup of fruit, and boil until jam is thick and clear, stirring to prevent burning. When sufficiently cooked, jam will sheet from spoon like jelly. Pour into sterilized glasses and seal.

✻ *The beach plum is found rooted in the dunes along the beaches of Cape Cod and Martha's Vineyard where excavations bring nothing to light but coarse beach sand. Where its nourishment comes from is a matter to marvel over.*

As beach plum pickers know, there is something of the grape, the plum, and the cherry about the beach plum. It is as though nature had combined the best features of all three. The thick tough skin of the ripe beach plum is much like that of the wild purple grape. There is a resemblance in the pulp and also in the shape of the fruit to that of the cultivated plum, although it is much smaller. And its firmness and bitter flavor are not unlike those of the wild cherry.

There is an old Indian legend that the Great Spirit created the beach plum especially for man because the birds flocked to eat all other fruits in their season, thereby depriving him of his just share. Be that as it may, in the autumn when the beach plum bushes hang full of ripe fruit, no birds sit among the branches to feast, although they devour the bitter wild cherry.

Beach plum pie was once a popular dish. The plums were not pitted. The diner might take a first tiny bite and finding it free from pits, sweet and toothsome, be misled to take a larger deeper bite. Often his entire skull would be jarred to its foundations when his teeth came together upon five or six bullet-hard obstacles concealed within the pink sweetness of the filling. Later, when pie makers went to the trouble of removing the pits, beach plum pie became much less common, and no wonder.

The beach plum is today considered primarily a jelly fruit.

Grape Conserve

4 pounds grapes
1 pound seeded raisins
2 oranges
3 pounds sugar

Cook the grapes until soft and sieve. Add raisins, the plup of the oranges and the skin, cut fine, and the sugar. Cook until thickened, stirring to prevent burning. Nutmeats may be added if desired. Makes about 6 half-pint jars.

Cranberry Conserve

4 cups cranberries
2 cups raisins
4 tablespoons chopped orange rind
1 tablespoon chopped lemon rind
2 tablespoons lemon juice
½ cup orange juice
6 cups sugar

Mix ingredients; let stand 30 minutes; boil quickly 10 minutes; lower fire and simmer until mixture thickens. Pour into sterilized jars and seal. Makes 6 jars.

If you like add ½ pound chopped walnut meats or slivered almonds.

Cranberry Ginger Relish

[*A modern Cape Cod recipe*]

2 tablespoons candied ginger
2 tablespoons orange rind
1 can cranberry sauce (2½ cups)

Chop candied ginger and cut orange rind in very thin strips. (Use only the orange-colored portion of the peel.)

Break the cranberry sauce with a fork and combine with the ginger and orange peel. Makes about 2 cups relish.

Cranberry Orange Relish

[*Uncooked*]

4 cups cranberries, washed and looked over
2 oranges
1¾ cups sugar

Put cranberries through food chopper; peel oranges, remove seeds, and put rind and oranges through chopper. Mix with cranberries and sugar. Let stand for a few hours before serving. Makes 4 cups relish.

Blueberry Jam

4½ cups blueberries
juice and grated rind 1 lemon
7 cups sugar
1 cup liquid pectin

Crush the berries; add lemon juice, rind, and sugar. Bring to a hard boil and boil 2 minutes. Remove from fire and stir in pectin. Skim and stir for 5 minutes. Pour into glasses; when cold seal with paraffin. Makes about 6 glasses.

Quince and Apple Preserves

1 pound of fruit—quince and sweet apple
1⅔ cups sugar
water

Peel, core, slice, and then cook quinces until tender in about 4 times their measure of water. Pare and core apples and cut into medium thick slices and cook in a small amount of water until tender. Drain off the juice from both apples and quinces, add sugar to the juice and boil mixture for 5 minutes. Add fruit and boil mixture until it is thick and clear. Pack immediately into hot jars and seal at once. Makes 4 to 5 glasses.

Raspberry Preserve

4 quarts raspberries
9 cups sugar

Wash berries, sprinkle with sugar. Let stand 12 hours. Cook about 10 minutes. Pack in clear glasses and let stand in the sunshine two days. Makes 4 half-pint jars.

Strawberries may be substituted for raspberries.

Rhubarb Jam

6 pounds rhubarb, cut in small pieces
6 lemons sliced thin
6 pounds sugar

Put fruit in a large bowl, cover with sugar and let stand 24 hours. Boil gently for about 45 minutes or until desired thickness is obtained. Do not stir more than necessary so that fruit will be unbroken. Turn into scalded glasses and cover with paraffin. Makes about 8 glasses.

Strawberry-Pineapple Conserve

2 cups fresh pineapple, cut in pieces
6 cups sugar
2 quarts strawberries, hulled

Combine pineapple and sugar; simmer slowly 10 minutes; add strawberries, and continue to cook until thick and clear. Makes about 6 glasses.

Heavenly Jam

[*A Rhode Island recipe*]

3 pounds ripe peaches
3 pounds sugar
juice and grated rind 1 orange
pulp and juice of 2 oranges
3-ounce bottle maraschino cherries

Peel and mash peaches with potato ricer, discarding pits. Add sugar and let stand overnight. Add orange rind, juice, pulp, and cherries cut in small pieces, also cherry juice. Cook until thickened. Makes about 6 pint jars.

Salem Currant Conserve

5 quarts currants, stemmed
1 quart red raspberries
juice 6 oranges
pulp and peel of 1 orange, cut in small pieces
2 pounds seeded raisins
5 pounds sugar

Wash fruit, combine ingredients and cook until syrup sheets from spoon. Remove from fire, cool about 5 minutes, stirring frequently to prevent floating fruit. Pour into glasses when cool and set, cover with paraffin. Makes about 15 glasses.

Sunshine Strawberries

Fine-flavored, large strawberries are most delicious when preserved in the sunshine. Hull, measure, and allow an equal quantity of sugar. Dissolve sugar in just enough water to melt it, then cook it almost to the thread stage (220° F.). Add berries and simmer gently about 10 minutes or until fruit is tender. Do not stir; try to keep the fruit whole. Pour strawberries onto large platters or shallow pans, cover with mosquito netting or glass and stand in the hot sunshine for 2 or 3 days when mixture should thicken and jelly. Bring in each night. Put into sterilized jars and seal with paraffin.

Sweet pitted cherries, raspberries, and blackberries may be preserved in the same way. Fruit may also be dried in a very slow oven (110° F.) instead of by sunshine.

Pumpkin Preserve

1 medium-sized pumpkin
1 pound sugar
½ cup lemon juice

Cut pumpkin in half, remove seeds, peel off the rind. Slice in ⅜-inch pieces. Pack the slices in a crock, alternating layers of pumpkin with layers of sugar. Pour the lemon juice over it. Let stand for 2 days. Drain. Make a syrup of 3 pounds of sugar and 1 pint of water. Boil the pumpkin in this until the pieces are very soft. Pour off the syrup, and boil the syrup until thick. Then pour the syrup over the pumpkin and seal in jars. If desired, boil with the syrup a little ginger root and fine lemon peel. Makes about 4 quart jars.

Sweet Pickled Pears

1 pint vinegar
2 pounds brown sugar
2-inch stick cinnamon
4 quarts pears

Boil vinegar, sugar, and cinnamon for 20 minutes. Stick 2 cloves in each pear. Place pears in the syrup and cook until soft. Can and seal. Makes about 4 pint jars.

Ginger Pears

10 pounds hard pears
3 lemons
5 pounds sugar
3 ounces Canton ginger

Peel pears, core, and slice thin. Cut lemon rind into strips and add rind and juice. Add sugar and ginger. Simmer about 3 hours or until juice sheets from spoon. Remove from fire, cool 5 minutes, stirring frequently to prevent floating fruit. Fill pint jars and seal at once. Makes about 8 pint jars.

Pickled Peaches

2 quarts peaches
2 cups vinegar
5 cups brown sugar, firmly packed
stick cinnamon (4 inches)
1 teaspoon whole cloves
½ teaspoon allspice

Scald peaches and remove skins. Boil vinegar, sugar, and spices (tied in a spice bag) for 10 minutes. Add peaches to the syrup (a few at a time) and cook until tender. Pack in clean hot jars, boil syrup 5 minutes longer, pour over fruit and seal. Makes about 4 pint jars.

Candied Tomatoes

[*Mrs. L. S. Hapgood, 47 Sparks St., Cambridge, Mass.*]

2 cups sugar
4 cups water
2-inch stick cinnamon
4 pounds tomatoes

Mix sugar and water, add cinnamon, and bring to a boil. Peel tomatoes, add the syrup and cook slowly about 45 minutes, or until thickened. Remove cinnamon. Makes 3 small glasses.

Preserved Citron

6 pounds fresh citron, weighed after preparing
3 pounds sugar
3 pints water
4 lemons, sliced thin

Peel citron and cut in sections, removing all the seeds. Slice the citron about ¼-inch thick and cut into 1-inch square pieces. Boil the sugar and water to a heavy syrup; add the citron and lemon and cook slowly until tender. Keep in crocks or seal in jars.

✱ *Candied angelica and sweet flag were among other early confections. Mountain cranberry, a small dainty species of bog cranberry, was used when the others were scarce.*

Watermelon Rind Pickle

8 pounds watermelon rind
1 quart vinegar
3 pounds sugar
several broken cinnamon sticks
2 teaspoons whole cloves
1 teaspoon allspice

Remove outer skin from rind and cut in medium thin slices. Weigh and cook rind until tender. In a second kettle boil together vinegar and sugar and a spice bag containing the cinnamon, cloves, and allspice. After the mixture has boiled, add the watermelon rind. Simmer slowly until rind is clear. Pack in clean hot jars, fill to overflowing with syrup, and seal. Makes about 4 quart jars. One or 2 sliced lemons may be added with the watermelon rind.

Beverages, Hard and Soft

Rhubarb Tonic

[*A drink children like*]

2 pounds rhubarb
3 cups water
⅓ cup sugar

Wash rhubarb and cut in small pieces. Add water and cook slowly, about 20 minutes. Strain. Add sugar, heat again to dissolve sugar. Drink when cooled.

Raspberry Punch

1 quart strong cold tea
1 quart water
1 quart raspberry shrub
juice 12 lemons
3 cups sugar

Combine all ingredients ½ hour before serving; add 4 pickled limes cut in slices, if desired. Strain and serve.

Raspberry Shrub I

4 quarts raspberries
1 quart vinegar
sugar

Add vinegar to berries and let stand 4 days. Strain. To each pint of juice add 1 pint of sugar. Boil 20 minutes. Bottle and keep in a cool place. A tablespoonful added to a glass of water makes a refreshing drink.

Raspberry Shrub II

1 cup raspberries
½ cup sugar
2 cups water
2 tablespoons vinegar

Crush the raspberries, add the sugar, water, and vinegar. Serve very cold with a few whole raspberries for garnish.

Haymakers' Switchel

1 gallon water
2 cups sugar
1 cup molasses
1 cup vinegar
1 teaspoon ginger

Stir the ingredients together thoroughly, "put in a stone jug," says the old recipe, and "hang in the well to cool."

* *Switchel—that good old Yankee drink—is nothing more than water seasoned to taste. It is thirst-quenching and inexpensive and the ingredients are always at hand; furthermore, it holds its own, lacking ice, better than most drinks of its kind.*

Soda Fizz

1 teaspoon lemon syrup
dash Angostura Bitters
sugar to taste
soda water

Put ingredients except soda water in chilled, tall glass; fill with soda water. Decorate with slice of lemon, lime, or orange.

Soda Beer

2 ounces tartaric acid
2 tablespoons flour
2 pounds white sugar
2 egg whites
2 quarts water
juice of 1 lemon

Mix cream of tartar and flour with the sugar. Combine all ingredients. Boil about 3 minutes. When wanted for use put ½ teaspoon soda in a glass. Dissolve in ½ glass water. Pour into it about 2 tablespoons of the lemon mixture and it will foam to the top of the glass.

Grape Juice

Wash Concord grapes and pick them from the stems. Barely cover with water. Boil until skins are broken and seeds are separated. Strain through a colander and then through a jelly bag. Measure the juice. Allow 1 cup of sugar to each 4 cups of juice. Boil the juice and the sugar for 15 minutes. Pour into sterilized bottles, cool, and seal bottles.

Uncooked Grape Juice

Wash Concord grapes and remove them from their stems. Place 2 cupfuls in a quart fruit jar. Add 1 cup sugar and cover with boiling water. Seal and allow to stand several weeks before using. When ready to use, strain the contents of the jar.

Yankee Mead

- 4 pounds brown sugar
- ½ pint molasses
- 3 quarts boiling water
- 4 ounces cream of tartar
- 1 ounce checkerberry
- 1 ounce sassafras

Mix the sugar, molasses, and boiling water; when lukewarm add the cream of tartar. When cold add the checkerberry and sassafras. Use about 2 tablespoons of this mixture to a glass of water and add ⅓ teaspoon soda, stir and drink immediately.

✻ *In grandmother's day mead was as common as ginger ale is today.*

Raisin Wine

2 pounds raisins, seeded and chopped
2 gallons boiling water
1 pound sugar
juice of 1 lemon
rind of ½ lemon, grated

Put into stone jar or crock and stir every day for a week. Strain and bottle. Do not use for 10 days.

Elderberry Wine

[*Mrs. Alice Richardson, Dover, N. H.*]

4 quarts elderberries
3 gallons boiling water
3 pounds sugar
½ ounce ground ginger
6 cloves
1 pound raisins
¼ pint brandy (if desired) to each gallon of liquid
1 yeast cake to each 4 gallons of liquid

Pour boiling water on berries which have been removed from the stalks. Let stand 24 hours. Strain through coarse bag or cloth, breaking berries to extract all possible juice. Measure and add other ingredients except yeast and brandy in proportion to amount. Boil for 1 hour skimming often. Let cool to "milk-warm" then measure again and add yeast in proportion to amount, and brandy if to be used. Let ferment with yeast 2 weeks and keep several months before using.

Elder Blossom Wine

1 quart elder blossoms
3 gallons water
9 pounds sugar
3 pounds raisins
½ cup lemon juice
1 yeast cake

Pick blossoms from stems. Pack measure full, pressing firmly. Boil water and sugar 5 minutes, add blossoms, and mix well. Cool to lukewarm. Add raisins, lemon juice, and yeast. Put in crock for 6 days. Stir 3 times each day. Strain and let stand till December in covered crock. Bottle or put in fruit jars.

Beet Wine

8 pounds beets
12 quarts water
5 pounds sugar
2 pounds raisins
2 yeast cakes

Wash, clean, and cut beets into small pieces, boil in 6 quarts water until soft. Drain and put the liquid in a crock. Put the other 6 quarts of water on beets and boil until they are white. Drain again and to all the lukewarm liquid add the sugar, raisins, and yeast. Let stand 3 weeks, then bottle.

Dandelion Cordial

3 quarts dandelion blossoms (remove stems)
3 quarts water
6 cups sugar
2 oranges
2 lemons
½ yeast cake
½ pound raisins
½ cup dark rum

Scald 3 quarts dandelion blossoms in 3 quarts boiling water. Let stand 3 days, then strain. Put into stone jar with sugar and the grated rinds and strained juice of lemons and oranges; add yeast and let stand 3 days. Strain into jars to ferment, adding water every other day to keep jars full. Do not cover. Bottle in 6 weeks. Add 2 seeded raisins to each bottle. Cork tightly. Do not add additional raisins as this will cause bottles to pop their corks.

Quince Liqueur

quinces } pound for sugar } pound	1 quart whiskey preferred

Wipe off fuzz from quinces using a dry cloth, then grate coarsely. Sprinkle 2 cups sugar on quinces, let stand 1 day. Press quinces to extract all juice and filter through jelly bag or clean stocking.

For each quart of juice obtained add 1 quart whiskey and 1 pound sugar. Pour mixture into a large bottle and let stand 2 weeks in warm spot. Shake vigorously every day.

After 2 weeks the liquor can be drawn off and bottled.

Concord Grape Wine

[*Minnie M. Laing, 9 Winter St., Penacook, N. H.*]

Stem grapes, crush, measure, add an equal quantity of sugar and water. Let stand 3 or 4 days, stirring occasionally. Strain, put in crocks, let stand 6 months. Syphon off, bottle, and cap. This wine improves with age.

One-half bushel grapes makes about 6 gallons wine.

Rhubarb Wine

4 pounds rhubarb cut fine	4 pounds sugar
1 teaspoon almond extract	½ yeast cake
1 gallon boiling water	¾ tablespoon gelatin

Combine rhubarb, extract, and water. Let stand 3 days and strain. Add the sugar and yeast, and the gelatin dissolved in a little water. Let stand for 2 days. Put into jug and cork. After 3 months strain and bottle. Makes about 3 quarts.

Spruce Beer

1 gallon boiling water
¾ teaspoon oil of spruce
¾ teaspoon oil of sassafras
¾ teaspoon oil of wintergreen
4 gallons cold water
3 pints molasses
2 cakes yeast

Pour boiling water over oil of spruce, sassafras, and wintergreen. Add cold water, molasses, and yeast cakes. Let stand 2 hours, bottle, let stand 48 hours before using. Place on ice before serving. Makes 25 quart bottles.

Potato Wine

[*Mrs. Donald Shirtcliffe, Turners Falls, Mass.*]

10 medium-sized potatoes, grated or ground
2 gallons warm water
6 pounds sugar
4 pounds seeded raisins
1 yeast cake

Combine and stir twice daily for 2 weeks. Strain and bottle. Makes 7 quarts.

Home Made Root Beer

Mix the contents of 1 bottle of root beer extract with 4 pounds of sugar. Dissolve this mixture in five gallons of lukewarm water. Dissolve ½ yeast cake in 1 cup lukewarm water. Stir well and strain through cheesecloth. Bottle at once. Fasten corks securely and fasten with a crown cap or stoppers. Set in a warm place away from draft for 3 or 4 days. Before serving put on ice. Makes 20 quart bottles.

Grandma's Ginger Beer

2 cups sugar
2 lemons, juice and rind
6 quarts boiling water
1 yeast cake
1 tablespoon cream of tartar
1 tablespoon Jamaica ginger

Put sugar and scraped (or grated) rind and juice of lemons into a large bowl. Pour the boiling water over them and let it stand until milk-warm. Dissolve the yeast in a little warm water with the cream of tartar and ginger. Add to first mixture and stir thoroughly. Bottle and tie down corks. Lay bottles on their sides in a cool place for 3 days. Fasten corks in securely or the working beer will force them out. Beer should be put into stone bottles if you have them. Two tablespoons of ginger powder may be used instead of the extract, but makes a slightly cloudy drink. Makes 6 quarts.

Hot Buttered Rum

Heat medium-sized tumbler and dissolve therein 1 teaspoon powdered sugar in a little boiling water. Add one wineglass New England rum and 1 tablespoon butter. Fill glass with boiling water. Stir well and sprinkle grated nutmeg on top.

* *Generations ago when the early settlers of New England, due to the rigors of the climate and the hardships of life, required fortifying and stimulating beverages, rum was the most popular and beneficial drink. In the eighteenth century the rum industry was well established in New England and a flourishing business was carried on between the West Indies and the states of Massachusetts, Connecticut, and Rhode Island. The rum trade played an important part in the economic and social life of early New England. Molasses imported from the West Indies*

was converted into rum in the many New England distilleries not only for local consumption but large exports of rum were sent to the African coast in exchange for slaves who were transported to the West Indies for labor.

Mint Julep

Using a silver mug (very important in order to obtain condition of proper frosting) place ½ teaspoon granulated sugar in the mug. Add enough water to make a paste. Grind fresh mint leaves into paste. Fill mug up to the top with finely scraped ice. Add 2 jiggers Bourbon, pouring it through the ice. Stir with spoon until mug is frosted. Add sprigs of fresh mint.

Champagne Punch

- 2 bottles champagne or dry sparkling white wine (Saumur or Vouvray)
- 1 large bottle (28 ounce) sparkling water
- 1 jigger (2 ounces) cognac or other good brandy*
- 1 jigger (2 ounces) curaçao or other orange cordial*
- 1 jigger (2 ounces) maraschino or other cherry cordial*
- 2 lemons, sliced
- 2 oranges, sliced
- ½ basket fresh strawberries

Have all ingredients thoroughly iced. Mix a short time prior to serving. Place block of ice in bowl or, better still, have ice outside, surrounding bowl. The proportion of champagne to water may vary from equal parts of each to champagne alone, according to taste. Makes about 24 4-ounce glasses.

* One, two, or all of these may be used; the total should be 6 ounces.

Old-Fashioned Eggnog

Beat separately the whites and yolks of 12 eggs. Mix yolks in punch bowl with 2 quarts cognac, 1 pint New England rum, 1½ pounds sugar. Add slowly 2 gallons milk. Stir constantly to prevent curdling. Place beaten whites of eggs on top. Sprinkle with grated nutmeg. Place in tub of ice 2 hours before serving. This recipe makes approximately 3 gallons.

* *Every Christmas Eve Boston's Beacon Hill turns back the pages of history and offers an enchanting scene.*

From the brilliantly illuminated State House to Charles Street, from aristocratic Beacon Street right over the Hill into the slum districts, old houses beam holiday tidings to all and hospitality reigns.

Caroling groups stream up and down the Hill past Bullfinch mansion fronts which are gaily illuminated with varicolored lights. Good fellowship flourishes as luxuriantly as Yuletide greetings. At Louisburg Square, the focal point of the celebration, guests toast each other with eggnog.

Householders come to their doors as the carolers halt outside. With them, as a gesture of democracy, the servants are permitted to stand. A few homes invite small groups of carolers to enter and warm themselves before the open fire. The custom of Beacon Hill carols was originated by Frederick W. Briggs, of Newtonville, Mass., in 1895 after spending a merry and musical evening in an English town. In recent years some 150,000 Christmas Eve celebrators have joined the wandering minstrels.

New England Baked Apple Toddy

Dissolve 1 teaspoon of sugar in 2 ounces boiling water. Pour into medium-sized tumbler and add 1 wineglass applejack and half of a baked apple. Fill glass ⅔ full of boiling water. After stirring well, sprinkle with grated nutmeg. Serve with spoon.

Tom and Jerry

Beat separately the whites and yolks of 12 eggs until the whites are stiff and the yolks lemon-colored. Mix in a punch bowl. Add 2 ounces Jamaica rum, 1 teaspoon ground cinnamon, ½ teaspoon ground cloves, ¼ teaspoon ground allspice. Stir well. Add sugar until the mixture reaches the consistency of light batter. In order to prevent the sugar from settling, use a dash of soda or cream of tartar.

To serve, place 1 tablespoon of the mixture in a small glass and add 3 ounces brandy. Fill the glass with boiling water and add grated nutmeg.

A mixture of ½ brandy, ¼ Jamaica rum, and ¼ Santa Cruz rum may be substituted for the straight brandy.

Sherry Cobbler

A great summer drink, refreshing as an east wind, is a Sherry Cobbler.

To make:
Half fill a tall glass with cracked ice
Add 1 tablespoon of powdered sugar
Add 1 sherry glass of sherry
Stir with a spoon until glass is frosted
Decorate with fruit, sliced orange, sliced lemon, sliced pineapple, cherries, etc.
Serve with straws.

Claret Punch

2 bottles claret
2 large bottles sparkling water
1 jigger (2 ounces) cognac or other good brandy
1 jigger (2 ounces) curaçao or other orange cordial
1 jigger (2 ounces) sherry
¼ pound sugar
rind of one lemon
4 slices cucumber (not peeled)

Mix claret, sugar, lemon, cucumber, and ice for several hours. Place block of ice in punch bowl, pour in the iced mixture and the remaining ingredients. Stir gently. Makes about 25 4-ounce glasses.

Rum Punch

1 bottle rum (New England Rum or Jamaica Rum may be used. The New England makes a less heavy punch)
½ pint Virgin Island rum (for added flavor)
½ pint cognac or other good brandy
½ pint claret
½ pint cold strong tea
1 bottle sparkling wine (champagne or Sparkling Saumur, etc.) or 1 large bottle sparkling water
3 oranges, sliced
1 pineapple, sliced
¼ pound sugar (½ pound if a sweeter punch is desired)

Mix all ingredients except sparkling wine or water at least 12 hours before serving. Place block of ice in punch bowl. Add previously mixed ingredients and sparkling wine or water. Stir well. Makes about 22 4-ounce glasses.

Cider Champagne

Make cider about November 25th from perfect apples without rot. Do not use apples that have been frozen. Delicious or Baldwins are best. Put cider in a new whisky barrel. To a 50-gallon barrel add 10 pounds white sugar and 10 pounds light brown sugar. Be sure to have 2 extra gallons of cider to fill in barrel as pumice works out. Keep a piece of burlap over bung hole while cider is working. Cider should be kept in a cool place at all times. It will be ready to bottle in about 8 weeks. Do not draw it from the bottom of the barrel but syphon it out.

The Mulls

- 3 bottles wine (usually claret, port, sherry, or madeira)
- 6 teaspoons mixed powdered cloves, cinnamon, and nutmeg
- 6 cups water
- 12 fruit sugar cubes, assorted flavors

Boil spices in water until steam becomes pungent. Stir in sugar cubes and wine and bring to a boil. Serve steaming hot. Makes about 25 4-ounce glasses of hot punch.

Brandy Punch

- 2 bottles cognac or other good brandy
- ½ bottle orange curaçao
- 2 jiggers grenadine
- 2 bottles sparkling water
- 1¼ pounds sugar
- juice of 15 lemons
- juice of 4 oranges

Place a large block of ice in punch bowl. Add above ingredients. Stir well. Makes about 35 4-ounce glasses.

Whiskey Punch

2 bottles whisky (rye or bourbon)
1 bottle sparkling water
½ pound sugar
juice of 3 lemons
2 lemons, sliced
1 orange, sliced

Place large block of ice in punch bowl. Add above ingredients. Mix well. Makes about 25 4-ounce glasses.

Champagne Cobbler

⅓ glass fine ice
½ teaspoon powdered sugar
1 piece orange peel

To the ice add the sugar and orange peel. Fill with dry champagne or great western. Decorate with fruit. Serve with straw.

Hot Brandy Sling

1 lump sugar dissolved in hot water
1 wineglass brandy

Fill glass with hot water, grate nutmeg on top. Serve at once.

Cherry Bounce

Fill a gallon jar with wild cherries and pour in enough whisky to cover. (Rum is preferred by some Yankees.) Let stand for 3 weeks. Then pour off the clear liquor and set aside. Mash the cherries, breaking the stones, and drain in a jelly bag. Add this to the first pouring off. For every 2 quarts of liquor from the cherries, take 1 pound of white sugar dissolved in a gill of water, bring to boil, and mix with the liquor, stirring well. Then bottle and let stand several weeks before using. As the lady who gave this recipe used to say:—"Hifalutin people call this cherry cordial, but I say it's cherry bounce."

Old Ironsides Rum and Soda

Into a large bar glass put the juice of 1 lemon, 2 dashes orange bitters, 1 wineglass New England rum, and 3 small lumps ice. Fill up with plain soda water. Mix and remove ice.

Fish House Punch

* *The following is believed to be the authentic recipe for this famous old punch as served at the famous Fish House Club in Philadelphia. This punch was often served in New England.*

Dissolve ¾ pound of loaf sugar in a little water in punch bowl. When it is entirely dissolved, add a bottle of lemon juice. Next add 2 bottles Jamaica rum, 1 bottle cognac, 2 bottles of water, and a wineglass of peach cordial. Put a big cake of ice in the punch bowl. Let punch stand about 2 hours, stirring once in a while. In winter, when ice melts more slowly, more water may be used; in summer less. The melting of the ice dilutes the mixture sufficiently. Makes about 60 4-ounce glasses.

Planters' Punch

½ bottle (12 ounces) fresh lime or lemon juice
1 bottle sugar syrup (or 1¼ pounds sugar)
1½ bottles rum
2 bottles water (or its equivalent in ice-and-water or ice alone, about 3 pounds)

Mix all ingredients well. Decorate with fresh fruit as desired. Makes about 30 4-ounce glasses.

* *The basis for nearly all West Indian rum drinks is:*
1 of sour, 2 of sweet, 3 of strong, 4 of weak.
Any of the best West Indian rums may be used in mixing this punch.

Old Salem Smash

Into a large bar glass put 2 tablespoons sugar, 2 tablespoons water, 4 sprigs fresh mint, rubbed to bring out the flavor, ½ glass shaved ice, and 1 wineglass New England rum. Mix well.

Hot Applejack

⅓ applejack
⅔ boiling water
juice ¼ lemon
2 teaspoons sugar
1 slice lemon

Stir together.

Mulled Cider

½ teaspoon allspice
2-inch stick cinnamon
6 whole cloves
1 quart cider
⅓ cup brown sugar
nutmeg

Tie allspice, cinnamon, and cloves in a cheesecloth bag. Drop bag into kettle of hot cider with sugar added and let it simmer until cider is spicy enough. Serve in mugs with dash of nutmeg. Serves 4.

"Sap's Risin'"

Sidney Wooldridge

The manufacture of maple syrup is not a process, but a ritual—a ritual of mysticism that has all the appurtenances of paganism and the Black Arts. The very metamorphosis of a thin, colorless, insipid, sweetish liquid of no particular character into a rich and delicate flavor, a distinctive table personality, partakes of alchemy. It could not be more marvelous were it done with the aid of unicorn horn, mummy dust, and bezoar stone. The mysterious offering of the trees, thousands, each its patient drip and drip; the attendance of the weather, its rhythm of freeze and thaw by night and day; the votive fire, its bottomless nap of coals endlessly devouring eight-foot logs, its roaring draft dominating and seemingly activating every movement within the sap house for days and weeks on end, constantly attended, never allowed to die; the oxen; the patchwork of snow in the naked orchard; the spiles and buckets, expressive symbols—all these are the trappings of a cult. A whole building, one of the most important and best loved on the farm, is set aside, a chapel, for the exclusive use of the god of sapping and his priests.

Priests is the word, for any one who once participates in the rites of sugaring-off becomes a quiet fanatic who yearly, at the season of Easter and the Passover and the pagan festivals of the rebirth of the world, returns to the sap house with a lilting heart, or, far away in years or miles, feels twinges of nostalgia.

Weeks before the first thaw, when the frost is still six feet in the ground and marbles are unthought of, when Christmas and New

Year's are barely gone and the seed catalogues have only begun to arrive, old weather wiseacres, knowing better even while they say it, try to wish the season into the present by remarks of, "Well, it'll soon be time for sugarin'-off," and, "Sap's about due to rise," remarks accompanied by wistful gazings over the hills on the horizon, introduced into conversations without preamble or apparent motivation and accepted by the hearer with the same momentary religious exaltation. Buckets are repaired and washed and set by the evaporator so long they have to be washed again before they are hung. Spiles are counted and furbished; wood, twenty, thirty cords of it, is piled in the open end of the sap house to form a fourth wall while the snow still lies heavy on the side hills. Spontaneously the fervor rises and, lacking the encouragement of the weather, dies, to rise and die again.

And then one morning, when, perhaps, no one about the farm has mentioned or thought of sapping for a week or more, Matt, the son of the family, wakes. Still wallowing in the warmth of sleep, he realizes suddenly (how he does not know; the knowledge springs into his head full born) that this is the day. He's off through the house spreading the tidings with a shout, and out to the big maple in the yard in his pajamas—making the first tap before sunup, when the sap will hardly start to rise before noon.

The ritual begins. The oxen, Buck and Broad, trace through the orchard with the sledge load of buckets and spiles. Father and the hired man and Uncle John and Allie from back of the mountain, the Coffin boys and Pops Talley and Jean, the Canuck, bore and hang, estimate the run, hazard weather predictions—there is no lack of willing hands during the sapping season.

Matt sucks the first drops from the first spile and, although it is hardly worth the effort from an economic point of view, once more Buck and Broad trace through the orchard, this time drawing the fifty-gallon gathering tank while the crew collects the few hours' offering. There is no profit in kindling the great fire to boil down these few gallons of sap that will make a scant quart of syrup—but farmers would sap if there were no profits at all; many do. The first run is sacred; the first born upon the altar, the wine upon the ground. Profits or no profits, the fire is lighted; the draft roars; steam rolls under the ridge ventilator, steam that sweetens hair and stiffens clothes with a sizing of sugar. Duke, the setter, sleeps under the fire box. Stories of runs almost forgotten fly while the sap bubbles and froths. A dozen pairs of eyes, not trusting the watcher's, needlessly inspect the thermometer in the last tray of the labyrinthed evaporator a dozen times every five minutes.

And when the first run is drawn off—

Tomorrow night the syrup will be clear, golden, light, delicate, fancy. Tonight it has served to wash the conduit pipes and the evaporating trays. It is brown, sluggish, almost dull in taste. It would hardly test B.

There is an adage that the first run is the best run. It is true, if you can be in the sap house when it is drawn off. The tin cup passing silently and reverently from hand to hand, from the straining bucket to the woodpile, is an orgy as truly as any ancient revel of Dionysus. Not a man in the sap house then will admit that this is not the choicest brew of the season.

When the farmer assures you that the syrup he sells you is the first run, do not believe him. The first run is gone as soon as it is cool enough to drink. You would not have liked it, anyway; but it was the best of the season.

It was.

How to Make a Rose Potpourri

First of all the roses should be just blown, of the sweetest smelling varieties and gathered as dry as possible. After each gathering spread the petals out upon a sheet of paper and leave until they are free from all moisture. Then place a layer of petals in your jar, sprinkling with very coarse salt, and so on, alternating layers of petals and sprinklings of salt until jar is almost filled. Leave for a few days until a froth is formed, then mix thoroughly, adding more petals and salt and repeat mixing operation daily for a week.

The next step is the addition of various aromatic gums and spices, such as benzoin, cassia buds, cinnamon, cloves, cardamon, and vanilla beans, all of which may be obtained at any drug store. Five cents each of benzoin, cassia buds (or ½ teaspoon ground cinnamon), and 5 cents worth of cardamon beans will be sufficient for an ordinary jar. Cloves should be used sparingly, probably half dozen whole ones bruised in a mortar, or not more than a half a teaspoon of the ground spice. One vanilla bean will suffice.

After these have been added, mix again and leave for a few days more when you may add the essential oils. Those of the jasmin, violet, tuberose, and attar of rose are best, with just a hint of ambergris and musk, and all of these must be procured from a perfumer, although a druggist could get them for you if he chose to. Ten cents worth of each of these is enough, with the exception of attar of roses, these drops being so exceptionally pleasing for a rose jar that twice the amount may be used.

Mix the oils in thoroughly and keep covered except when you wish to perfume your room.

If these directions are followed carefully, you will have a rose jar that will be a joy forever.

Candies, Sweetmeats, and Popcorn

Old-Fashioned Butterscotch

2 cups brown sugar
¼ cup molasses
½ cup milk
2 tablespoons water
2 tablespoons vinegar

Combine ingredients; cook until mixture cracks when tried in cold water (290° F.). Pour candy into buttered tins and mark into squares as it hardens. Makes 18 squares.

Candied Cranberries

[*A Cape Cod recipe*]

½ cup firm cranberries
½ cup sugar
½ cup water

Wash and dry berries and prick each with a needle. Boil sugar and water until syrup spins a thread (234° F.). Add berries and continue cooking until syrup forms a hard ball in cold water (250° F.). Lift berries from syrup, remove to wax paper, and let stand until well dried. Roll in granulated sugar. Use like candied cherries.

Fudge

2 cups sugar
¾ cup milk
⅛ teaspoon salt
2 tablespoons light corn syrup
2 squares chocolate
1 teaspoon vanilla
¾ cup walnuts, broken in pieces

Combine sugar, milk, salt, and corn syrup. Place over low heat, bring to a boil and boil gently until mixture forms a soft ball in cold water (238° F.). Remove from heat and add chocolate. (It is not necessary to cut chocolate in pieces.) Cool fudge for 10 minutes. Add butter and beat until fudge is thick and begins to lose its glossy appearance. Add vanilla and nuts and pour into buttered pan (8″ x 8″). Cut in squares while still soft.

Applets

[*A modern Yankee recipe*]

- 8 medium firm cooking apples or
- 2 cups unsweetened apple pulp
- ½ cup cold water
- 2 cups white sugar
- 2 tablespoons unflavored gelatin
- 1 cup chopped walnut meats
- 1 tablespoon lemon juice
- powdered sugar

Peel and core apples; cut in small pieces. Cook in saucepan with ¼ cup of the cold water until tender; force through sieve; add white sugar, cook until thick, about 30 minutes, stirring occasionally to prevent burning. Soak gelatin in remaining ¼ cup cold water; add to apple mixture, stirring until dissolved. Cool slightly by placing pan in cold water for 15 to 20 minutes; add walnut meats and lemon juice; mix well. Pour into flat pan to ½-inch thickness. Place in automatic refrigerator or let stand on ice overnight. Cut in squares and roll in powdered sugar. One tablespoon cornstarch added to each ½ cup sifted powdered sugar will prevent stickiness.

Molasses Taffy

[*The kind children love to pull*]

- 1 cup sugar
- ¾ cup brown sugar
- 2 cups molasses
- 1 cup water
- ¼ cup butter
- ⅛ teaspoon soda
- ¼ teaspoon salt

Cook white and brown sugars, molasses, and water together until brittle (272° F.), stirring frequently to prevent burning. Remove from heat, add butter, soda, and salt, stirring just enough to mix. Pour into large greased pans and allow to stand until cool enough to handle. Butter fingers, and pull taffy until firm and light yellow. Stretch into a rope, twist, and cut into 1-inch lengths. Makes 50 pieces.

Molasses Brittle

2 cups sugar
2 cups molasses
⅛ teaspoon soda

Boil sugar and molasses in a heavy iron skillet (295° F.) until it cracks when tested in cold water. Remove from fire and stir in soda. Don't revel long in the beautiful blending of color, but pour immediately into well-buttered tins. Cool, crack up, and munch. If you are fortunate enough to have butternuts, place a layer of nut-meats on the pans after they are buttered.

Butternut Panocha

[*A Vermont recipe*]

3 cups light brown sugar
¼ teaspoon salt
½ cup milk
2 tablespoons butter
1 teaspoon vanilla
⅔ cups coarsely chopped butternuts

Combine sugar, salt, and milk and cook over low heat until a soft ball can be formed (238° F.). Remove from stove; add butter, set aside to cool without stirring. When cool, stir in vanilla. Beat until candy becomes creamy. Stir in nut meats. Turn into buttered dish when candy is thick. Cut into squares when cold. Makes 24 large pieces. Walnuts or pecans may be substituted for butternuts.

Maple Caramels

¼ cup white sugar
¾ cup maple sugar
½ cup heavy cream
¼ cup brown sugar
¼ cup corn syrup
⅛ teaspoon salt
1 tablespoon butter
⅓ cup whole nut meats

Cook the first five ingredients until a soft ball is formed when a little of the mixture is dropped in cold water (250° F.). Remove, add the salt, butter, and nut meats and pour into buttered pan. When cold, cut into squares.

* *Today, thirty per cent of this country's maple crop comes from Vermont. There is a tendency for maple sugar to become stronger in flavor the farther north the region in which the trees grow. Why, no one can say. But Vermont is happily located so that its syrup carries a distinctive flavor that is neither flat nor too strong.*

Taffy Apples

[*Often called Lollipop Apples*]

1 cup brown sugar
½ cup granulated sugar
½ cup light corn syrup
½ cup water
1 tablespoon butter
¼ teaspoon salt
1 stick cinnamon
few drops red vegetable coloring
6 red eating apples

Cook sugars, corn syrup, water, butter, salt, and stick cinnamon until syrup crackles in cold water (300° F.). Remove from fire, take out stick cinnamon, add red coloring. Stick a wooden skewer in the stem end of applies, dip one at a time into the hot syrup, coating thoroughly. Place on oiled paper to cool. Makes 6 apples. Apples may also be colored green and flavored with mint or wintergreen.

Maple Syrup Cakes

Boil maple syrup down to 231° F., or until it forms a very soft ball in cold water. Beat with a sugar beater, made for that purpose (or an egg beater if cakes are made in small quantities). Pour into molds 1½ x 3 inches. Do not wet molds.

A Sugar-On-Snow Party

[*A Vermont recipe*]

A maple-sugar-on-snow party is a unique way of serving refreshments to a group. Such a party is most satisfactorily managed when fresh, clean snow is available.

Preparing the Snow

Gather a quantity of snow, providing a panful for each couple. Pans ten to twelve inches in diameter are best. Pack the snow solidly in the pans. In cold weather these pans may be prepared with the snow beforehand and left out of doors. Soup plates packed full of snow may be used in place of pans, if preferred. In this case, prepare one dish of snow for each person.

Preparing the Syrup

Allow one quart of syrup for six people. Pour the syrup into a large kettle; when it begins to boil it will bubble up and boil over rapidly. Boil the syrup until when dropped on the snow it remains on the surface and becomes waxy. Until it is of the right consistency it will dissolve into the snow. If a thermometer is used boil until 236° F. It is well to boil down the syrup partially before the party as it takes quite a time before it reaches the proper consistency.

Serving

Provide each person or couple with a pan of snow, a small pitcher of hot syrup and a fork. Pour the syrup on the snow, a little at a time. Some will prefer to make hollows in the snow and fill them; others will string the syrup out in fine lines. Some people call the syrup "sheepskins"; others refer to it as "leather aprons" or "maple wax." As soon as the snow cools the syrup, each person takes his fork and gathers up the syrup to be eaten and then the process is repeated.

MENU FOR SUGAR-ON-SNOW PARTY

Sugar on Snow
Plain Doughnuts—Sour Pickles—Coffee

For a real Vermont maple sugar party, doughnuts and pickles are necessary to complete the menu. The tartness of the pickles makes it possible to enjoy and consume more "leather aprons." Coffee clears the taste and doughnuts naturally follow along with coffee. Some Vermonters insist on cheese and at "elegant" parties butternuts are rolled with the sugar on the fork.

Sugaring Off

When the enthusiasm for the waxed sugar begins to wane, usually someone begins creaming what he has left in his dish. If this syrup is still warm it may be stirred until a nice creamy consistency and then picked up in the fingers and eaten as candy. Any syrup which has been boiled down and not served may be restored to its original consistency by adding water and bringing to a boil. It may then be used in cooking or served with pancakes.

✱ *A good maple sugar season is characterized by several good "runs." A "run" simply refers to the flow of sap which is fostered by alternately cold and warm periods.*

Those who like to get outdoors in the early spring to witness the fascinating phenomenon usually take a trip to a genuine sugar camp. It may be necessary to drive over a rutted muddy road, but the experience amply repays the effort. If they are "boiling" at the camp, a profusion of escaping steam will greet the eye and the essence of maple is readily apparent. Inside the shelter someone is tending the evaporator, an iron monster with a rather confusing series of pans and siphons and valves.

When the syrup in the finishing pan boils, it is drawn off and passed through a very fine felt strainer. The strained syrup is then ready for market.

Butternut Sea Foam

[*A Vermont recipe*]

- 2 cups sugar
- ¼ teaspoon salt
- ⅔ cup light corn syrup
- ½ cup water
- 2 eggs, stiffly beaten
- 1 teaspoon vanilla
- ½ cup butternuts or pecans

Combine sugar, salt, corn syrup, and water; cook over low heat until mixture boils, stirring constantly. Continue cooking, without stirring, until mixture spins a long thread (240° F.). Pour very slowly over egg whites, beating constantly, until candy holds its shape. Add vanilla and nuts, cut in pieces. Turn into greased pan. Cut in squares. Makes 18 pieces.

Herbs, by Marjorie Mills

No Yankee cook book would be complete without a chapter, however brief, on the herbs and simples that were cherished by early New England settlers, some of the seeds brought in little packets by the Pilgrims. Bees worked among the thyme and hyssop and hung in the tall sprays of lavender under the hot July sun that first summer in Plymouth. Women, a little homesick perhaps for the gardens they had left behind, saved the medicinal herbs to dry carefully, sage and winter savory and dill for seasoning the coriander seeds for seed cakes, and the leaves of innumerable herbs for tisanes both medicinal and refreshing to weary human-kind.

The Indians taught the Pilgrims the medicinal and culinary uses of the plants, roots, and berries in the New World, and the early settlers guarded their herbals by Tusser, Culpeper, Coles, and John Parkinson. They also clung to a sturdy belief in the benign effect of certain herbs, southernwood or Lad's Love, rosemary, lavender, hyssop and angelica. The herbs that invoked the evil spirit were vervain, betony, yarrow, mugwort, and St.-John's-wort.

Oil from the plants of sweet marjoram and lavender was used to polish the oaken tables and chairs, which must have left a spicy scent about the rooms even if the sprays of herbs, laid away with linens and with woolens to guard against moths, had not kept the rooms fragrant.

From the seventeenth to the nineteenth century New England women depended for the most part on their home-grown herbs and condiments for seasoning foods, for medicines, for the fragrant potpourris and lotions which they must have loved then as now. Parsley, thyme, and celery root seasoned their stews; rose water gave flavor to pound cake. The first edition of *The American Frugal Housewife,* published in Boston in 1829, mentions nasturtium and peppers from Mexico as new and desirable condiments.

Not until steamships replaced clipper ships were spices like mace, cloves, and allspice available to more than a few, so patches of pot herbs flourished near the doorway of every New England home or gave off their fragrance under the summer sun in clumps along the garden wall.

And there you'll still find herbs growing with the lilacs, the cinnamon roses, and Queen Anne's lace near the crumbling cellar holes of many an old New England homestead. For herbs have a mysterious vitality and tenacity; they ask little encouragement to flourish and they persist as though they knew we needed their quiet healing and refreshment in a hurried and harried generation.

Perhaps we are beginning to realize our need of the simples, the pot and nose herbs of another day, for herb gardens flourish again the length and breadth of New England. You may read any one of a dozen fascinating books on herbs, their history, their culture, their use and significance. The legend, fantasy and superstition clinging around herbs is endless. We read again and again "Herbs and the Earth" by Henry Beston whose herb garden, growing against an ancient stone wall beneath a gnarled apple tree in Nobleboro, Maine, is one of the pleasantest spots we have ever visited. The book is sheer poetry.

Start an herb garden and you'll find yourself treading a fragrant path to adventure and discovery. You'll make rose geranium jellies, herb soups and salads and fascinating beverages; you'll strew herbs in omelets and stews and fricassees; you'll miss basil if it's lacking in tomato dishes and your cottage cheese will be aromatic with chives; you'll candy mint leaves and sweet flag and perhaps blue borage blossoms. You'll inevitably make your own potpourri and insist all your friends sniff it while you look on proudly as though you had invented the idea.

In case you haven't a tiny plot of ground for a herb garden, or the quiet, gentle little plants seem too dull for you, blended herb powders or the dried thyme, basil, chervil, marjoram, mint, sage, and savory may be bought. The secret of success in using fresh or dried herbs is subtlety. One should never be conscious of the lusty flavor of herbs, only of a mysterious enhancement of savor and aroma in food or a beverage.

In spring, country women find their pot herbs and savory greens along every New England roadside and in every marsh and field. No one needs tell them that narrow-leafed dock, bright new shoot of dandelion, gray-green, furry sprouts of milkweed, mullen, and the first cowslip, chicory, kale, and sorrel can go into a round-bellied pot with a piece of salt pork, ham hock, or lean bacon and come out good beyond the telling.

Gathering field greens you sniff the fragrance of moist brown earth in springtime, sense the rhythm of life stirring around you, and feel as renewed as the earth itself. Eating properly cooked tender shoots of New England greens, you'll enjoy one of the savoriest foods Nature spreads out on her green tablecloth.

If you're a cliff dweller in a city apartment and neither the patch of home-grown herbs nor the sprightly waifs of the field are available for your gathering basket, do grow a small window box of spicy plants to lend zest and romance to urban menus. Mint, cress, marjoram, basil, chives, and rose geranium will flourish on a sunny window sill and supply both the savor to food and the poignant link with old New England ways which herbs, wherever grown and cherished, can't fail to yield.

The recipes listed are a few of our favorites, one or two from Helen Morgenthau Fox's *Garden with Herbs,* one from Helen Noyes Webster of Lexington who is a sort of patron saint for herb enthusiasts in New England, and the candied mint leaf recipe from Caroline Torry of the Wenham Herb Center.

CANDIED MINT LEAVES

Thin gum arabic with water and brush each fresh green mint leaf with the mixture, using a good-sized firm, clean paint brush. Then dip the leaves in sugar and let them crisp and harden on wax paper. Pack in air-tight tin boxes in layers with wax paper between each layer—and you can regale your friends with your own candied mint leaves next winter at tea, or adorn a huge layer cake with pink peppermint icing and a wreath of candied peppermint leaves.

TARRAGON VINEGAR

Pick fresh green leaves of tarragon herb, wash, dry slightly, fill a jar with them, cover with a good grade of vinegar. Cover the jar closely and let it stand 2 to 4 weeks, strain and bottle.

MINT VINEGAR

[*Elinor Beckwith*]

2 quarts mint leaves | white vinegar

Fill a bottle with mint leaves puréed in blender. Pour in as much vinegar as a gallon jug can hold. In 5 weeks it will be ready and can be strained into another bottle. Green vegetable coloring enhances its appearance.

CUCUMBER VINEGAR

[*Elinor Beckwith*]

Wipe 9 large cucumbers, slice them thinly into jar with 3 large sliced onions, a clove of garlic, ½ tablespoon salt, ½ tablespoon white pepper, ½ teaspoon red pepper, and 1 quart vinegar. After 4 days, strain through flannel bag and bottle, putting a few white peppercorns in each bottle. Excellent flavoring for salads, cold meats, or added to mayonnaise.

CORIANDER SEED ROLL

Roll rich pie pastry very thin. Spread it with butter, brown sugar, spices, and coriander seeds. Roll up and cut into slices. Bake in hot oven (400° F.) until pastry is brown.

CORIANDER SEED CAKES

2 cups flour
1 cup sugar
2 egg yolks
1 tablespoon coriander seeds
1 tablespoon sour cream

Combine and roll, press mixture into shapes like little pretzels or any shape desired. Bake in moderate oven.

CHIVE OMELET

1 tablespoon flour
½ cup milk
6 eggs, well beaten
¾ teaspoon salt
pepper
⅓ cup chives, finely cut

Stir flour into milk until mixture is smooth; add eggs, salt and pepper. Turn into a buttered hot frying pan and place over moderate heat. As omelet cooks, lift edge toward center and tip pan so the uncooked mixture flows under the cooked portion. When portion is lightly browned, sprinkle chives over top. Fold over and slip on to hot plate. Serves 5.

CARROTS WITH LEMON JUICE AND MINT

[*Helen Webster*]

Melt a generous piece of butter and add juice of 1 lemon, 1½ tablespoons chopped spearmint. Combine well with 1½ quarts cooked and diced hot carrots.

MINT SAUCE FOR GRAPEFRUIT OR FRUIT CUP

½ cup mint tips packed hard
½ cup water
1 cup sugar

Boil about 5 minutes, strain and add green coloring as desired. When cool add to fruit and let stand at least 2 or 3 hours. If you prefer a sweeter sauce add more sugar when making syrup. Vary with different kinds of mint.

GREEN PEA SOUP WITH MINT

[*Helen Fox*, Gardening with Herbs]

- 1 quart of fresh peas
- 1 onion
- 1 large or 2 small sprigs of mint
- 1 teaspoon spinach juice
- 1 teaspoon salt
- 1 teaspoon sugar
- 4 tablespoons butter
- 2 egg yolks
- ½ cup cream

Shell the peas, and break up the pods; wash the pods and boil for two or three hours in the water in which other vegetables have been cooked if possible. Strain and add the peas, the onion, mint, salt, and sugar, and three pints of water in which the pods were cooked. Cook until the peas are tender, then rub through a sieve, add butter, spinach juice (for color), and bring to boiling point. Season more if needed, and just before serving add the egg yolk diluted with the cream. Cook, stirring constantly for five minutes, but do not allow the liquid to boil. Strain and serve with croutons. Serves 4 to 6.

PERFUME AGAINST MOTHS

[*Elinor Beckwith*]

Use equal parts peppermint, rosemary, thyme, and wormwood. Dry these and rub leaves off stems. Add 6 tablespoons freshly ground cloves and ginger to each cup. Mix well and keep in tightly closed containers until wanted. Place a bit of the mixture in small cheesecloth bags and put in with the winter clothes you are storing away.

✱ *Grandmother Shepard used this for her clothes and her daughter's clothes, but for Grandpa Shepard and the boys, she sprinkled Grandpa's pipe tobacco over the woolens. This imparted a nice masculine odor to their clothes and chased away the moths.*

ORANGE AND LEMON FRAGRANCE

Peel 4 lemons and 4 oranges. Chop the peel into very small pieces. Mix with 2 tablespoons of orris root and 1 teaspoon cinnamon. When dry put in small cheesecloth bags. This is extremely pleasant when used in your linen closet.

HERBAL BATH

For an aromatic bath, tie a large bunch of herbs in a cheesecloth bag and let steep in boiling water for about 10 minutes. Strain and add to bath water. Lavendar, mint, cardamon, anise seed, rosemary, marjoram, thyme, rose geranium are a pleasant combination. But you will probably evolve your own. You may also add flower heads of roses, clove pinks, and honey locusts if you desire a unique fragrance.

Another way is to put the herbs in a quart of rubbing alcohol, being sure to get a brand that does not have a strong odor. It will take 10 days for the chlorophyll in the leaves to give it a nice green color. Strain and re-bottle.

Three tablespoons of the dry herb mixture in a bowl of boiling water makes a cleansing steam bath for the complexion. Cover your head with a turkish towel as you lean over the brew.

Instructions for Bayberry Candles

Remove berries from twigs; pick them over again to remove any leaves or small pieces of twigs. Put a few berries in colander and shake back and forth to remove all dust. Put berries in kettle filled with water. Use a large kettle so wax will float to the top. Set in middle of stove (not over direct heat else sediment will cook into wax) and leave overnight. In the morning, set in a cold place, preferably out of doors, and wax will form in a solid cake. This will take all day.

Remove wax and brush or pick off any sediment, and put in

a small kettle filled with water. Set it on the stove again (not over direct heat), and when entirely melted, pour through strainer, then through cheesecloth. Set out of doors again to harden. If it is not clean enough, melt it again in water and strain. Be sure to have wax perfectly clean. In straining warm wax, work in a warm place, else wax will begin to harden. Work over the back of the range but be careful not to get too close to the fire.

Now your wax is ready for the molds, or to dip by hand. If you use a mold, have wicks longer than mold, so you can pull out candles. Put wick in mold, and dip the tip of wick into warm wax and let it harden (this will take but a moment). Then pour your wax into the mold. If you use a teapot, wax will be easier to handle. Hold the mold in upright position or tie it to faucet. Let this stand in a cold place half a day. Then take a sharp pointed knife and loosen candles at the base, and pull out. Here is where a long wick is handy. If candles do not come out readily, it is because your wax was not clean enough, and you will have to pour boiling water over the molds to loosen them. Then hold them until they are firm enough to lay down.

10 pounds bayberries makes 1 pound wax
1 pound wax makes 2 good-size candles.

Index